FEB 2 0 2017

Pretend I'm Not Here

Pretend I'm Not Here

How I Worked with Three Newspaper Icons, One Powerful First Lady, and Still Managed to Dig Myself Out of the Washington Swamp

Barbara Feinman Todd

WILLIAM MORROW
An Imprint of HarperCollins*Publishers*

HarperCollins books may be purchased for educational, business, or sales promotional use. For information please e-mail the Special Markets Department at SPsales@harpercollins.com.

FIRST EDITION

Library of Congress Cataloging-in-Publication Data has been applied for.

ISBN 978-0-06-244510-0

17 18 19 20 21   LSC   10 9 8 7 6 5 4 3 2 1

For Dennis and Sasha

Contents

Pretend I'm Not Here

Chameleon

We go through life. We shed our skins.
We become ourselves.
—PATTI SMITH

In the summer of 2014, my brother called to tell me he'd just heard that our ninety-one-year-old father was being taken to a Miami emergency room by ambulance because he was having trouble breathing.

"Find him and figure out what's going on," my brother said, explaining that the aide who called from the assisted living facility didn't have any additional information. "I know you can find him faster than I can," he repeated. "That's what you do."

So I identified the hospital closest to my dad's address and tracked down the ER nurse tending to my father. She said they were running tests on him and they would have some answers shortly.

"Is he in pain?" I persisted.

"He can tell you himself," she said and handed him the phone.

"Hello there," I heard my dad say, with a forced cheerfulness punctuated by wheezing.

"Dad, what's wrong?"

"I don't know. Do I have a medical license?" he said, sounding more like his ornery self.

"What are your symptoms?"

"They've got me on a gurney in the hallway."

"Dad, your symptoms—do you have pains in your chest? Your arm?"

"They say I was having trouble breathing..." He launched into a long story about how he hadn't felt "quite right" after lunch and had sat down in the lobby when a friend came along and noticed his color wasn't good . . . So they called over someone else to see if they agreed that he was a little pale . . .

I interrupted, trying to get him to tell me exactly what he was experiencing.

"Listen," he said, "Harriet called me this morning and said there was a story in the paper about Hillary, and it mentioned you." I didn't know who Harriet was. I did know the story he was referring to. The *Washington Post* had run something about Hillary Clinton's latest book, *Hard Choices*. The day before, Paul Farhi, a reporter at the paper, had contacted me for a comment. Nearly twenty years earlier, I had worked with Mrs. Clinton on her first book, *It Takes a Village*, when she was First Lady. The reporter wanted a quote from me that would provide context for the standard story he was probably writing—*Hillary Clinton has a new book out and this time she's given her ghost credit.*

"Did you see that story?"

"Yes, Dad, the guy e-mailed me, and I said what I always say: 'No comment.' Dad, can we *please* get back to your health?" I tried to keep the mounting exasperation out of my voice.

"I guess you'll be the only one in the family who doesn't vote for Hillary," he said with a sniff. I realized then what my father was doing. It wasn't that he was faking this medical emergency; he was exploiting it, holding his condition hostage. I knew how this would end; he was a lifelong Democrat, and he wanted me to promise I would vote for Hillary Clinton in 2016.

"Right now, Dad, I'm worried about your health."

"No need to worry about me. I will be fine. It's this country you need to worry about. Which brings me back to my original question: Who will you be voting for in the next election . . . ?"

EVEN AS EARLY AS HIGH SCHOOL, like Woody Allen's Zelig character, I found myself orbiting on the periphery of people in the public eye. Maybe it's in the genes, as I can trace a through-line back to my great-grandfather, who was a stable groom to Czar Nicholas.

My first brush with celebrity was Elisabeth Kübler-Ross, whose "five stages of grief" theory gained world renown in 1969 with the publication of her groundbreaking book *On Death and Dying*. One of my high school classmates was Dr. Kübler-Ross's son, and in the mid-1970s, I hung out frequently in the Kübler-Ross home in the suburbs of Chicago. It was a big house and we didn't go into parts of it. I knew that was because terminally ill patients stayed there some-times. One day we went into a part of the house we didn't usually go, a room that had a sort of teepee-shaped structure, made from what looked like giant Legos. My friend said I could sit inside the structure and see if I felt anything. I sat there and sat there, waiting for something to happen. You'd be right if you thought this was a good description for my whole high school experience.

These were also the years when Dr. Kübler-Ross was be-ginning to participate in some unusual activities such as out-of-body experiences and spiritualism, but all I knew was that she was helping dying people and that seemed like a worthy cause. After graduation, when I was leaving to go to Occiden-tal College in California, Dr. Kübler-Ross gave me an auto-graphed copy of *On Death and Dying*, which she'd inscribed "To Barbara, with good wishes for your trip to California. Elisabeth K. Ross Sept. 1977."

My next brush with fame didn't even involve real con-tact, and I wouldn't know it until many years later. At age twenty, after my sophomore year, I transferred to UC Berke-ley, leaving Occidental four months before a young Barack Obama would arrive there. I left behind some (extremely bad) poetry, which found its way into a student literary pub-lication. I had no memory of the poetry journal, until thirty years later, when I received an e-mail from David Maraniss, whom I had known when we both worked at the *Washing-ton Post*. The e-mail said he was working on a biography of Barack Obama and that during his research he had found the Spring 1981 volume of Oxy's literary journal, *Feast*, which contained three of my poems along with one written by

Obama. "Yours were better," Maraniss wrote to me. And then he quoted a line from one of my poems: "Ashes sleep with ashes but people dream alone." "Anyway," his e-mail continued, "I would love to talk to you about Oxy, that time and place, whether you actually knew Barry or not . . ."

I wrote back, explaining that I hadn't crossed paths with the future president. Later, when I read Maraniss's book, I learned that my best friend at Oxy had become close with Obama, serving as inspiration for "Regina," a key female character in his 1995 memoir, *Dreams from My Father.*

IN MY EARLY TWENTIES, I got an amazing opportunity—to work for Bob Woodward of Watergate fame. I hadn't thought about becoming a book researcher, but once the seed was planted, it grew with abandon. After my stint with Woodward, research jobs on additional high-profile books quickly followed, and soon enough, with a few books on my résumé, I was under the illusion that I was running with the big dogs; I was part of the game, inside the power structure. The role I played was as varied as the books I worked on: the gig with Woodward turned out to be the first stop on a long ride that would take me from researcher to book doctor, to collaborator, to ghost—a publishing insider's taxonomy that I will flesh out later. For now I'll just use "ghost" as shorthand to refer to my role as someone who worked behind the scenes on other people's books. I couldn't know it then, but before I would lay to rest my ghostwriting career I would masquerade as, among others, a U.S. senator with a "female problem" (in a project that had failed to launch), a congresswoman who took on the male-dominated Congress, a second U.S. senator who had also been a presidential candidate, a tire magnate turned presidential candidate, and, most notably, a First Lady (who would later become a two-time presidential candidate) who wanted to reshape her image.

Few occupations allow you to see how famous people act when they aren't on the public stage. My clients were people I saw on television or read about in newspapers and magazines. I was only twenty-three years old when I began working for Woodward, and the proximity to fame and power was intoxicating. I suddenly found myself interesting to people who I thought were more interesting than I was. It slowly became clear to me that—in Washington at least—my appeal was more about who I knew than who I was.

I was someone who was constitutionally camera-shy, both literally and figuratively, so being a ghost offered me cover. I could hide behind the celebrity of prominent people. Being offstage was a relief, but at the same time it was disappointing to realize that someone at a dinner party was talking to me because of whichever famous person I was associated with at the moment, that I was just a conduit to a Big Name. This had an eclipsing effect on me during a decade—that of my twenties—that was defining. "As a twentysomething, life is still more about potential than proof," writes psychologist Meg Jay in her book *The Defining Decade*. "Those who can tell a good story about who they are and what they want leap over those who can't." By yielding to others' stories, I neglected to live and to tell my own.

Once I saw a TV profile of a woman who had received

a kidney transplant, and though a lifelong vegetarian, after the transplant, she began to crave fried chicken. In the predictable tearful meeting between the donor's family and the recipient, she learned that the deceased had loved—you guessed it—fried chicken. For me, taking on a ghosting gig was like getting that person's kidney—or maybe their heart—transplanted into my body. I'm sure plenty of ghosts don't feel that way. But for me, my experience was that the act of writing in the voice of others, in addition to being taken away from my own writing, meant that I was being taken away from myself. My subjects seeped beneath my skin. Their blood and marrow commingled with mine, and ultimately I found myself absorbed. Their problems became more important than mine, their dreams more alluring. Their mental stuff took up all the room in my head and my heart, pushing mine to the periphery.

It was alarming to me when I realized my subjects' histories had become intertwined with mine, so much so that I began to date things in my mind with their touch points instead of mine. *The Gulf War, that must have been in 1991 because that's when the senator was doing such and such . . .* instead of *That must have taken place in 1989 because it was the same year my mother died.* My vocabulary changed, and I began to swear like a truck driver when I worked with the famously profane, legendary newspaperman Ben Bradlee. I even appropriated my clients' mannerisms, nodding my head to show concern as though I were Hillary Clinton on a listening tour.

After my honeymoon period of being a ghost and that first flush of adrenaline that accompanied it, I experienced a long, slow trajectory of feelings that ultimately settled into sadness and regret. I felt that I had let myself down by giving up my own voice, identity, and precious time. All along I kept reassuring myself that ghostwriting was a good training ground for what I really wanted: to write my own book and try to make it as a novelist. Someday, I told myself, thanks to the skills I acquired ghosting, I would resurrect my long dormant unpublished novel and be equipped, at long last, to turn it into a masterpiece. Studying how to calibrate and construct the voices of others would teach me how to shape and refine my own. I once confidently told my students in a creative writing class that learning to modulate, sometimes appropriate another's voice, was useful. But even as the words were coming out of my mouth, they sounded hollow and forced. I had actually come to believe that ghostwriting was an exercise in ventriloquism and nothing much else. I learned, above nearly all else, that everyone has a story to tell, but the version they are willing or able to tell is not necessarily the story most worth telling.

Despite how I feel about ghostwriting, the fact remains that it can be very interesting work, and it is often a lucrative profession that has kept food on the table for a lot of out-of-work journalists and aspiring novelists, myself included. But few aspire to become a ghost, and in my case it certainly wasn't premeditated. As a child I didn't pose my Barbie at a miniature typewriter and have her ask Ken insightful questions with a toy tape recorder running. I don't think I even heard the word *ghostwriter* until a half-dozen years into my career as a Washington journalist, when, uncertain about my future, I encountered a New York literary agent who proposed I become one. The fact that anyone had any sort of an idea about my future was a relief, and the fact that this agent had a writer-related job in mind for me was exciting. It wasn't the sort of writing that I ultimately wanted to do, but at least it was writing.

My identity, the way I approach everything, is and always has been about being a writer. One of my earliest, sharpest memories is of writing a poem in fourth grade. We were studying poetry forms: haikus and limericks, that sort of thing. My teacher was Mrs. Baker and I loved her. She wore her pitch-black hair in a *Madmen*-ish bouffant updo, was always dressed in crisply tailored suits, and never raised her voice. She was the first person I can remember who thought my writing showed promise.

I was born in Chicago, but when I was six we moved to Jenkintown, Pennsylvania, an unremarkable bedroom community ten miles north of Philadelphia, because of my dad's job. There weren't a lot of Jews in Jenkintown. In fact, my memory is that I was the only Jewish kid in my class. Seared into my mind's eye is the humiliating scene of being chased home from school one day by a gang of kids yelling, "Go fly a kike."

I didn't know what the word *kike* meant, but the mob's tone was menacing enough that I didn't stick around to ask questions. When I arrived home, breathless and with tears streaming down my freckled cheeks, I told my mother what had happened and she explained what the word meant. It hadn't occurred to me up until that moment that being Jewish was a liability. This is my first memory of being branded as an outsider, a theme that has recurred throughout my life, in

many ways, sometimes by choice but more often by circumstances.

This came on the heels of Mrs. Baker assigning us to write
Easter poems one afternoon. Nowadays, of course, a teacher
in a public school couldn't get away with an Easter assignment, but this was 1970 and holiday-specific activities were
still standard fare. Since I was a people pleaser from the get-
go, when Mrs. Baker asked for volunteers to read aloud their
Easter poems, my hand shot up and in a proud but tentative
voice I went first:

> *It's that time of year again*
> *To dye Easter eggs all different colors*
> *I like to dye them*
> *Purple, green, yellow and blue*
> *Even though I am a Jew.*

It makes a better story to say I read with purpose, that I
had a political point to make, that this was my big Norma
Rae moment. But I think I just was proud of the rhyme and
wanted to show off; my poem's ironic value was, I'm sure,
totally lost on me and all my little classmates.

Whatever was in that ten-year-old head of mine, Mrs. Baker
looked horrified and my classmates giggled when I finished
my recitation. She kept me after class, and, thinking I was in
trouble, I felt a rush of relief wash over me when she apolo-
gized. Though this moment was long before political correctness had entered our collective consciousness, it must have
been obvious to Mrs. Baker that her assignment, while well
meaning, was problematic.

After I grew up, influenced by the ways of Washington, I spun that anecdote into a lesson about the power of the pen as persuasion, editing and improving on my own life to suggest that as a precocious schoolgirl I was a master of irony. It wasn't until I found the original document that I realized that I had superimposed my adult's interpretation onto a child's much more innocent motivation. I rediscovered the actual poem upon my mother's passing, in 1989, when I was twenty-nine. My father had asked me to go through her things and keep what I wanted, divide up the rest among my siblings, and give away the unclaimed possessions to Goodwill.

I found folded up in her jewelry box a piece of lined notebook paper. There was my poem, in my shaky cursive, the ink faded by time. And below my words, a string of a half-dozen little Easter eggs I had drawn with pastel-colored pencils. They seemed to be dancing across the page, hopeful oval shapes filled with zigzags and stripes. This was not a polemical manifesto but rather a child's art project. *Shut up, Memory,* I told myself.

So there it is, my life in an eggshell: my desire to be a writer, my desire to please, my complicity in my own disappearance, and my meek protest against that very fact.

ONE

Moses and Me

The most courageous act is still to
think for yourself. Aloud.
—COCO CHANEL

I graduated from Berkeley with a degree in creative writing
and a vague notion about wanting to pursue a career that involved writing. But before surrendering to adulthood, I spent
a mostly magical summer in Italy and Greece, first attending
a college buddy's wedding in the Italian Alps and then roaming around the Greek Isles with another friend. As Labor Day
approached and my funds dwindled, I booked a ticket from
Athens to D.C., landing in the nation's capital with not much
more than a duffel bag of dirty clothes and a travel journal.

I decided to head to Washington because that is where my
siblings were and I didn't have a better idea. First my sister
and then my brother—both government lawyers—provided
me food and shelter and helped me put together some semblance of a résumé for my job search. This wasn't easy, given
my spotty work history: babysitter, camp counselor, greeting
card author (a college roommate's father owned a greeting

card company and had employed me to write sappy verses to accompany cloying animal photos), and singing-telegrams entrepreneur (another college buddy had talked me into going into business with her).

A friend of my brother's who was an editor in the *Washington Post* Style section passed along my résumé to the woman at the *Post* in charge of hiring fresh-faced college grads (read: easy prey) willing to work menial newsroom jobs. "You'll have to take it from here," Ellen, my brother's friend, had said when she told me she had gotten my résumé to the right people, adding that if I got the job I shouldn't tell anyone she had recommended me until I had proven myself.

I was hired as a part-time "copy aide"—the phrase had recently come into use as a concession to the women's movement but even I knew it was just a verbal sleight of hand for "copyboy." Whatever the title, I was thrilled to have a real job though I was still too young to appreciate the sheer serendipity that my first foray into the professional world was going exactly according to my hastily devised plan. My main duty was to answer phones and fetch whatever anybody on the Style section staff needed—anything from clip files from the newsroom's library, which I was disappointed to learn was called the morgue only in the movies, to deliveries from bike messengers left at the front desk.

The best part of the job was the phone answering. The copy aides were the reporters' lifelines to the outside world, with missed calls from elusive sources, needy children, and annoyed spouses rolling over to our phones. I liked taking messages because it gave me a sense of how the reporters actually worked. After a while, I began to figure out which ones were merely waiting for some PR flack to call, and which ones were working the phones themselves and developing their own sources. As lowly as the position was, the pace was frenetic with phones going off all the time, reporters constantly barking out requests, and the unsettling feeling I was supposed to be in two places at one time, especially when a deadline loomed.

The one thing I didn't like in those early weeks was the way the head copy editor, whose job it was to lay out each page of the section, would yell, at the top of his lungs, for whichever one of us who was up next to grab the dummy, a long, thin sheet of paper, and run with it through the newsroom and down two floors via the creepy stairwell to the composing room where typesetters were waiting to lay out the next page.

He would holler, "Dummy to go!" and if you were next, you had to jump up like you'd just heard a bullet shot out of a gun. I didn't object to the running, and I liked getting away from the chaos at the copy desk, but it was demeaning that we had to respond to someone yelling commands at us, like we were dogs being told to fetch. Also, it made us all nervous that we might hear someone scream out "Dummy to go!" at any moment, and we might not be ready to go.

Other than that, I didn't mind the grunt work. I basked in the reflected star power around me. The *Washington Post* newsroom in 1982 felt like a grand social science experiment being conducted on hundreds of idiosyncratic journalists with IQs north of 130. I was assigned to the highly regarded Style section, a new, modern iteration of the women's pages, birthed in 1969 by the newspaper's famous editor, Ben

Bradlee, who came up with the idea of a section for an edgy, in-your-face kind of writing that would push the boundaries of where soft newswriting could go, stylistically, tonally, and topically.

Style would become an incubator for some of the most innovative and voicey and daring feature writing of its time, including that by Nicholas von Hoffman, Myra MacPherson, Tom Shales, and Henry Allen. And there was Sally Quinn, who famously penned biting profiles of assorted Washingtonian types—social climbers, players, takers, movers and shakers. Even more famously, perhaps, Sally married Bradlee (more on that later). But I didn't have much of a sense of this recent history, arriving with just the most cursory understanding that the newspaper and its charismatic editor were household names because of Watergate, and because of the movie chronicling that era, *All the President's Men*, which had come out just six years before I stepped foot in the newsroom.

Though the Style section had little to do with the paper's Watergate coverage beyond proximity, it shared a sense of collective self-importance and an aura of excitement that felt like a current of electricity was always running through it. Pulitzer Prize–winning journalists milled about, asking if so-and-so government official had returned their call, or if I knew where the empty notepads were (I did eventually), and I was making every effort to answer them without letting on that I was as overwhelmed as I was. I could barely breathe those first few weeks and spent much of my time avoiding eye contact and trying not to stumble over my words. Even though I certainly did not have a glamorous job there, I had landed myself in a glamorous spot.

We copyboys were young and female—Charlotte, Ann, Kathryn, Elaine, Diane, and me—and that was enough of a draw for many of the middle-aged male reporters who, battling writer's block, would often get up from their computers and come over to shoot the breeze. Usually three of us were on duty at a time, and we sat just outside the glass wall of the managing and deputy editors' offices, in a perfect row like shiny new sedans on a car lot.

The assignment editors sat in the next row, parallel to us, and they talked among themselves or to the writers they were currently editing. But we were able to hear what they were saying and just sitting in such close proximity to great editors editing great writers was worth as much as a year or two at the best MFA program or journalism school in the country. They would sometimes look up and realize we were there, hanging on their every word. Occasionally they would dole out a little mercy, offering advice to us about our (mostly imagined) writing careers.

"Let me give you a little piece of wisdom," Harriet Fier, one of the assignment editors, said one morning, apropos of nothing, yawning and stretching. "Don't get too fat and happy in any job."

I looked at her blankly, and she sighed at my lack of understanding.

"Always move on to the next challenge," she continued. I nodded, though I still didn't completely understand what she was telling me.

Harriet's last name was pronounced "fear" and she *was* a bit scary, in the sense that she was more confident than any woman I had ever encountered, and also louder. She wore black leather boots and tight sweaters and exuded an unapologetic sensuality. She had come to the *Post* from *Rolling Stone*, where she'd been a managing editor who had worked her way up from switchboard operator. I like to think we copy aides reminded Harriet of her salad days, but I can't imagine she was ever as tentative as I was, and it's doubtful she saw any glimmer of herself in me. She was gutsy, brassy, of the original lean-in generation decades before anybody was using that phrase.

The *Post* was filled with characters like her, and the more I figured this out, the more hooked I was on the place. The smell, the noise, the hustle—all of it worked on me like an aphrodisiac. I loved it in its entirety though each section had its own vibe, rhythm, and philosophy. As soon as you moved from the "hard news" newsroom (Metro, National, Foreign, Business, Investigative, and Obits) to "soft news" (Style, Sunday Magazine, Food, Home, and Weekend), the climate changed. The hard news sections were quieter—there was much less banter and clowning around. Reporters talked in hushed tones on the phone and I always imagined shadowy figures on the other end of the line, sources deep within the bowels of the Pentagon or the FBI. Their desks were messier with stacks of files and documents, and the national reporters tended to have fewer personal artifacts like family photos or cartoons tacked up in their cubicles.

The "soft news" sections were segregated from the rest of the paper. The cubicles of the soft news reporters were set apart from those of the hard news reporters by a mere forty yards, but the hallway that separated them was like a demilitarized zone, and when you moved from one to the other, you felt like you had crossed a border into another country. People would look up from their word processors, warily eyeing you, openly eavesdropping if you started a conversation with someone nearby.

I learned quickly that reporters had no use for social graces or nuanced manners. Men loosened their ties—the few who bothered to wear them in the first place—women kicked off their heels, and everyone spoke loudly and over each other. The exception was Judith Martin. She was the woman behind the popular etiquette column "Miss Manners," and it's possible that she took her job too seriously, floating around the newsroom in a royal haze, wearing white gloves up to her elbows. It was a cacophony of acerbic, inappropriate humor, deadline tension, free-floating anxiety, and not infrequent glimpses of genius.

Here, in Style, each person's workspace was a miniature art installation of personality: bulletin boards with labor union bumper stickers, "You can't eat prestige"; tattered strips of outrageous headlines—HEADLESS BODY IN TOPLESS BAR (now a cliché but then a tabloid news story about a hostage forced to decapitate a strip club owner)—and, when seasonal affective disorder became a thing, "Happy Light" boxes popped up on desks, casting their negative-ion therapy rays. Reporters often wore headphones, listening to music on their Walkmans, which had just become a thing a few years earlier. Others shouted at each other across the rows of heads, sometimes in jest, occasionally in anger, always on deadline.

The copy editors were the grown-ups of the newsroom, and they sat by themselves, in a bay of terminals off to the side. Their shift started around 4:00 P.M. and lasted long into the night, often past 1:00 A.M. Each day, they saved the newspaper from embarrassment and legal action and saved the writers from themselves, from errors of both judgment and fact, not to mention grammar. They grumbled about the collective lack of attention to the newspaper's in-house style guide for grammar and language, but secretly they were pleased because it was a constant validation of their existence.

I marveled at how bold and pushy the reporters acted, but eventually it became clear that much of their bravado was covering up a lot of garden-variety insecurities. It wasn't unusual for a reporter to get up in the middle of a contentious editing session and stomp off to have a cigarette or, even worse, disappear across the street to pout in the Post Pub, nursing a bruised ego with a beer. In high school they'd been the ones who had taken refuge in the school newspaper, or, if they were late bloomers, hadn't found their passion and tribe until they'd arrived at college, where they had stumbled into a campus newsroom and never left. They spent the next four years socializing exclusively with other student journalists, the closest facsimile to a band of brothers that civilians can join. And they continued this camaraderie when they found their way to the *Post* newsroom, albeit a bit tempered by what Ben Bradlee famously called "creative tension," the friendly, competitive pitting of newsroom staffers against each other for bylines and "gets." The newsroom crackled with a collective ambition that demanded you subscribe to or risk being left behind.

I hadn't been one of those J-school types. While my peers at the *Post* had hung out in campus newsrooms writing stories about their university's administration wrongdoing and learning about the inverted pyramid, I was scribbling bad poetry under eucalyptus trees on the Berkeley campus or in crowded, smoky coffee shops. Besides the core curricular requirements, I took creative writing workshops where I worked on plays, short stories, and novellas and talked about narrative arc and craft and voice. Not only had I never been involved in campus media, I had never even considered a career in journalism until I arrived in Washington. I wasn't yet sure where I ultimately wanted to go, but I knew I wanted it to involve words and stories, and people who cared about both.

Style was a great section for me to start my career in because it was a place where women had risen to the top ranks. I was surrounded by confident, competent newspaperwomen who didn't look to men for approval or permission: Harriet Fier; Mary Hadar, the Style section managing editor; and her deputy editor, Ellen Edwards. Also, working for a company headed by Katharine Graham—a legendary figure who had taken over leading the paper after her brilliant but mentally unstable husband killed himself—mitigated my overall sense that journalism was largely the realm of powerful white men. Nearly two decades later, in a collection of pieces about Washington that Mrs. Graham edited, she would observe: "Washington is a tough town for women—and especially for wives. This is in large part because, since its inception, Washington has been and remains a man's town. For most of the decades of my Washington life, it was men who were in charge."

It never occurred to me that it was unusual that a woman

was at the helm of a ship as hulking as the *Washington Post*. The few sightings I'd had of Mrs. Graham in the newsroom my first year left me with the impression that she was untouchably regal, even unearthly in her sense of confidence and command. I knew only the briefest of outlines of how she had gotten there. I didn't know about the decisions she made, the risks she took, and—what would be for me, when I did finally school myself in her personal history, the most resonant—the fears she thwarted or at least managed. I had no idea that in her own way she felt as much an outsider as I did in my lowly position. Despite her place at the center of power, Mrs. Graham also felt oddly on the sidelines and wanted so much to be in the game.

Though in my salad days, I also wanted to be in the game, and my perch on the periphery of the Style section was as good as any to figure out where I might begin to build a career.

I worked about twenty hours a week those first few months, hoping they would give me more hours while I struggled to save enough money to get my own place. I was living in my brother's brownstone at Fifteenth and Q Streets NW, a neighborhood on the edge of Dupont Circle that was slowly becoming the gentrified, trendy mecca it is for young professionals today. My brother, David, was then a happy bachelor, and he good-naturedly put up with housing me temporarily. The deal was that once I saved enough for first and last months' rent I would find my own place. He helped me navigate Washington and the beginning of adulthood. Right after I arrived he took me out on the front stoop and pointed in the direction of the *Post*.

"When you walk out the door, you can go that way. Don't go that way," he said, wagging a finger in the opposite direction. "The methadone center is two blocks over. Unless you're secretly an addict, you don't want to go there. And if you work late, after dark, you have to take a cab home. No exceptions, ever."

David was secretly proud of my job, I could tell, but he had a weird way of showing it. His favorite gag was to creep up on me just before sunrise, when I was still deeply asleep, and yell in my ear, "DUMMY TO GO!" I would leap out of my bed and run toward what I believed in my stupor was the direction of the copy desk. He did this day after day for a month, and I fell for it every time.

Copy aides were allowed to pitch stories, and if their idea was approved, they could go ahead and pursue it, as long as they did it on their own time. If a story actually made it into the paper, the aide was paid a freelancer's fee, usually a couple hundred bucks.

The Food section was particularly open to freelancers, and even though my idea of a meal was a tuna sandwich or a can of smoked oysters on crackers, I volunteered to write whatever they needed. Soon enough they gave me my first assignment, a medley of pumpkin recipes, and I turned David's kitchen into my own test lab. That's making it sound too sophisticated because my performance was more *I Love Lucy* than *Julie & Julia*. I also thought David and I might both throw up from eating too many pumpkin muffins, pies, and bread, but that concern disappeared the morning I picked up the paper off the front stoop and, spotting my very first byline in bold black typeface, ran into the house shrieking with delight.

AFTER A FEW MONTHS, just as my brother's patience was beginning to wear thin, the *Post* gave me a full-time position. I was still a copy aide, but now I was working a forty-hour workweek. That pay, along with what I made freelancing, meant I'd be earning just enough money to support myself. I was still writing for Food and Home (hard-hitting stories like how a Redskin offensive lineman decorated his bachelor pad and when to refinish your hardwood floors), but I also began to get assignments covering parties, mostly political fund-raisers.

I moved to a studio apartment in Foggy Bottom, close to the White House and the State Department and the Corcoran Gallery of Art. It was also walking distance to work. The building was art deco-ish and, if you squinted, it had a shabby elegance except for the occasional cockroach in the kitchen. My apartment was small but serviceable and sunny, being on the sixth floor facing east. It had parquet floors I would hate now but loved then and a Murphy table that unfolded from the wall in the unlikely event that I cooked dinner for anyone.

I was now truly on my own, gainfully employed, and my life was taking shape. My routine was to work the day shift, 9:30 A.M. to 6:00 P.M., and as winter approached and the temperature dropped, I was able to fit ice-skating into my regular schedule on the nights I didn't get assigned to cover a party. I had figure-skated since I was a kid, though I was never good enough to compete. But now that I had established myself in Washington, I started to explore the city's outdoor rinks and a few nearby indoor ones, too. There was an adequate outdoor rink on my way home, and I would bring my skates with me in the morning and stop there for an hour or two before heading home for a late dinner.

One day I was walking through the Style section with my skates slung over my shoulder, and Henry Allen, a Vietnam vet with a gruff voice that bordered on a growl, yelled out, "Hey, Blades." Not realizing he was talking to me, I kept walking. "Hey, BLADES!" he yelled louder. And then, in a cheesy Mexican accent, he hollered, "Senorita *Blahh Daze.*"

After that, whenever Henry saw me, skates or no skates, he would bellow from across the newsroom either "Blades!" or "Senorita Blahh Daze!" He would chuckle to himself every time as if the clever nickname had just then come to him. It was a friendly hazing, the first sign that I might someday get keys to the club of *Post* insiders. I turned bright red and fumbled and sometimes walked into the nearest desk, but secretly I was thrilled by the acknowledgment.

Henry didn't have much of a filter when communicating with other people, and he was slightly deaf so there could be little subtlety in any conversation with him because you both ended up yelling. But as eccentric as he was in person, his journalism was another story. A feature writer, he also wrote essays and criticism on whatever struck his fancy. He won a Pulitzer for criticism in 2000, and he put in thirty-nine years at the *Post* before leaving under a strange cloud of media attention when he got into a fistfight with a young reporter. This was in 2009, and Henry, in his late sixties and by then an assignment editor, was within weeks of retiring. The fight with a Style section reporter, Manuel Roig-Franzia, with whom he'd had a growing conflict over several days, culminated in Henry's critique of a piece that he deemed "the second worst story I have seen in Style in forty-three years." It involved a "charticle" (a hybrid genre of journalism that marries a chart or graphics with an article and is often the object of disdain by old-school journalists because it is viewed as a threat to the traditional narrative) about the history of inadvertent disclosure of sensitive information.

"Back when I got into journalism, the idea that a fistfight in a newsroom would turn into a news story was unthinkable," Henry told Politico. "The guys in the sports department at the *New York Daily News*, they had so many, you wouldn't even look up." (If this story isn't emblematic of the tensions between old and new media, I don't know what is.)

In 2013 Henry wrote an opinion piece for the *New York Times* about the *Washington Post*. He described the earlier days, before the Internet and media conglomeration and all those evil things that aging journalists like to pull out of their complaint boxes, but he also acknowledged that people, almost from the beginning of his tenure at the *Post* in 1970, had been asking him, "Didn't the *Post* used to be better?"

Publishing this rebuke in the *Post*'s chief rival must have been satisfying, though the loving nostalgia was what was powerful. "The *Post* that questioners remembered had yet to grow into its greatness," Henry wrote, "but its happy few gave it style, a sexy, ironic edge. It was liberal and Ivy League, Kennedy and Bogart. The hip female reporters strode around the newsroom and swore a lot—an F-bomb had to be dropped at every dinner party, it seemed. I had the feeling that any young man who showed up in Levi's, loafers and a Harris tweed sportcoat would be hired instantly."

Throwing a punch was not a professional move, but I certainly understand the impulse, and I like to think that if I had been born a man, I might be the type to throw more than a few. But it was Henry's talent that interested me a lot more than his temper. Being around writers of this caliber made me hungrier to write something worth reading. I wanted to produce journalism myself, but I also longed to develop the fiction writing I had worked on at Berkeley. The problem was that, at age twenty-two, I didn't have much to write about. I carried around a small notebook and jotted down ideas and impressions, hoping that one of them would incubate.

One rainy afternoon, a short, stocky reporter with a permanent snarl and possibly a Napoleon complex—I'll call him "Bonaparte"—was late to an interview across town. Until recently, Bonaparte had been the rock critic, but at his own request, he had switched to general assignment reporting. He declared that he had run "out of adjectives." I was particularly intimidated by Bonaparte's gruff manner. Everyone referred to him by surname, without the honorific, just "Bonaparte." He and Harriet Fier were chums, and their theatrical swaggering and sparring often commanded the collective attention of the Style newsroom.

He approached the copy aide station that day and pulled out his wallet. The three of us manning the phones were lost in our own thoughts.

"Hey, do any of you have change for a twenty?" Bonaparte barked. "These D.C. cabdrivers never have change."

Bonaparte was the type who regularly seemed to compare D.C. to New York—always unfavorably.

The other girls shook their heads but I dutifully reached for my purse, scrambling for my wallet. I pulled out a messy wad of one-dollar bills and started unfolding them, smoothing, organizing, and counting them into a neat stack. Bonaparte shook his head, tapped his foot, and sported his signature sneer. I came up short, at eighteen bucks. I looked at him, silently apologetic.

He snatched the bills from my hands, threw the twenty in my lap, as though I were a panhandler, and said with a sniff, "Poor girls always have singles."

Before I could answer—not that I had a real comeback—he turned and strode off. The other girls giggled nervously. My eyes clouded up, and I mumbled something before running off to the ladies' room. It was the first of many times I cried at the *Post*, but that time was the most pathetic.

As humiliating as the Bonaparte exchange had been, within hours I realized he'd given me an enormous gift. Skating around the rink that night, doing my warm-up crossovers, I brooded over Bonaparte's comment. *Poor girls always have singles*. At first it rang in my ears like a recrimination, but the longer and faster I skated, the more mesmerizing it became, transforming itself from an accusation into an incantation, almost a kind of prayer.

As I walked home in the dark, exhausted from my workout, *Poor girls always have singles* was still playing in my head, becoming a musical riff. Bonaparte meant *singles* as in *single dollar bills* but really *poor girls* had single rooms, single beds, singleton status. I stayed up most of the night. By the next morning, I'd sketched out the rough outline of a plot about a philosophy student working her way through school by waiting tables in a Chinese restaurant.

One night, when a new shipment of fortune cookies turns up empty, Rachel O'Reilly, daughter of a Jewish mother and an Irish Catholic father, cannibalizes Yiddish aphorisms and the wisdom of the great philosophers to improvise.

Her fortunes prove to be wildly popular ("Trust in God but tie up your camel," "It is better to eat vegetables and fear no creditors than to eat duck and to hide from them," "Hell shared with a sage is better than paradise with a fool," "Love your neighbor, even if he plays the trombone," and "The fortune you seek is inside another fortune"). It wasn't a stretch from my odd jobs during college writing greeting-card text and singing-telegram lyrics. Before I knew it, I had half a dozen chapters written. I titled it *Poor Girls Always Have Singles.*

DURING THAT FIRST WINTER, when I wasn't working, I spent most of my time either writing my novel or skating at the rink. As the months wore on, I was slowly becoming more comfortable in my own skin and less awed by those around me. I made some friends, mostly other copy aides, and we'd get a drink or burger after work, though we eyed each other through the competitive lens of Ben Bradlee's "creative tension." We all wanted to be journalists, but given our lowly station there were just two traditional ways to score bylines and move up.

The first was rewriting the news wires about breaking

entertainment news for what's now called "The Reliable Source," but back in the day was called, unimaginatively, "Personalities." It was the bottom-feeder of writing assignments, but you got a tagline at the end of the column. The second avenue to promotion was party reporting, and as the months went on I got the hang of it and began to get the better assignments.

I quickly discovered that very little that went on in Washington was actually fun for fun's sake, and parties were no exception. Politicians, lobbyists, and consultants all flocked to these events, conducting business, pressing cards into each other's hands, plotting power moves between the bar and the bathroom. I understood their motives, but there were other people who seemed to be hangers-on who had no clear function or goal but showed up decked out and pumped up.

President Roosevelt at a 1942 press conference noted that a lot of social types were hanging around Washington and yet contributing nothing. "I suppose if we made it very uncomfortable for the—what shall I call them? Parasites? in Washington," he said, "the parasites would leave." But forty years later, the parasites were still there, and they all had to do something in the evenings. Balls, benefits, fund-raisers—you name it—anything with pigs in a blanket, a mic, and a crowd, and politicians and parasites would show up in cocktail attire.

The Style section was determined to cover it all. If one of Washington's A-listers, such as the president, First Lady, a Supreme Court justice, or, even better, a Hollywood celebrity, was scheduled to make an appearance, a real reporter would be assigned to cover the event. But if the party was a strictly B-listers affair, one of us copy aides would be sent.

When we had one of these assignments, we waited until the day shift ended, and then we'd go to the bathroom, put on big-girl clothes and the strand of pearls that our parents had given us for graduation. We'd grab a reporter's notebook and take a cab to the hotel or banquet hall where the event was happening. If the assignment editor had given us advance warning, we would have gone to the newsroom library and read any clips on the prior year's coverage of the annual event, and if the paper had been given a guest list, the editor would go over it with us so we knew which people to get quotes from.

Covering parties is much harder than it sounds and significantly less fun. First of all, you're the only one at the table who can't drink. That is, unless you think getting loaded is going to help you when you get back to the newsroom and have an hour or ninety minutes max to bang out an eight-hundred-word piece that hundreds of thousands of *Post* readers are going to see the next morning. Everyone at the *Post* was aware that the publisher, Katharine Graham, might read your story in her paper. Just the idea that she might spot an error I made was enough to make a temporary teetotaler out of me.

Another challenge is that if you're twenty-two and short and look lost or disgruntled (which I've been told on occasion is my resting face), "important" people aren't likely to talk to you. Or even register that you exist. You are completely and utterly invisible. Then, when the important people find out you're from the *Washington Post*, they want to talk to you, but that doesn't mean they are necessarily going to say anything interesting. And taking a break to visit the ladies' room is a risk because actual news only seems to happen when you are in there.

This famously happened to my friend and colleague Liz Kastor in 1985, when she was covering a formal banquet for the *Post* and had the misfortune of going to the bathroom when Washington Redskins fullback John Riggins drunkenly said to Supreme Court Justice Sandra Day O'Connor: "Come on, Sandy baby, loosen up. You're too tight."

That line was delivered just before he passed out on the floor under the table.

The absence of breaking news doesn't mean that party reporting is without value. Covering parties gave me an education I wouldn't have found anywhere else. Important Washington business—networking and fund-raising—was conducted at these parties and at private ones closed to the press.

In addition to learning how political Washington works, the young party reporter also gets on-the-job journalistic training. Nothing makes you think faster or more creatively on your feet than having a rapidly approaching deadline, a tired and grumpy editor expecting copy, and a news hole reserved for your yet-to-be-written story. I developed a love-hate relationship with the process. I loved it because it forced me to construct a narrative quickly, accurately, and engagingly, even if its main characters were dull senators with canned responses and photo-op blown hair. I hated it because it meant talking to strangers, ones usually much older than I and always full of themselves.

The *Washington Post* press pass dangling on a thin chain around my neck—and constantly entangled with my pearls—

helped to legitimize me, but still, I had to come up with a compelling question. In those first few months, I sometimes fell short and the list of interviewees who responded to me with contempt is long. Zbigniew Brzezinski, Jimmy Carter's national security adviser and master of disdain, was among the top—if not *the*—most unforgiving of those I tried to wangle a quote out of, his cold eyes boring into me after I stumbled through an inane question.

I learned you couldn't predict who would be generous with their time and their wit, but no one was as gracious as Moses. That first spring, in May 1983, after having covered a dozen or so smaller parties, I was sent to cover the Folger Shakespeare Library's annual benefit. The guest of honor was Charlton Heston. All I knew was that he'd parted the Red Sea in *The Ten Commandments*.

I was assigned to the party two days before the event, a luxurious amount of time in the pre-Internet age to read up on the Folger and Heston. Additionally, I wasn't on the schedule to work the day shift because the Folger affair was a late-afternoon event. That meant I could sleep in and be well rested. I was intent on writing a great story. The only problem was I woke up speechless. Literally. I had a bad case of laryngitis, prompted by my newly acquired allergies, which the allergist had described as inevitable.

"Washington is a swamp," he noted in a way I could tell was part of his regular spiel. "No one gets out alive." He handed me a prescription. (Many years later I discovered that this often repeated cliché that the city was built on actual swampland was untrue, but as a metaphor it captured the essence of political Washington.)

No way was I calling in sick. This was the best assignment I'd gotten to date. I stayed in bed all morning drinking tea and slurping Campbell's chicken noodle soup. When it came time to get ready, I dressed up and waved down a cab, notebook in hand, voice still nowhere to be found.

Heston couldn't attend the matinee performance of *All's Well That Ends Well,* and he got there just as the 150 guests swarmed into the Folger garden, munching on Renaissance meat pies and chicken morsels. In my story I described him as standing, "casually chatting, sun-tanned and towering majestically above a few reporters." Somehow, after a few minutes, it was just Moses and me. The other reporters had gotten what they wanted, and now Heston was looking at me expectantly. I scribbled on my notepad that I had laryngitis.

Heston smiled and said, "Oh, that's a shame." He motioned to a waiter who was carrying a tray of wineglasses. "Sir, this young lady is under the weather. Do you think you could scare up a hot toddy for her?"

He then explained exactly how to make the drink as I stood nearby, stunned. Within minutes I was seated at one of the Folger's intimate café tables for two, sipping my hot toddy with the man who had led the Israelites out of Egypt. He suggested that I write down my questions for him on my pad while he watched: *What Shakespeare roles have you played? Is Macbeth your favorite role? Do you have a connection to the Folger . . .*

I took down his answers, excited and filled with gratitude, basking in the curious stares of the other reporters and the female guests who were obviously wondering what my secret was. He rose from the table, still smiling his biblical smile, and said, "And now I have a question for you. Did the hot toddy do the trick?"

I nodded and then managed to utter a throaty "yes" and "Thank you, sir."

He bowed and returned to the rest of the guests. I continued on the party circuit and met all sorts of Washington types, from presidents to princesses, but no one ever came close to showing that sort of kindness or class.

I wrote about everything from how to get your rugs cleaned (I didn't have any, but it seemed like a useful piece of information) to the perils of sleepwalking (I'm a lifelong sleepwalker). Being a young reporter is a humbling experience, mainly because you quickly learn how much you don't know. Luckily, I had good editors who saved me from my huge gaps of knowledge and lack of worldliness, which on one particular afternoon made itself painfully known to the entire Style section.

I was on the desk and took a call from the White House press office. I hung up and yelled over to one of the assignment editors that Nancy Reagan was having Jane Wyman over that afternoon for tea. Wyman was a popular film actress in the 1940s and 1950s, but recently around Washington she was known as President Reagan's first wife. Suddenly, reporters were jumping up from their seats and fighting over who would get the story. Editors were close to screaming "Stop the presses," while they excitedly figured out how to rip up the front of the Style section layout to make room. "Above the fold, for sure!"

But then Ellen, my brother's Style editor friend who had been my connection to the *Post,* looked at me and shook her head. "Robin," she said, turning to Robin Groom, the salt-of-the-earth Style social events editor. "Could you call your White House contact and confirm this?"

Then, with laserlike intensity, she turned back to me, "Are you sure they said Jane Wyman? The actress? Ronald Reagan's first wife?"

"Uh, I think so . . . I mean . . ." I have to admit that I didn't know Reagan *had* a first wife. I knew of Nancy, and that was it. And as for Hollywood actresses, I was lucky if I could tell an Audrey from a Katharine Hepburn.

Robin hung up the phone and smiled. "Barbara, Barbara, Barbara," she said, shaking her head. "What are we going to do with you? It's Jane *Wyatt*, the actress who played the mother on 'Father Knows Best,' not Jane *Wyman*, movie star and ex-wife of the president. That's who is having tea with the First Lady right now."

This was followed by a group eye roll and from-the-gut groan as I shrank down in my seat, shamed into silence for the rest of the week.

I did learn the first lesson of journalism: Double-check all names. The second lesson: Triple-check.

This wasn't the last time I had to learn the hard way what it feels like to make a mistake that could end up being in front of hundreds of thousands of people. I had a knack for rewriting the wires, which we did a lot for the Personalities column, and I began to get assigned to this frequently. One day I noticed something interesting from the wire service and refashioned it into copy suitable for the *Post*, then hit "send," moving it through to the editor. It was a particularly busy news day and though the copy desk was first rate, it didn't catch every error. After the paper's first edition was published, one of the copy editors came over and informed me I had written "Marvin" instead of "Melvin" in an item about the famously litigious defense lawyer Melvin Belli. When the editor explained who Belli was, I was terrified. If you haven't heard of him, Wikipedia notes that he was known as the "King of Torts" and "Melvin Bellicose."

"Would he sue me?" I asked.

The editor laughed and fixed it for the next edition. "He's got bigger fish to fry than you. But next time don't take your eye off the ball," she responded, walking off jauntily.

And then, perhaps my most horrifying mistake came when I was the wingwoman to Donnie Radcliffe, an old-fashioned social reporter who had covered the White House for many years. Donnie was the sweetest, most gentle person I met in that newsroom. And she was also one of the hardest workers. Careful, nervous, meticulous, she was a wonderful mentor and guide through official Washington. She was the go-to person for the Style section whenever the White House hosted a state dinner.

Covering state dinners sounds glamorous, and in a way it was, but it was mostly just nerve-racking. At one point, while Donnie was downstairs filing an early version of the story, she stationed me at the entrance where the guests arrived to note anyone of significance. A White House staffer was on hand to help the reporters identify people as they came in. When I saw a woman who looked to be in her sixties come down the line accompanied by a young man in military garb, I asked the White House press woman for the names of the couple.

"I don't know," she said. "I'll check."

I wrote down the names, but they didn't mean anything to me. Donnie came up and relieved me of my post, asking me to go file any quotes and updates I'd gotten. We had to file several versions of this story for the paper's many editions throughout the evening.

When we got back to the office later that night to file the final version of the story, Donnie read the first edition, which had been out for hours. When she got to the sentence about the woman, she let out a squawk. The woman was the widow of a former congressman and a well-known socialite and expert on manners, Donnie explained in a panic.

"He wasn't her date!" Donnie cried in distress. "He's half her age, if that!"

She ran over to the copy desk and had the copy chief correct it for the next edition. When she returned, Donnie told me that the White House provides a military escort for all unaccompanied female guests at state dinners. That's who the young man was.

Horrified, I couldn't sleep, certain that the next morning I would be summoned to the eighth floor where Mrs. Graham would excoriate me for my carelessness and then fire me for embarrassing her, the newspaper, and her friend.

The reality was much less dramatic. I dragged myself in and learned that the woman had already called the Style section and told them she hadn't laughed so hard in years. She loved imagining herself as the topic of scandalous conversation over cornflakes from Georgetown to Capitol Hill.

Journalism lesson number three: Never assume.

And then there are the mistakes not of fact but of judgment. I was sent out one night to cover the Washington premiere of one of the Indiana Jones movies, which was doubling as a benefit for Save the Children. Harrison Ford was to be there, and my marching orders were to return with a quote from the great man himself. I definitely knew who he was and was particularly pleased with the prospect of meeting him, but when I got to the event, I was herded into the press pool and we were cordoned off behind ropes as though the movie star were the president of the United States. (He later played one in *Air Force One*.)

"Can't we talk to Mr. Ford, just for a minute?" one of the other reporters asked.

"I'm afraid not," replied one of the young Hollywood types assigned to body-block us, the unruly, unwashed press.

"But that's why we're here," another protested. "To get a quote from him. We wouldn't have come if you'd told us we wouldn't have access."

The Hollywood type shrugged and tossed her highlighted hair over her shoulder. "Sorry," she said, sounding not very.

This led to a heated discussion between the reporters and the handlers. I could tell there was no winning this so I slunk away to review my options. My editor had been pretty clear about not coming back empty-handed. I finally decided to go for it, raised the rope, and did a limbo maneuver. The next thing I knew I was right beside Harrison, who was sipping his drink and talking to a Save the Children executive. I waited patiently and then opened my mouth. But nothing came out. It wasn't laryngitis this time. It was stage fright. He was just as good-looking in person as he was on the big screen, handsome in that weathered, rugged, attractively aging male way.

He was also short on patience for young, wet-behind-the-ears, starstruck reporters. Finally I mumbled something he obviously considered lame—I can't remember what—and he answered me in a tone that made me want to dig a hole in the floor. The only thing I can remember he actually said was: "I think your first question precludes your second one." Right then, one of his handlers spotted me and rushed over, grabbed me by the upper arm, and hauled me away, yelling at me about breaking protocol. Then another one appeared and soon it felt like a whole posse reprimanding me. Embarrassed, I escaped back to the newsroom.

One of Ben Bradlee's favorite quotes was "Never pick a fight with someone who buys ink by the barrel." That is true, but it's also true that it's not a good idea to use that ink to settle personal scores (journalism lesson number four). In the story I wrote I referred to Ford's handlers as "pit bulls in evening gowns." The editors loved it and thought it was a hilarious characterization. After all, don't journalists love every opportunity they have to put down a flack?

The paper never got any pushback from anyone about it, but this was before the days of Twitter. Before social media made it easy to widely disseminate your opinion, it took a lot for someone to write a letter to the editor or make an angry call to Mrs. Graham. But looking back, I regret that line. It just doesn't sit right with me. My redemption is that I use it as a teaching tool to remind my students that it's better to be fair than to be clever.

Lesson number five—First do no harm—applies to journalism as well as medicine.

TWO

The Man Who Knew Too Much

Those who tell the stories rule society.
—PLATO

Washington is a city steeped in a history that has been re-corded, documented, chronicled, and celebrated. But this city also has its share of invisible history—stories that remain untold and are forgotten and neglected. They haven't been captured in books or movies or newspapers because their retelling doesn't stand to profit anyone, or at least not the right people. The history of slaves who built the Capitol, for instance, or immigrants who drive our cabs and care for our children—this is not the sexy stuff typically memorialized by monuments or movies.

On the other hand, the Watergate scandal was sexy. It was about a president and power and his abuse of that power, and the main players were all white men: Richard Nixon, H. R. Haldeman, John Mitchell, and others. It was also a story about what happened to journalism in the early 1970s and key fig-ures like Bob Woodward, Carl Bernstein, Ben Bradlee, and others. They redrew the map of modern journalism, moving the *Washington Post* from the margins to the center, sharing prime media real estate only with the *New York Times.*

I don't think I fully appreciated my close proximity to this eminence when I was twenty-three, just a year into my Washington adventure. Like many of my peer group, I knew the rough outline of the Watergate story, that two young, male reporters stumbled onto the aftermath of a break-in at the Watergate office complex and that their reporting led them all the way to the president of the United States. And I knew that this story had resulted in a book, a Pulitzer Prize for the *Post,* and a Hollywood movie. It also inspired a generation to forgo law school and instead attend journalism school because being a reporter was suddenly elevated to a noble calling rather than a low-paying job for borderline alcoholics.

My intersection with Watergate's legacy came thirteen months into my stint in Style, in the fall of 1983. Though I was amassing bylines, I was getting antsy. We were told repeatedly that copy aides rarely moved up to reporter jobs. So, reluctantly, I began to look beyond the *Post.* I applied for a job to write photo captions for *National Geographic,* and just as I got through the first tier of a rigorous vetting process, I heard that Bob Woodward was looking for someone to help him and his investigative reporting staff of about ten reporters.

This research position on Woodward's investigative unit was highly coveted; anything to do with half of the Watergate duo was. But working in this elite section of the paper without the specter of daily deadlines carried a particular newsroom cachet. Reporters had months, even years, to report out highly complex stories. I can't say that I fully understood what a once-in-a-lifetime opportunity it was to work for Woodward. I'm not sure I even knew the investigative unit existed until I heard about the job opening.

Luckily the newsroom den mother who oversaw all the copy aides, an ebullient woman named Nancy Brucker, took me aside and explained the significance of working for Woodward, and so I raised my hand, putting my name on the list of internal applicants. When I got the call confirming my interview date, I became nervous. My brother had recently traveled to Paris and brought back a movie poster for *Les Hommes du Président,* featuring Robert Redford and Dustin Hoffman as Woodward and Bernstein, causing me to daydream about the dashing movie star looking over my résumé and hiring me on the spot.

The application process wasn't as glamorous as that, nor did it go as smoothly. First, it was more competitive than I'd imagined, and my credentials came up short. Second, I had been out of college for just a little more than a year, my degree was in creative writing, and what I'd learned so far about journalism was soft news. Geographically and temperamentally, the Style section and the investigative unit were at opposite ends of the newsroom. The closest I had gotten to investigative reporting was helping the classical music critic look into some alleged financial wrongdoing involving the Kennedy Center.

I just wasn't an obvious candidate for this job. I didn't like bothering strangers, which seems to be a prerequisite for becoming an investigative journalist, and I didn't have a driving interest in government, politics, or the economy. And

I had no familiarity with Bob Woodward's Washington, the one that is fueled by power and secrets. Nonetheless, after submitting my résumé, I got a call saying Woodward wanted to meet me and that I should come over to his office the next day for an interview.

Woodward was much more approachable than his character in the movie. Though he didn't look like Redford, he dressed more neatly than most reporters, in a suit and tie, and he had an open and friendly smile that immediately put me at ease. I had been raised in the Chicago suburbs so his midwestern accent was familiar, and I had anticipated the questions he asked, mostly about my work in the Style section and why I wanted the job. I watched him take a few notes on the résumé. He smiled and said he would be in touch. I got up from my chair feeling more hopeful than when I had sat down.

On my way out of Woodward's office, I recognized many of the other applicants waiting to have their interviews. Most of them were more senior. By now I realized how much I wanted the job, but I also knew enough to figure I wasn't going to get it.

This emboldened me to return to Woodward's office several times in the days after the interview. I concocted newsroom errands that would bring me into his orbit. If his door was open, I poked my head in and reminded him that I *really* wanted the job. I hammed it up and smiled. It was risky because I didn't know him enough to know how he'd receive this. He glanced up from his computer each time, smiled, and nodded his head in a cordial, if distracted, sort of way.

I was at the copy aide station when I got a message that

Woodward wanted me to stop by when I had a moment. On my break I hurried through the newsroom and approached his office. He saw me through the window and motioned for me to enter. He smiled. Was it a "sorry you didn't get the job" smile?

I stood there nervously. "The job is yours if you'd like it," he said finally, grinning.

"Yes," I managed to utter. "That's great. Thank you so much." I told him I had to get back to work and he said he needed to let the other applicants know so I shouldn't share the news with anyone just yet. It seemed inconceivable to me that the wind had blown away all the other applicants, leaving me still standing: Woodward chose me, the kid from Style, the one who knew nothing about national security, the intelligence community, foreign policy, and so much else.

I went into the ladies' room, the same one I had cried in on previous occasions, and I locked myself in a stall. Was fist-pumping a thing in 1983? I can't remember. I do remember I indulged in some version of a silent happy dance, then composed myself, and returned to my station at the Style phone bay.

A few weeks later I moved over to the investigative unit. Woodward said he chose me because I was the most persistent candidate, and he hoped I would pursue potential sources with the same sort of doggedness. But first, I had to learn the basics.

My job was to answer Woodward's phone and do research both for him and for the team of investigative reporters who reported to him. It was also my job to answer the main line for the investigative team. Anyone calling the general *Post* number with a tip even vaguely investigative got transferred to Investigative. Anything that sounded "interesting" I was supposed to let Woodward know about.

The problem was I didn't know what "interesting" in this context meant. The calls we got in Style were mostly drunk people in bars who wanted us to settle a bet: "Did Cher have a last name?" "Which sold more: Chia Pets or Pet Rocks?" We were supposed to be Siri before Siri existed. If it was a slow news day, sometimes one of us would go to the newsroom library and research the answer, if only to amuse ourselves.

But playing the trivia game didn't prepare me for answering Woodward's phone. I quickly learned that any tipster claiming that he had a story "bigger than Watergate" was most likely—as in 99.9999 percent—not in possession of a story bigger than Watergate, equal to Watergate, or even actually newsworthy in any sense of the word. Not only were most of the tips we got in Investigative not viable, they were not plausible. They were often, in fact, crazy.

It took me a few days to catch on to this. Maybe my fourth or fifth day on the job a voice on the other end of the phone confided that she found herself in a very bad situation. She was well-spoken. She said that she had extremely valuable information, so much so that the government was interested. It had to do with national security. She said that the government—she believed it was the FBI specifically—was following her, monitoring her every move. I started furiously taking notes. Then she said that the FBI had approached her gynecologist and persuaded him to implant her with recording and tracking devices.

My pen froze, midsentence. Her story sounded crazy but

she didn't. And remember, a lot of true stories sound crazy. Watergate, in fact, sounds a little crazy (five guys in business suits wearing latex gloves are caught in the middle of the night breaking into the DNC headquarters and one has links to the CIA and another to the White House?). In any event, I took down her number and said I would get back to her. Before you judge me too harshly, remember I was only twenty-three, a year and a half out of college.

I hung up and looked over my shoulder into Woodward's office. He was on the phone. I looked over the top of my cubicle wall at one of the male reporters who was transcribing an interview, headphones on and eyes trained on his word processor. Two other reporters, both male, were talking about their Rotisserie League baseball picks. The guys on the investigative unit were much more serious than the folks in Style; sports was just about the only chitchat they engaged in. Mostly they were focused on whatever story they were chasing, and these veteran reporters had a certain swagger that marked them as members of the Big Swinging Dick culture, a term originally ascribed to Wall Street types but that now applied to this mostly male newsroom culture as well. While everyone had been friendly and welcoming, I couldn't imagine asking any of these guys about this caller's claims about her gynecologist. But I didn't feel I had the authority yet, after just a few days on the job, to reject her out of hand.

The one woman on the team, Athelia Knight, had told me on my first day to come to her if I needed help with anything. Tentatively, I stood up and approached her. She looked up from her screen and smiled. I grabbed a chair and pulled it up beside her desk and told her about the phone call.

She looked around, leaned over, and said something to the effect of, "A lot of people will call here because of Bob and Watergate. Some of them may have useful information. But some of them, most of them, like this woman, just need someone to talk to. They don't have a story, but they are human beings so be polite and thank them. But don't encourage them." She looked at me and paused. "And don't mention the call to anyone else," she added. Her expression—a mix of kindness and sympathy—told me everything. She saved me from being a laughingstock.

I tried my best to get up to speed quickly, determined to prove to myself and to Woodward that he had made a good choice. Soon enough I saw an opportunity. At my first investigative unit staff dinner, in the Capital Hilton Trader Vic's Tiki Room, during a brainstorming session for story ideas, Woodward politely turned to me and asked if I had anything to contribute.

No one expected anything from me. After all, I had just started, and what could this rookie, this girl who was just over five feet tall, with a wild mop of curly hair, who knew nothing about investigations into the intelligence community, possibly offer up as a worthy lead for the *Post*'s venerable A1 section?

The Tiki Room fell silent. Eight or nine hard-bitten males and a sole female reporter looked on, waiting as I played with the little pink paper umbrella in my cocktail. Finally, I opened my mouth, and words came out, forming improbable and unorganized sentences.

"My sister, a tax attorney for the IRS, is married to a woodworker-sculptor. They live in Reston, Virginia," I said, before pausing to take a sip of my piña colada and looking over in Woodward's direction. In the short time I had worked for him, I had come to recognize that Woodward always seemed to be engaged in some kind of internal struggle between his midwestern politeness and his innate impatience with anyone who wasn't a potential source. Now his face was saying, *Where are you going with this, Barbara?*

I continued, "Recently, my brother-in-law was working in his studio when the phone rang. He answered, 'Rick Wall' and heard a female voice say, 'Don't be alarmed, but this is the CIA calling.'"

Though Rick started out as a furniture maker, he had expanded his repertoire to sculpture, and his recent work featured larger-than-life objects, like giant Mont Blanc pens and fire extinguishers constructed of wood with secret compartments. Rick's work was being featured in local Washington galleries, and he had been favorably reviewed in the *Washington Post*. The woman on the phone said they wanted to explore the possibility of hiring him, but he wasn't interested in building shelves at the CIA.

"But that's not what they wanted," I said. "The CIA needed someone to build spy furniture."

I paused after "spy furniture." They were just two words, but together they made a dangerous and enticing phrase. Everyone was listening now. I continued my narrative. After that initial phone call, the CIA arranged two interviews in an unmarked building in Foggy Bottom. They wanted a woodworker to build chairs with hidden compartments for cameras, lamps with antennae, tables with microphones. The agency's plan was to fly my brother-in-law around the world to different diplomatic outposts where he would install drop boxes for secret documents. They wanted to know, for instance, if he could make a secret compartment in the trunk of a tree in the middle of a forest.

Woodward's eyes were illuminated. It was an expression I would come to know, but this was the first time I'd seen it. I kept talking as he scribbled on his notepad.

Confidence momentarily replaced my jittery, eager-to-please demeanor. I was mimicking the sort of swagger that made it okay for the Bonapartes of the world to dismiss the girl Fridays of corporate America with lines like "Poor girls always have singles." Swagger was a by-product of the predictable pedigree of a white male who had graduated from one of the Ivies, who had interned in the most prestigious newsrooms, and who had never shown any self-doubt (that is, if he even had any).

I had graduated from UC Berkeley, one of the finest schools in the country, but it never occurred to me that that gave me bragging rights. I looked at my life thus far as a series of happy accidents. If there is anything I want my female students and my own daughter to learn from my story, it's that you have to claim what is yours.

The entire investigative unit was paying attention now, and before you could say "pupu platter," my brother-in-law was slated to become front-page news. Woodward assigned the piece to one of the reporters, Chris Williams, who would later go on to Hollywood to write for TV. The story appeared soon after on the *Post*'s front page and was subsequently picked up by the international press. Rick was a guest on Charlie Rose's middle-of-the-night show, *Nightwatch*. Two decades before the Internet became a thing, Rick went viral, and I had made it happen.

I hadn't known what real Washington currency was until I found myself in possession of information others deemed interesting. This possession was exhilarating; the best description of it I discovered years later in Richard Ben Cramer's iconic campaign book, *What It Takes*:

> Alas, it is the surest sign that official Washington remains a precultural swamp that it has not offered mankind any refinement of language to illuminate its own constant preoccupation, the basic activity of its single industry, the work of its days and the spice of its nights, which is *knowing*. There are, in the capital, a hundred different ways to know and be known; there are fine gradations of knowing, wherein the subtlest distinctions are enforced. But to discuss this art and passion, we have only the same bland flapjack of a verb that flops each day onto our plates, along with the morning paper: To Know.

My bringing the spy furniture story, literally, to the table was my rite of passage, my entry into the kingdom of knowing. In Hollywood or New York you had to be something special: beautiful, or talented, or rich. In Washington, you just had to know. I was hooked.

Too distracted by the lure of investigative reporting to think about fiction, I completely abandoned my novel.

IN THAT FIRST YEAR WORKING FOR WOODWARD, I helped him and his reporters with research for their stories, getting clips from the newsroom library, reading through documents, transcribing tapes—basically whatever anyone needed. My gaps of knowledge about history, politics, and government were pretty big. I tried to make up for this by working really hard. The reward was that when I did a good job, they gave me a tagline—a sentence in italics at the end of the story that said "Researcher Barbara Feinman contributed to this report." I collected them in a scrapbook and showed my parents when they came to town.

One December day, after I had been working for Woodward for several months, he came out of his office and said he had a little project for me. A book by Laurence Barrett revealed that in the final days of the 1980 presidential race, Ronald Reagan's team had mysteriously obtained Jimmy Carter's briefing book for the October debate. Barrett reported that William Casey, Reagan's campaign manager, had had a hand in stealing the briefing book. James Baker, who had prepped Reagan for the debate and later became Reagan's chief of staff, swore under oath that he had received the papers from Casey. Casey denied it.

Woodward's curiosity was piqued, and he wanted to look into the conflicting accounts and try to determine what had happened. The FBI's investigation appeared to be incomplete, and the matter remained unresolved. Woodward wanted to know if the FBI had interviewed Reagan campaign staffers to see what they knew about Carter's stolen papers.

The first hurdle was finding a list of people who had worked on the campaign. I have a memory of talking to a source on deep background—meaning I couldn't quote him, but I could use the information he gave me. Woodward had sent me. I'm pretty sure it was for the Debategate story, but I don't have a name for the source nor can I summon his face. I can, however, clearly see his office: the gray metal regulation desk, the messy stacks of files, a bookshelf behind the desk with reports haphazardly piled. An air of overwhelming bureaucracy and a sense of resignation permeated the room. The source was pleasant but inscrutable, giving me nothing to take back to Woodward.

I returned to the newsroom and said it was a bust. "Try again," Woodward directed.

"Okay," I said, even though I didn't think it would do any good.

The second visit was as fruitless as the first, and that's what I reported to Woodward.

"Go back one more time," he said, his voice flat and his expression unsympathetic.

Woodward read my face, which was telling him I thought this was a waste of time.

"People rarely tell you everything they know in the first meeting," he said.

I was silent, unconvinced.

"Or the second meeting, sometimes," he added.

I was nervous when I showed up for the third time that the guy was going to call security. Instead, just like in the movies, he pushed a file toward me. "There's a copy machine in the next room," he said, nodding the direction with his head, pushing his glasses up the bridge of his nose. "No one is around. I'm going to lunch. Put the file back on my desk when you're done."

I returned to the office triumphant, as though it had been my idea to go back again and again. To Woodward's credit, he congratulated me. Then he told me to get to work on the list.

"Me?"

Woodward laughed and nodded.

My mind flashed on that scene in *All the President's Men* where Woodward had a list of names that had been found in one of the Watergate burglars' address books and started calling people. In his version he calls the White House and gets Howard Hunt. In my version, people hung up, numbers were changed, people weren't home.

I began to feel discouraged until Woodward heard me on the phone and he patted my shoulder and said, "You're doing great." All that mattered to me then was living up to his expectations. I stayed late the next few evenings to work the phones for the story some more. Woodward stayed late, too.

At 9:30 P.M. one night Woodward got ready to leave and I was still dialing. He started to walk away after saying good-bye, but then he turned around and came back. He stopped and I stood up.

"I'm really impressed with you," he said, "I haven't seen someone work like you do—in a long time. You cast a big net over everything and draw it all in."

I just stood there, afraid I would say something stupid—finally I uttered a thank-you.

That weekend I went to a colleague's party and one of the guys on the investigative unit gave me a ride home. "Woodward's a nice guy," he says, "but he thinks he's got a patent on reality."

I laughed, but it scared me. I felt like Woodward had my future in his hands and that this was a safe place. It surprised me that someone who worked for him would speak about him with anything but reverence. Someone should have told me to stop acting like I was a hurricane victim and that Woodward was the Red Cross.

In those days, Woodward was known for his sharp reporting, and less so for his news analysis. But in an opinion piece accompanying the news story, he wrote, "Even though this is no Watergate, Debategate offers some troubling echoes of the past. There are questions about some top administration officials, about the attorney general's conduct of the inquiry, about the FBI's performance and about collective memory loss that is almost a contagion."

The other piece that ran that day in the same section, headlined THE FBI DIDN'T EVEN RING ONCE, described the agency's investigation into the briefing book scandal, and after pointing out some of the bigger names they hadn't contacted, the story noted:

> *Washington Post* research assistant Barbara Feinman, working with Reagan campaign staff lists available to the FBI, last week found another nine people from the Reagan operation not contacted by the FBI, including Louise Bundy, the correspondence officer whose office handled all incoming mail; Kathryn Ahem, who worked at the front desk, and these others who worked in the campaign headquarters: Clifford Heverly, Anne Graham, Laura Genero, Karen Ceremsak, Donna Eiron, Penny Eastman and Anne Brooks.

A congressional investigation was launched, and the predictable partisan sniping and blaming ensued with the usual scapegoats and intrigue, and the matter was never conclusively put to rest. It certainly was no Watergate, but Woodward's interest in it became obvious to me in November 1984; about six months or so after the *Post*'s coverage of Debategate had died down, I learned that Woodward was gearing up to write a book about Casey, who by this time was Reagan's CIA director. Debategate proved to be an early case study of Casey's tactics. Woodward traditionally hired a researcher to work with him solely on his books, and given my role as his researcher for his newspaper stories, I was next in line for this position. This was an exciting prospect, but almost as soon as I found out about the book, I also found out I wasn't going to be the chosen one.

One morning I arrived in the newsroom to see Woodward interviewing a stream of young people. When I approached him to ask what was going on, he looked guilty and uncomfortable. He told me he was looking for a research assistant for his next book, and it had something to do with Central America and he really needed someone who spoke Spanish. I had had two years of French and two years of Italian and could barely ask for directions in either language.

My head started to spin. I couldn't believe I was going to miss out on the opportunity of a lifetime because I had studied the wrong languages.

I asked Woodward if I could take a crash course, at Berlitz or something? He shook his head. He told me not to worry, that my job working for the investigative unit was safe. I was great at that, he assured me, and things wouldn't change.

Devastated, I went home and crawled into bed before the sun set. The next day I didn't get up; instead, when the morning light started to intrude, I pulled the covers over my head.

Recently I had moved from my Foggy Bottom apartment to a Capitol Hill row house that I shared with a couple of guys. I was tired of living alone so I had moved, happy to have more space and companionship. My male roommates were good people, but neither had had much experience consoling a distraught female. So one of them, a police reporter for the *Post*, unbeknownst to me, called the only other woman on the investigative unit, Athelia Knight, who was soon standing over my bed.

"Okay, so this is how you're going to handle it?" she said, addressing the room since I was submerged in the sheets. "You're giving up. Defeated. Okay, that's fine. You can just stay in bed with the covers over your head. Or you could get dressed and go in to work and tell Bob why you have earned this job. Why you are the best person for this job."

Athelia didn't suffer fools. Which in her world included people who gave up without a fight. Not only was she the sole female reporter on the investigative unit but she was also one of just two African Americans on it.

This was 1984, and she was one of only a few people of color in the newsroom, and she had made a name for herself covering cops in the nation's capital. At the time, she was working on a series about drugs being smuggled into the local prison by girlfriends and wives of inmates. She was fearless.

I slowly pulled down the covers, exposing my sad little,

tearstained, cowardly face. Her eyes bore into mine. I got out of bed, got dressed, went down to the newsroom, and asked Woodward if we could talk.

"Sure," he said, not making eye contact.

"I can do this job," I said. "What's more, I deserve it," I went on, summoning up in my mind Athelia's speech. "I've worked hard. I can learn Spanish."

I wasn't really sure, but I thought I saw a flicker of guilt when I said "Spanish," which, given the fact that the whole "needing to know Spanish" thing was bullshit, made perfect sense.

"Okay, let me think it over," he said.

The next day, I went into work and he told me the job was mine if I still wanted it, and he hoped I did. So we found a replacement for me as the staff researcher, and a few weeks later I began working solely as his researcher on a book that chronicled the CIA's covert wars in Central America during the Reagan administration.

For the next three years, my responsibilities included researching, reporting, and editing for the book that would be called *Veil: The Secret Wars of the CIA 1981–1987*, as well as for occasional breaking news stories about the unfolding Iran-Contra scandal.

Every young woman trying to find her way needs to have an Athelia in her life.

THIS WAS MY FIRST TIME researching anything longer than a newspaper series, and predictably Woodward's standards were high. My confidence had been shaken by his charade of needing a Spanish-speaking assistant, and I also felt some shame at having retreated into the fetal position. I was relieved he had relented but also a bit shell-shocked. His reluctance to hire me had the effect of making me bound and determined to prove him wrong, which was useful because working on a book with him would prove to be an endurance test.

The hours were long because they could involve everything from conducting background research Woodward would use to prepare for interviews, to transcribing the tapes he brought back and synthesizing the information from different sources, to reading through interviews to find discrepancies or patterns among sources. I had to get up to speed fast on a raft of complex national security issues. Woodward suggested reading material to help with that, and soon I was carrying around books like *The Man Who Kept the Secrets: Richard Helms and the CIA,* reading them on the subway or before I fell asleep at night.

We worked on the third floor of his beautiful Georgetown brownstone, our offices across the hall from each other's. We were close enough that we could hear the tapping of each other's keyboards, a sound that signified a challenge to see who could work longer. I always lost; Woodward could outwork anyone I had ever known then or have ever met since. And I've known my share of workaholics.

We established a steady routine, and after a few months, the book was taking shape. Though I seemed to be performing well enough, I still felt insecure because of the rocky way I got the job. Woodward, perhaps overcompensating, tried to make me feel more like "one of the guys," even buying me a set of expensive golf clubs for Christmas because I had (half) jokingly noted that he and the other investigative reporters spent a considerable amount of time discussing stories they were working on while they were on the golf course, and I wasn't a part of that general male bonding.

To no one's surprise, golf was not my thing, and after schlepping the clubs from apartment to apartment through a series of moves, I finally sold them. Over the years, Woodward was very generous with gifts. I knew I wasn't expected to reciprocate, but one Christmas I found the perfect present for him, a movie poster, Hitchcock's *The Man Who Knew Too Much*, which he proudly displayed in his den.

It was an endless blur of long days and nights that bled into each other. I felt part of the family, and over the three years I helped Woodward on his book I spent more time on Q Street than I did in my own apartment. I was fond of Elsa, a gifted writer and reporter who would become Woodward's third wife in November of 1989. She made sure we took meal breaks and she insisted they take vacations, which meant I got time off. Also, I had grown close to his young daughter, Tali, whom I often picked up from her mom's house or school. Working as a researcher on the book was lonely, and Woodward wasn't much for chitchat so I found spending time with a lovely and engaging child a pleasant diversion. Looking back, I see that the bond I forged with his daughter probably didn't help my campaign to be taken seriously. It was my choice, but it wasn't a strategic one. It reinforced an image that was counter to what an ambitious young journalist should be presenting. And yet, the time I spent with her became a precious memory.

The work on the book was interrupted only when Woodward unearthed information that couldn't wait for the book's
publication and necessitated a front-page article. I was grateful for breaking news—anything that brought me back
among people. I missed the newsroom—the hum of working reporters, the collective messiness of notes, documents,
and cassette tapes stacked everywhere, an obstacle course
for anyone moving quickly on deadline. Working on Woodward's book was a mostly solitary endeavor, and his orderly
and well-scrubbed house felt sterile and eerily quiet in com-
parison.

Loneliness aside, the education I was receiving from
Woodward was priceless. I learned the importance of meticulous organization in the face of copious amounts of material.
Woodward would ask different sources the same set of questions. Once I had the interview tapes transcribed, I would
print them out and cut them up, pasting together the different answers, writing the name of the interviewee in the margins. Patterns or narratives would emerge when, say, twenty
people provided the same answer to one question—or when
they all gave different answers.

Transcribing Bob Woodward's interviews—usually drudge-
work in other contexts—was a master class in technique,
persistence, and finesse. I would learn, by osmosis, the value
of the poker voice. If he hadn't come by his flat midwestern
affect by birth, I think he would have appropriated it anyway.
He scrubbed his questions of any adjectives that might reveal
judgment. Stick to the chronology. When did this happen?
Who else knew about the arms sale? When did they know?

Above all else, I learned, sometimes the hard way, to

meticulously check and recheck information. Talk to everyone who attended the meeting. Don't assume anything. Don't connect dots that you can't confirm are connected.

Though we spent most of our time at his home office, we occasionally went into the newsroom, which is where we were one day when Woodward asked me if I had a dress suitable for a black-tie event. He said he was sending me to the Watergate hotel to crash CIA director Bill Casey's private forty-fifth wedding anniversary party, to be hosted by Casey's daughter, and it was strictly off-limits to the press. He said it was going to be a little tricky. I didn't know what he meant by "a little tricky," but it soon became clear to me.

As we were standing there, Woodward spotted Ben Bradlee, the newspaper's legendary executive editor, and called him over to us. Woodward told Bradlee about the party and said he wanted me to get in the room somehow. They agreed it would be really interesting to know who was there and what they said.

I didn't understand why Woodward was involving Bradlee in this. Bradlee was looking at me and sizing me up. He acted like he'd never seen me before, and he probably hadn't other than to recognize me as Woodward's girl.

He laughed and said "Sure," giving Woodward the thumbs-up, but then he instructed Woodward to stay by the phone in case I needed to get "bailed out." That's when it hit me that they thought I might actually get arrested or detained. Bradlee was still staring at my face, which must have been registering horror. He laughed again, rapped his knuckles against a filing cabinet, and sauntered off toward the center of the newsroom.

That night as I got dressed in my black velvet, off-the-shoulder cocktail dress, I kept picturing myself behind bars. What would the charge be? Trespassing? Impersonating an invited guest? I briefly considered calling Woodward and telling him I had food poisoning. But I summoned my nerve, got in a cab, and headed for the hotel at the Watergate complex.

When I arrived, I asked at the front desk where the party was. I went down a spiral staircase and found myself alone in a hallway that led to the various party rooms. It was then I realized I was probably among the last to arrive. I hurried past a row of Secret Service guys, mumbling something about always being late, fully expecting them to ask for an ID. But they didn't; they just smiled and I smiled back.

By Washington standards, it was an intimate affair, meaning there were about seventy people there. I was the youngest by at least a few decades. I tried to blend in and stay away from the Secret Service guys, while also trying to look like I belonged. With a club soda in one hand and my little black clutch purse in the other, I hovered on the periphery of small clusters of chatting Washington power brokers.

I kept busy memorizing the names on the place cards for the dinner that was to follow the cocktail party. I would commit as many names as I could to memory and then rush to the bathroom, where I scribbled down the ones I could remember. I went back and forth so many times the Secret Service agents started making jokes about the size of my bladder. Otherwise, they didn't seem to be interested in me or the least bit suspicious. I guess a twenty-six-year-old young woman in a cocktail dress didn't appear to pose much of a security threat.

At one point, I was standing just outside a group of chit-chatting guests, including a cabinet member and a White House speechwriter, when I suddenly felt the cold grip of a small-handed person on my bare shoulder.

"I'll bet I know who you are," a woman's voice said in a singsongy teasing way.

"I bet you don't," I singsonged back, terror welling up from my gut as I turned around, steeling myself.

Woodward had told me that if anyone interrogated me about who I was or why I was there that I should fess up and then call him if there were any problems.

"Aren't you Suzy Garment?" the woman said.

I didn't know who Suzy Garment was, but I later learned she was a *Wall Street Journal* writer who focused on Washington. She was married to Len Garment, who had been Nixon's special White House counsel. Never mind that she had to be fifteen or twenty years my senior. I was still young enough that I wanted to look older.

"Look! There's Henry!" I responded and made a beeline over to Henry Kissinger, who was holding forth to a group of adoring women.

What I knew about Kissinger was that he had been involved with Nixon's foreign policy and that Ben Bradlee's wife, Sally Quinn, had written a famous Style profile of him in which she got him to admit he was "a secret swinger," something he'd never completely lived down.

A few minutes later, I called Woodward from a pay phone outside the party room to tell him I had a notebook full of information, but I was getting nervous that the hotel security, if not the Secret Service, would soon be on to me.

"Can't you stay a little longer, just for the toasts?"

I told him the seats had all been assigned and that surely I'd be caught if I sat down in front of someone else's name card.

"You'll figure out something."

Taking that as an order, I hovered in the back of the room as everyone else was seated and the first course was served. I nervously shifted from one foot to the other and then decided to kill some time visiting the ladies' room.

When I returned, I saw that people were finishing up their entrees. I listened as people clinked on their glasses to silence the room for the delivery of speeches. Bernadette Casey rose from her seat and said, "I wanted this to be at least a semisurprise. But you all know how hard it is to keep a secret, from Dad especially."

Everyone laughed and someone yelled, "That's what the Allies said," referring to Casey's intelligence work during World War II.

More people got up to speak, and I tried to take mental notes on what they were saying since I couldn't whip out my notebook. Even so, I felt the steady gaze of one of the hotel's staff. Finally, she walked over and asked if everything was all right, a polite way of getting at why I wasn't sitting down. I started coughing and told her I had this darn cough I couldn't shake and didn't want to be a nuisance to the toast makers. She disappeared momentarily and returned with a cough drop. I thanked her profusely, popped it in my mouth, and stood there smiling and sucking.

A few minutes later, I saw her looking at me and leaning over to another woman, who then went and fetched a man who appeared to be from the hotel's security staff.

As the toasts continued, I slowly backed out of the room and into the hallway, where I saw several Secret Service agents. I quietly kept walking until I rounded the corner and saw the stairs. I took off my heels and flew up the staircase to the lobby, out the door, and down the street, running as fast as I could, my stockinged feet cold and sore on the pavement.

I hailed a cab, jumped in, and before I even slammed shut the door asked him to step on it. The cabdriver sized me up in his rearview mirror and, reassured I wasn't a bank robber, headed toward Capitol Hill to take me home.

Woodward included a paragraph about the party in his book, listing about a dozen of the A-list guests and quoting Reagan's attorney general, Ed Meese, who noted in his toast that without Casey's 1980 campaign efforts, "most of the people in this room might not be here today."

NINE MONTHS AFTER THE PARTY, in late 1986, as we were heading into the book's final stages, Casey had a seizure and was taken from CIA headquarters to Georgetown Hospital, where he was operated on for brain cancer. Six weeks later, Woodward decided it was time to interview Casey, who had just resigned and was languishing in the hospital. Woodward told me to go over to the hospital and do some advance work for him, to try to find Casey, who was staying there under tight security and an alias.

I was unsettled by this assignment. It was one thing to crash a festive party, and another to enter the hospital room of a sick man uninvited. Still I went and roamed halfheartedly around the halls for a bit. I had met Casey's wife before (at a legitimate event, not when I was party-crashing), and the idea of running into her when I was hunting down her dying husband was an unseemly prospect. Of course she would have no reason to remember me, but still, just the possibility of that encounter gave me cold feet. So instead, I went to kill time in the hospital's chapel and thought about what it meant to be a reporter, at least the kind that gets the big stories.

I wondered whether I had what it takes, and whether Woodward had ever asked himself that question. For me it was a tangle of self-doubt and uncertainty about the profession itself. This was four years before Janet Malcolm's famous first line of *The Journalist and the Murderer*, the one so often quoted by journalists and journalism professors: "Every journalist who is not too stupid or too full of himself to notice what is going on knows that what he does is morally indefensible."

That's what was dogging me about journalism: Could it be done well, and by well I meant ethically and thoroughly, without doing harm? I didn't answer that question for myself then, and I'm still trying to answer it for my students, even now, nearly thirty years later in my role as a journalism professor.

But the self-doubt was also a problem, bigger than I was equipped to face. I remembered something we had learned about at Berkeley in one of my literature classes when we read *The Madwoman in the Attic*, an idea of feminist theory the authors called the "anxiety of authorship." It was the idea that women and men approached authorship differently, that women had too few role models and that this resulted in a fear of creating. In the classroom it was all so theoretical and scholarly. Here, in the moment, it was too real. To be bold enough to do what investigative reporters do—to challenge, to uncover, to create? To fight back the anxiety, the fear—I didn't see others grappling with that. It felt like a problem unique to me, my failing.

I left the hospital, went back to Woodward's house, and told him I couldn't find Casey. He went over to the hospital himself and was gone for a few hours. When I heard him open the front door, I came out of my office and met him on the stairs. I could see immediately that his usual veneer of calm and control was eclipsed by an uncommon excitement. He said he had found Casey and that they had a brief conversation, during which he asked the CIA director if he had known about the diversion of Iran arms sales to the Contras and when Casey nodded affirmatively Woodward asked him "Why?" The exchange was in a shorthand; Woodward had interviewed him more than four dozen times for the book and this last encounter was limited by the circumstances of Casey's illness—his speech was affected by the brain tumor—and the fact that Woodward had entered the room without permission so he needed to be brief. The implication in that one-word question, "Why?," was significant—that to know of illegal activity was to be complicit, and so how did he justify that? He said Casey had whispered, "I believed."

This became the last scene of the book, and it made headlines everywhere. And it sold a ton of books. Many had no problem with what came to be referred to as "the deathbed scene" and valued the insight that scene, and the book in its entirety, offered.

But Woodward also took considerable heat for including the bedside conversation. Some people thought he had invented the exchange. And many who believed him didn't approve of his sneaking into a dying man's hospital room. Mrs. Casey said Woodward made up the scene and was outraged. Her husband died a few months later, on May 6, 1987, and the book came out the following fall.

THREE
Loyalties

Everything is copy.
—NORA EPHRON QUOTING HER MOTHER, PHOEBE

In early 1988, *Veil* had been out for a few months, and I was still on Woodward's payroll, tending to the loose ends of a bestseller: fielding interview requests and answering correspondence.

But with *Veil* launched, and Woodward not yet focused on a new project, the clock was ticking for me. Though I knew it was time to look for new employment, I was dragging my feet, reluctant to leave the nest. I felt part of the family, having spent more time at Woodward's place than I had in my own apartment over the past three years.

His former book researchers had gotten jobs back at the newspaper, but it was becoming clear to me that I was more drawn to the book business and that daily reporting wasn't for me. Though admittedly a lonely endeavor, the pace of a book project suited me much more. Even if I wasn't working on my own novel, it was still a luxury to immerse myself in research pursuits, to chase down leads and make connections that required patience and careful work. But I had only one book under my researcher's belt, and though it was a book by one of the world's preeminent journalists, it was still just the one.

Luckily, Woodward knew someone else working on a book who needed assistance and he recommended me. This is how I would get most of my future book gigs: word of mouth among writers, editors, and agents in Washington literary/journalism circles. The author who needed help was none other than Woodward's Watergate partner, Carl Bernstein.

I was relieved it was someone I already knew and liked. I had gotten to know Carl when he came to stay at Woodward's house in the fall of 1986 to get some traction on his own book, to be called *Loyalties: A Son's Memoir.* His book project had a long history. Carl had attempted to write it in the late 1970s but hadn't gotten very far and then put it aside, possibly because it involved digging up some painful memories from his family's past. He tried his hand at network news as ABC News Washington bureau chief and as an on-air correspondent. But when that didn't work out, he returned to the book, and on and off over several years had been working toward finishing it. He was writing the book for his and Woodward's Simon & Schuster editor, Alice Mayhew, who had worked with them on *All the President's Men* and *The Final Days.*

Loyalties had several layers. It was a portrait of the Red Scare through the lens of Carl's parents' membership in the Communist Party. At the same time, it explored how their political activities shaped his childhood and his struggle to understand the context and circumstances of the 1940s as a way of better understanding his parents' choices. As if that weren't enough, the story also addressed his parents' distress over the book's impending publication.

Carl had an uneasy relationship with them, particularly his father, Al Bernstein, a graduate of Columbia Law School, who had held various government positions and then worked for the United Public Workers of America as their director of negotiations. In that role, he represented more than five hundred public employees who had been accused of disloyalty and were called before government hearings. Carl's father appeared before congressional committees five times.

His mother led lunch counter sit-ins for desegregation and marches to protest the pending executions of Julius and Ethel Rosenberg, who had been found guilty of spying for the Soviet Union. When Carl was just ten years old, his mom was called to testify before the House Committee on Un-American Activities. A newspaper headline referred to her congressional appearance as D.C. HOUSEWIFE TAKES THE FIFTH. When the public scrutiny into their activities was over, Mr. Bernstein ran a laundry business to support the family.

So for three months, while we had worked on Woodward's *Veil*, Carl stayed in a nearby guest room. He arrived full of promises to make real progress on his manuscript, but he spent little time on the third floor, the designated workspace, where we were toiling away on Woodward's book. Carl was loud and messy, gregarious and funny: the life of the party who was still there the next day.

But as far as I was concerned, Carl was a welcome break from long days and too many nights hunched over my computer reading Woodward's drafts or transcribing taped interviews or trying to find some needle-in-a-haystack fact buried within an intelligence document. Carl brought some much-needed levity to our regimented work environment, even occasionally loosening up Woodward, who was otherwise completely focused on his reporting and writing. One day when I came to work with a raspy voice from seasonal allergies, Woodward convinced me to call Carl—I don't remember where he was, perhaps he had gone back up to New York for a few days—and pretend I was the bad girl movie star Debra Winger, whose signature husky voice mine apparently bore a temporary resemblance to. At Woodward's instruction I bantered a bit and then invited him to a party "I" was throwing. When Carl returned, he told us about the call and wondered if the actress was romantically interested in him. Woodward cracked up and I turned red and we fessed up to the prank. Carl good-naturedly joined in our laughter.

Pranks notwithstanding, Carl considered his stay a productive one, telling a writer at *Washingtonian* magazine: "I got a tremendous amount done at Bob's . . ."

Apparently, "tremendous" in Carl-speak meant "something," but in publishing terms it meant "not finished by any stretch of the imagination."

That was a year before *Veil* was published, and now Carl was more than a few years late on this book. I had gotten to know their editor, Alice, while I worked on *Veil,* and let me just say she is not someone whose wrath you want to incur. She terrified me, like she terrified most people. Barely five feet tall, Alice is a towering presence. If you were casting the part of a prison warden in a maximum-security women's prison, she would fit the bill. Peering out at the world over her spectacles, gimlet-eyed, Alice was anxious for Carl to finish his book.

I absolutely revered her. The way she talked about books, their conception and execution, her no-bullshit manner, her quiet confidence—she was one of just a handful of women I met early on who demonstrated a steely toughness I knew I needed to acquire.

Now she and Woodward had cooked up this scheme to get this elusive book out of Carl. They wanted to send me to New York to be the Enforcer. I immediately jumped at the chance. Working on Carl's book would solve two problems: my impending lack of employment and my desire to get out of Washington, at least temporarily. I was becoming tired of the city's focus on politics and government, which I found two-dimensional and single-minded. With my literary aspirations as strong as ever, I was excited about living in New York, the publishing center of the world.

But before this plan was set into motion, Woodward said he wanted to address a few issues. Woodward was going to bankroll my participation, at least for a while, and he'd make sure I was paid for all my time spent on the project.

And there was one more thing, and Woodward seemed nervous, even flustered as he prepared to address this. Though he could be personally awkward, he wasn't terribly self-conscious. I waited until he spoke. He said something to the effect of "I'm sure you've heard about Carl and women?"

I nodded.

"I just want you to know I've talked to Carl about this since you'll be staying in his apartment."

Woodward laughed nervously, clearly embarrassed. I was both mortified (picture talking about sex with your father) but also slightly pleased he thought that Carl might behave badly around me. It meant he thought I had game.

I was flattered until I remembered a line from Nora Ephron's *Heartburn*, her thinly veiled roman à clef about her disastrous, famously-imploding-on-the-gossip-pages marriage to Carl, who had cheated on her, while she was pregnant, with the British ambassador's wife, Margaret Jay. Nora described the Carl character as "capable of having sex with a Venetian blind."

Even though this was five years after her novel was published and two years after the movie version of the book premiered, Woodward was not sending his twenty-eight-year-old female assistant to live in this man's Manhattan apartment without a little chat. I can still feel my face flushing.

I happened to be a huge Nora Ephron fan. Secretly I hoped that during my time helping Carl I would get to meet Nora. I thought *Heartburn* was hysterically funny, and I admired her for her boldness and her vulnerability, and, of course, her writing talent.

Her take on Washington spoke to me: "So we got married and I got pregnant and I gave up my New York apartment and moved to Washington. Talk about mistakes . . . there I was, trying to hold up my end in a city where you can't even buy a decent bagel. I don't mean to make it sound as if it's all about being Jewish, but that's another thing about Washington. It makes you feel really Jewish if that's what you are. It's not just that there are so many Gentiles there, it's that the Gentiles are so Gentile. Listen, even the Jews there are sort of Gentile."

Eager to relocate to a city where I could find a "decent bagel," I bought a round-trip train ticket with an open-ended return date and headed up to Manhattan. When I arrived, with the same ratty duffel bag I had schlepped around Italy and Greece, I felt out of place in Carl's world. He lived in a two-story duplex on the Upper East Side. It was a big apartment by New York standards, though cramped by the rest of America's. It was nice and classy and light filled, but it was also kind of deteriorating in a shabby chic sort of way, with plaster falling, described in a 1989 *Washington Post* Sunday magazine profile of Carl as "faux decay. It's supposed to look old and flawed and just accepted. A lot like Carl."

It was also a bit crowded, the rooms filled with elegant furniture that didn't really accommodate the realities of Carl's life, which included joint custody of his two sons and an ongoing book project that relied heavily on documents such as twenty-five hundred pages of FBI files on his parents. Those files spilled out of filing cabinets and onto any free surface and could even be found stashed between pots and pans in the kitchen cabinets. His bicycle took up space in the hallway outside the bathroom.

I learned upon arrival that I would be occupying the bedroom where his two sons stayed during their weekend visits. It didn't strike me as a hangout for young boys, but something more suitable for the Empress Dowager of China. The full-size bed was encased in an ornate wood frame with carved gewgaws and a vase of tulips on the nightstand beside it.

Taking in my surroundings, I was reminded of how different he and Woodward were. I marveled that the two together had ever accomplished anything. Every magazine profile about them emphasized this contrast and certainly I had witnessed it in small doses when Carl had stayed at Woodward's, but now I was seeing it up close and all the time. It is impossible to overstate the yin and yanginess of what the late great *Washington Post* managing editor Howard Simons dubbed "Woodstein."

As Ben Bradlee would later write in his autobiography, "Carl loved the midnight glitter. Bob loved the midnight oil." Carl was fun. Bob was not. Carl cared about fresh, expensive cut flowers in vases carefully placed throughout his living space, and Bob not only failed to stop and smell the roses, I don't think he even saw them.

I was anxious to get to work, mainly because I felt like an awkward intruder and wanted to have a purpose. So I began to furiously organize his files, the ones in his kitchen, on his desk, and in random cabinets. We made a list of what I should look for in the documents in his possession, what other documents he might need, and what sections of the book he needed to produce or revise.

When he described this scene or that anecdote that he intended to include, I was hopeful. But after a few days of catching only glimpses of Carl on his way out the door to the gym or some unspecified "meeting," I began to despair, admitting to myself that salvaging the great book I knew was buried within Carl's brain was like hunting for a downed plane's black box at the bottom of the sea. I knew it had to be there, sometimes I could even hear it pinging, yet, day after day, no box. Of course it was significantly more fun for Carl to hang out with celebrities than it was to stay home and work on a book that had become an albatross.

I kept myself busy in his absence, poring over stacks of documents like *Hearings Regarding Communism in the District of Columbia*, fact-checking quotes from FBI files, editing and proofreading the chapters Carl had already drafted. When he was gone, his absence was a reminder to me that I was failing to do my job and I began to panic that Carl would never finish the book. I wondered why I had let myself get into this mess. Of course I thought it would be cool to be able to say down the road that I had worked with both parts of Woodstein. And the Red Scare era fascinated me, particularly Carl's personal approach: rather than a dry history tome, Carl's book was a compelling read that explored a family dynamic from within a culture that spoke to me personally.

But none of that mattered if I couldn't persuade him to sit at his desk and actually finish the book. I would hear the sound of his key turning in the lock and then his footsteps as he cheerfully bounded up the stairs. He entered the room with all the subtlety of a leaf blower. Looking slightly guilty, he would then make excuses about why he had been delayed or regale me with stories about his fabulous life.

Carl was a masterful storyteller. I just needed to get him to turn these talents to his book. I never knew where he was or when he would appear or with whom. One day he would show up suddenly at home with one of the Baldwin brothers (Alec, I think) in tow, the next, author Kathleen Tynan. I learned more about where he was when he wasn't at home by reading the gossip columns, which were full of photos and juicy items pairing him with everyone from Bianca Jagger to Martha Stewart to Liz Taylor.

My desire for him to buckle down and finish the book was

no match for the bigness of his life. Though I had come to witness firsthand that even legends in their own time are still just people, with hassles and ex-wives and flaws like everyone else, they are still different. Becoming "larger than life," as icons do by their very definition, means they often leave little space for others.

Case in point: Carl is particularly good at filling up a room and I got to see him in action one night when he invited me to dinner, noting I had been working hard and deserved a night out. He took me to *the* Manhattan restaurant of the moment, Indochine, a place to be seen as much as to get a meal. I was excited to go and felt flattered Carl was taking me. I was also more than a little bit curious to see what a typical night out was like for Carl and where it was he disappeared to for hours on end.

The maître d' showed us to a table in a section of prime real estate and people began stopping by to chat, people whose names I'm sure showed up in boldface in the gossip columns but whom I was unfamiliar with. I did manage to recognize the name of artist Julian Schnabel, who came over to say hello. The entire meal Carl fielded people stopping by to be acknowledged, introducing me, trading bits of news with friends and acquaintances.

Another time he took me out to lunch and I looked forward to talking about our progress on the book and to establish what else remained to be done. But as soon as we sat down, he pulled out that day's *New York Times* and started reading it, holding it up as a sort of barricade between us, seated across from each other at a small table. I wished I had had the nerve to ask Carl to put the newspaper away, but I didn't.

Looking back, I see that these small moments had defined my future, moments in which I should have staked out my own identity and demanded attention. Instead, I vanished into myself. Now I urge my students, particularly the timid females, to speak up, to assert, *This is mine, I am here. Put down the newspaper, please.* Time after time, I failed to do that, complicit in my own erasure. Maybe I'm being too hard on my younger self—is it too much to expect a young woman, working for an older, famous man, to speak up in a situation like this?

Though I had trouble speaking up for myself, I forced myself to lobby for the project. I brought up Alice a lot, that she was waiting for the manuscript and we didn't want to disappoint her. In the end, he did it. When Alice received the manuscript, she gave me a lot of credit, more than I felt I deserved. I later would tell people that having me around cramped Carl's famous party-boy style and that he finished the book just to get rid of me.

I regret having labeled what I was doing as "nagging." It was a way of devaluing my contribution before anyone else did. The act of nagging has a definite value as far as skill sets go, but unfortunately it is perceived historically as female and is therefore inherently diminishing. I didn't acknowledge that then and tried to wear the "nag" badge proudly, joking about it, even encouraging other clients to call me a nag. The etymology of the word *nag* is, unsurprisingly, pretty disheartening. Besides being a slang word for "penis" and "prostitute," the *Oxford English Dictionary* defines it thus: "To find fault, complain, scold, or urge, esp. annoyingly or persistently. Also (in extended use): to irritate; to demand attention or make one's presence felt in a marginal but persistent manner." Ugh. *Marginal but persistent.*

The truth is there is an art to collaborating with people, particularly with those in the limelight who are used to being surrounded by yes men. A good collaborator not only gathers, organizes, and shapes the material but also convinces the subject, through gentle persuasion or not-so-gentle cajoling, to confront the stuff that doesn't make it into the campaign speeches, photo ops, or television appearances—those private thoughts, marked by self-doubt, fear, and regret that render something authentic.

ON FRIDAY APRIL 1, 1988, with the completed manuscript out of our hands, Carl invited me to join his parents for Seder on the first night of Passover back in D.C. where his family lived. I was touched by the invitation, and I looked forward to meeting his parents who existed for me only as characters on the pages of Carl's manuscript.

I immediately felt comfortable with the Bernsteins because they easily could have been my parents or grandparents. Vintage Old Left, New Dealer sensibility, educated, Jewish, Yiddish-speaking: this was a demographic I shared. I could read in the lines of their furrowed brows a high level of anxiety, and I felt a wave of empathy for them. This book was going to stir up a painful past, one they had worked hard to leave behind, building a different, unpolitical, and quiet life from the one chronicled in *Loyalties*. I also had empathy for Carl. It struck me in that moment that the gulf created by celebrity between Carl and me was not as wide as I had perceived, because no matter how successful or famous you become, you still are forced to see yourself through the lens of parental disappointments, frustrations, tensions, misunderstandings, and bitter and bittersweet memories.

It didn't take long for his parents to start asking Carl about the book, and as he dodged the questions, they redirected them to me—When would the book come out?, How long was it?, What did I think of it? I fumbled through my answers, trying to be neutral or at least diplomatic. I spent most of my time trying to make small talk as it slowly dawned on me that Carl had brought me less for breaking bread (or matzo) with his loved ones and more because I could serve as an unwitting human shield on the battlefield of Bernstein family unresolved issues.

I was confused because I knew Carl had interviewed his parents for the book and also had access to his father's personal papers. And in the book's postscript Carl noted that his father had refused to read the final version of the book, that he was resigned to the book's publication and "to the certainty that the book would say my mother and he had been members of the Communist Party; nevertheless, he wanted to register his disapproval in the strongest terms."

If Mr. Bernstein had rejected an opportunity to read the manuscript, why all the questions now? The *New York Times* review later clearly articulated what I intuited that night: "While the very form of the book is a running argument between parents and son over the importance of the parents' membership in the Communist Party, their real quarrel appears to be something else. There is a hostility permeating the relationship that even Mr. Bernstein's eventual comprehension of his parents' political position does not dispel."

In the postscript, Carl recounted how his father had pulled from his bookshelf a copy of author, activist, and Communist Party member Jessica Mitford's memoir *A Fine Old Conflict* and read aloud: "My policy has been to use the real names of Communist [Party members] only with express permission of the individuals so identified in my book."

"'That is the decent thing to do,' he said. 'You didn't afford your mother and me that decency.'"

This gets at the heart of an ethical issue that fascinates and dogs me: *Whose story is it to tell?* If you are compelled to tell your own story, are you obliged to let others' feelings dictate what you do or don't document? What if changing names isn't an option because most any description of a person in the public eye is easily identifiable? After all, Carl had only one set of parents. He didn't have the option to do what Jessica Mitford suggested and change their names. Is it reasonable to expect a writer not to tell the one story he or she is most compelled to share? What if protecting other people's privacy is at the expense of being able to tell your own story?

I don't know if Carl wrote the book to heal or perhaps just to acknowledge old wounds or because it's the truth and sometimes that's enough of a reason. Or maybe it was just that he had a good story to tell and that's what writers do: tell stories. I was annoyed when reviewers and profilers focused on the backstory of the book's circuitous path to publication rather than how well it turned out. I thought the book was heartbreaking on a personal level—the toll the Red Scare took on Carl's family, his childhood, and an entire generation.

Whatever the critics and gossip columnists said back then, I do think it took guts, something I doubt I fully appreciated at age twenty-eight. Now, at twice that age, I have a better sense of how painful it must have been to write that book. Investigating a corrupt president and his administration is tough, but if you really want a challenge, try investigating your own parents.

Competing loyalties inevitably arise in the process of auto-biographical narration. Later, when I would actually write books for public figures, I frequently met resistance from the "author" about what I could include in the narrative; they were understandably worried about hurt feelings or, more often, about political expediency. Ironically, Nora Ephron, who wrote about her marriage to Carl in ways he objected to legally and publicly, makes a compelling argument for Carl's right to write about his parents, though she was talking about herself at the time. She suggested you have the right to take control of your own story, if you have the guts to do so.

She is quoted as telling a reporter, "I think what I learned from my mother was a basic lesson of humor, which is, if you slip on a banana peel, people will laugh at you; but if you tell people you slipped, it's your story—you are in fact the hero-ine of slipping on the banana peel."

Preach it, sister.

FOUR

Ben

Three things cannot long stay hidden:
the sun, the moon, and the truth.
—BUDDHA

My mother died of heart disease in late August of 1989. Like anyone who loses a loved one after a long illness, I felt many things at once. Guilty relief, overwhelming grief, and mounting anxiety about a future without her. And again I suddenly felt a bit adrift professionally. Though Alice Mayhew had been sending me occasional editing projects after *Loyalties* hit the bookstores, I didn't have a long-term, full-time gig and now, at age twenty-nine, I was without a mother, a family of my own, or a steady job, and that made me feel vulnerable.

Shortly after my mother's funeral in Chicago, I returned to D.C., and Woodward and Elsa invited me over to try to cheer me up.

We were sitting around the kitchen table eating dinner, where we had shared countless meals together, when Woodward put down his fork and grinned.

"Ben wants to hire you," he said.

"Ben who?"

I thought maybe he meant Ben Weiser, a reporter then on Woodward's investigative unit (who now writes for the *New York Times)*. Perhaps *that* Ben needed a researcher.

"Ben Bradlee," Woodward said, laughing, Elsa joining in.

He said Ben was in the process of signing a deal with Alice Mayhew and needed a researcher to help him produce an autobiography. I looked at Woodward in disbelief. Ben was perhaps the most famous newspaper editor in modern times, and his book would chronicle a life that included a close friendship with President John F. Kennedy, his role in the publication of the Pentagon Papers, and, most notably, his legendary reign as editor of the *Post* during Watergate, famously immortalized by Hollywood in the movie version of *All the President's Men*. I had seen Ben strutting around the newsroom like a proud rooster for several years, but my only interactions with him had been as a conduit to Woodward. I would have been shocked if he actually knew my name, much less wanted to hire me, as Woodward was claiming.

I knew if Woodward was being more precise, he would have said, *Ben needs a researcher, doesn't want the hassle of interviewing candidates, and I told him he should hire you.* He added that Ben's secretary was expecting my call.

Within a few days, I found myself having lunch with Ben at the McPherson Grill, a nearby restaurant he frequented when he didn't just go down to the *Post* cafeteria, grab a tray, and go through the chow line like the rest of us.

I was nervous because this was the first time my exchanges with Ben would go beyond him asking me about Woodward's whereabouts and me supplying that information. This meeting was about me. Or at least it was about me in relationship to Ben rather than in relationship to Woodward. So we were having an actual conversation. Ben Bradlee and me (!).

Inside I was giddy. Outside, I was monosyllabic, petrified of saying something deal-breakingly stupid. By this time I had met countless famous people, through covering parties for the Style section and in the course of working for Woodward, then Bernstein. But Ben was in another league. For starters, he was movie star handsome; he was more handsome than Jason Robards, the movie star who had played him on the big screen. And, at age sixty-eight, he still *had it going on*, as my students would say. He had a kind of "animal magnetism," which had been noted in countless profiles about him over the years.

But beyond his physical appearance, or maybe in a complementary sense, there was something intangibly and incredibly compelling about Ben. He had made his name in Washington but was not a product of the place. He had the razzle-dazzle of Hollywood and the sophistication of New York and the pedigree of Boston. And above all else, he never seemed to depend on anyone else for his happiness, his buoyant spirit powered by a self-generating energy.

Even a charmed life such as his had its share of challenges and disappointments, but I never saw him break down or even flinch, nor was there any evidence as such in his very public life. He possessed a true resilience that, more than anything else, I would marvel at and try to understand as I got to know him.

But right then, during this conversation, Ben was talking and I was nodding, like one of those bobblehead dogs in a car's rear window. I had gone from monosyllabic to mute, and I couldn't stop my mind from replaying that newsroom scene in the movie *All the President's Men*, when Woodward, Bernstein, and Bradlee talk about Deep Throat.

"How much can you tell me about Deep Throat?" Bradlee asks them.

"How much do you need to know?" Woodward responds.

"Do you trust him?" Bradlee says.

"Yeah," Woodward replies.

"I can't do the reporting for my reporters, which means I have to trust them. And I hate trusting anybody," Bradlee says, then pauses. "Run that baby."

I had to shake myself out of it and focus and also try to exhibit something resembling a personality. *You're blowing it, Barbara*, I told myself. *Speak now or forever kick yourself.*

I knew I had better ask a question so I asked him about his project—What did he need a researcher to research? He said he had been thinking for several years about writing a book he would call *How to Read a Newspaper*. He would give his insider's view of the news. He told me he was about to sign a two-book deal for that book and also for his autobiography. He rolled his eyes when he said the word *autobiography* and mumbled something about Sally Quinn, his wife, and Alice Mayhew thinking this was a good idea. He would write the autobiography first, he speculated, because that was the book the publishers would be interested in. He looked at me expectantly.

This conversation wasn't exactly a job interview, so its rhythm didn't follow any logical progression or provide any obvious prompts. Was this the moment I was supposed to make my pitch? Was I supposed to sell myself? I just started to talk, describing how I had worked with Woodward, and then Bernstein. I told him that every book takes on a life of its own (I had heard Woodward say this on occasion, and it sounded good to me). I said we would figure out a process that would accommodate his schedule and work habits, and I would be there to facilitate it all. He could worry about the writing, and I would take care of the research and organization and preliminary editing.

The waiter removed our dishes and served coffee.

"So when can you start?" he said, looking at me intently.

He seemed almost nervous when he said it, though I knew enough to know that I couldn't make Ben Bradlee nervous. If it was tentativeness I detected, it was nothing more than the self-realization that hiring a researcher was a tangible commitment to moving forward with the book rather than just talking about it.

I looked at my watch. "How about in an hour?"

Ben laughed. He told me to call his secretary, and we would work out details like the "money thing." I should come over to his house in Georgetown and meet Sally, and I could look through his files and get acclimated. He explained that before he could start writing hc needed me to organize and make sense of all the papers and other things he had accumulated over the course of his larger-than-life life. And there would be people to interview, to fill in memory gaps or information that other people knew that pertained to his life but that hadn't been shared with him previously.

Not long after that meeting, I showed up early one morning, as instructed, at the Bradlee mansion, which takes up about half a square block in Georgetown and was once owned and occupied by Robert Todd Lincoln. Standing on the front porch, I hesitated. I wasn't sure I was in the right place because there was a mezuzah, a piece of parchment with Torah verses inside a decorative case, on the door frame.

Finally, I sucked it up and pressed the buzzer. The door swung open, and there was Ben, in one of his signature Turnbull & Asser shirts. He saw my eyes dart back and forth between his face and the mezuzah and he laughed. "You're in the right place. Buchwald gave it to me." He was referring to Art Buchwald, whose humor column ran in Style. Buchwald, I would learn, held a special place in Ben's heart.

Ben led me into the foyer. I expected elegance, but what I saw was opulence, with a *Gone With the Wind* sweeping stairway and grand ceilings that made me feel like I had wandered into *Architectural Digest*. Ben introduced me to Sally, who was sitting at the dining room table, drinking coffee and reading the paper. She was Ben's third wife, twenty years younger than he, and she had made her name writing provocative celebrity profiles in the Style section; though she was no longer on staff, she still wrote occasional pieces and wielded considerable power.

Ben showed me up to the third floor where he had a sprawling, messy, comfortable office that looked out on a pool and tennis court. Papers and accordion files and boxes were piled everywhere. Looking around, I figured it would require at least a month just to get his papers organized, and that had to happen before it made sense to do any additional research. Ben left me to it and I dove in, finding things like an adoring letter from a high school student seeking an autograph or a quote for a term paper next to a memo about Watergate or something related to the Pentagon Papers or his friendship with President Kennedy. That first day I sat on the floor lost in Ben's past, poring over everything, organizing nothing. Usually, a job like this would be tedious, but given the subject, the time flew by. I was fascinated and didn't realize that three hours had passed and it was already lunchtime, my stomach growling to remind me. Just then, Sally popped in and asked me if I wanted lunch.

"Um, no, thank you," I said. I have to admit I was terrified of her. She was portrayed in gossip columns as a social climber and backstabber. "I'm, uh, on a diet and skipping lunch these days."

Sally shrugged. "Okay, if you change your mind, come downstairs to the kitchen."

As the afternoon wore on and my hunger gave way to a headache, I told myself that this was not a sustainable plan. Given my fondness for eating, I was going to have to get over my fear of Sally.

In the meantime, I had my work cut out for me.

With Woodward I was implementer more than architect: he knew how he wanted information organized. And his book covered a relatively manageable chunk of time: William Casey's tenure at the CIA during the Reagan administration. With Carl, given that the FBI files were sharing space with the frying pans, anything I did in the way of organizing was an improvement. And Carl's book was a memoir—a discrete era chronicling the Red Scare years.

Ben's book was more epic and would cover his life, sixty-eight years and counting, and spanned many historic events and decades. Organizing papers for someone who has led such a big life takes care and thought. Archiving takes expertise, which I didn't have, and so I improvised. A degree in library sciences would have come in handy because I quickly realized that cross-referencing was important. For instance, should JFK's clandestine relationship with Ben's sister-in-law go in the JFK years or topically under "lying"—one of Ben's pet obsessions—or for the *How to Read a Newspaper* book maybe it would go under "Sources: conflict of interest"?

Soon after that, *Dossier* magazine, which covered social Washington, ran a few sentences in a column called "Eyes Only" about Ben's two-book deal. He was quoted as saying he had hired me to sort "years of accumulated junk into two piles, one about our business and the other anything you want to call it." I was disappointed that he characterized my role as merely "sorting," but I reminded myself how lucky I was to have the job. I told myself it didn't matter what anyone else thought, and, after all, I *was* "sorting," even if that was just the first of many stages in producing a book.

I focused on the work in front of me, preoccupied with the enormity of material and what a Herculean effort it would take to get it cataloged into some sort of usable system. I quickly got over my fear of Sally and soon looked forward to eating lunch with her on the days she was home. She was funny and welcoming and took an interest in me. Once Ben and I began working mostly at the *Washington Post* offices, I missed seeing Sally. But occasionally I needed something from the files at home, and I was happy to get a chance to catch up with her.

IT TOOK LONGER than I had first estimated but finally, after a few months, I had all the existing material sorted into some semblance of an order. Ben and I were then able to take stock of what we had and could identify gaps in his chronology and unfolding narrative. We made a list of people to interview, and Ben decided whom he would interview, whom I would, and whom we would tackle together. One of the reasons I did some of the interviewing alone was because it's hard to get people to be honest about someone, especially someone as legendary as Ben was, when the legend is sitting right there in an armchair. Ben knew that and he decided it would be more effective if I talked to some people about their memories of him without him present.

Ben also felt he needed to interview some people himself, and he took me along primarily to run the tape recorder. But I was also there in case the interview turned into a bull session, and at that point, he instructed me, I should gently nudge things back on track. It happened a few times, mainly because Ben was so much fun to talk to and whoever we were interviewing was eager to reminisce with him. But sometimes they veered off into topics that had nothing to do with the project. Then I would speak up and ask a question to try to get things back on track.

Over the next year, we worked our way through the list.

One of the first people on my list was an old war buddy of Ben's from World War II when Ben had been a naval officer. Ben hadn't wanted to do the interview because he thought it would devolve into two old guys sitting around telling war stories. It would be more efficient if I went alone, he thought. In the book, Ben would later describe Robert Edmund Lee as "my best pal and my model, probably because he was so many things I was not." One of those things he was turned out to be easily insulted. After I conducted the interview with him, he wrote a letter to Ben that began by praising Ben for his illustrious career and saluting him for his achievements. But then the letter got to the part about me and a line that I cherish to this day. "I must say I was a little pissed off," he said, "when you sent a little girl around a couple of months ago to interview me in aid of your autobiography." At the time I felt Gloria Steinem and Betty Friedan rising up in me but now it just makes me laugh and roll my eyes.

I was thirty-one years old in 1991. Not exactly "a little girl." But I am a girl. Ben and I shared a laugh, after my initial flash of consternation. Ben just shrugged and rolled his eyes. I inferred from this—and from how he reacted (or didn't react) to practically every other unpleasantness that came across his desk—that you can either let things get to you or you can shake them off. Sure, it's easier to shake them off when you're blue-blood Harvard educated, but I told myself the letter writer was revealing more about his own insecurities than any true deficiencies of mine.

Later in the letter Mr. Lee made a pitch for ensuring that their glory days together found their way into Ben's book. He asked if perhaps it was neither Watergate nor the Pentagon Papers that had been Ben's finest hours but rather their shared experience on Treasury Island: "There you had no phalanx of lawyers, publishers and other editors backing you up: only a simple microphone that enabled you single-handedly to direct 40 Marine pilots how to keep more than 100 Japanese planes from fucking up the landing and deny-

ing Treasury's role as the air staging point for the Bougain-
ville Invasion. There's one for the autobiography."

I understood his point—even if Ben hadn't meant to come
off as dismissive, it must have stung that Ben didn't interview him himself. They had been through hell together. But
still. *Little girl.* It irked me.

That momentary slight was easily eclipsed by the many
highlights of the job. One of those was being invited to join Ben
when he interviewed Katharine Graham for his book. I suspect
he took me along because the prospect of interviewing "Kay,"
his boss and perhaps his biggest champion, was a little bit awkward. Here they were, two newspaper legends, whose lives and
personal histories were inextricably linked; Mrs. Graham was
also working on her autobiography and so they found themselves in the strange situation of simultaneously being major
characters in each other's unfolding literary narratives.

As I listened to them talk, I wondered how they could not
feel at least a little bit competitive and even a bit nervous
about what each would say about the other. Ben's book, *A
Good Life*, came out first; she joked she was going to call hers
A Better Life.

She could have also joked she would call it *A Better Book*,
because it got more laudatory reviews and even won the
Pulitzer Prize for biography. Plenty has been written about
their friendship and working relationship. What I remember
witnessing is the genuine affection they had for each other,
and Ben's deference to her, out of admiration and respect. I
hadn't seen him defer to anyone else, not even Sally. But his
bond with Mrs. Graham was immutable and, at least to me,
largely impenetrable.

I was reminded of this private world that just the two of them inhabited a few years after I left Ben's employ. It was 1997, just after Mrs. Graham's book was published. I had moved on to other book projects and was also teaching part-time. As busy as I was, I missed working with Ben so I convinced him to coteach a class with me at Georgetown University. I pitched him the idea of teaching a course that would cover the material that was supposed to be the basis for the second book he had agreed to write: *How to Read a Newspaper*. I told him that teaching the class would help him organize his thoughts and generate new material. (It was a good idea, but even after a semester of teaching, he still didn't write the book. I suspected that book writing required more focus than he felt like summoning up, and it wasn't much fun. At age seventy-five, he didn't have anything to prove.)

Mrs. Graham visited our class that April. It was clear that still, after all these years, and so many successes, they both felt really lucky. They shared the strange combination of confidence and a sense of having good fortune. The bond between the two of them was as strong as ever. We all sat in a circle, about fifteen students, Ben, Mrs. Graham, and me. Mrs. Graham talked about meeting Ben and hiring him, how he tread gently at first, not wanting to barge into the newsroom and be perceived as a heavy-handed manager who didn't understand the existing culture.

"He wasn't very pushy or anything. It was a good beginning," she said.

This was nearly the end of the semester, and Ben had enjoyed teaching and was very fond of the students. "Kay was right. I didn't really know her very well but . . . this is some-one whom I love. And someone who is such a fine person. So gutsy."

I remember the classroom was silent. Everyone under-stood that just to be in their company in such a small, private space was a gift. For journalism students, this was as good as it gets.

AFTER A WHILE we realized that Ben wasn't producing pages very quickly or consistently. We came to the conclusion that one way to get a book out of him would be for me to inter-view him. The interviews, if we went chronologically, would provide an organic structure, and as we amassed anecdotes and events we would be able to determine what to include and where to fill in material we got from the interviews we did with other people. I would then transcribe the tapes and provide him with all the material he needed to write each chapter and then the chapters would come back to me for editing, proofreading, and fact-checking before we sent them up to Alice.

So we set up a schedule of appointments and met at the designated hour over several months. We started with no ground rules: I could ask Ben anything I wanted, and he could answer any way he chose. This is one of the vexing things about being a researcher or book doctor or ghostwriter; you have amazing access to material but little editorial control.

But it was enough for me, plenty in fact, to be in his pres-ence and to have license to sate my curiosity. And, like anyone familiar with Ben's history, I was curious about his friendship with President Kennedy. They had become friends when the young senator and Jackie moved in across the street from Ben's Georgetown house.

Ben had written a short book called *Conversations with Kennedy* that was published more than a decade after the president's assassination. It left me with more questions than it answered, particularly about Kennedy's infidelities, which spoke to a lapse in judgment and his basic decency as a spouse. I wondered if that affected Ben's view of this man he professed to admire so greatly?

Much has been written about whether Ben knew about his friend's infidelities while they were going on. Ben told me time and again that he hadn't known, not even that his own sister-in-law, the sister of Tony Bradlee (Ben's second wife), had had a two-year affair with Kennedy when he was in the White House. While that shocked Ben, he told me what shocked him even more was learning later about the president's involvement with Judith Exner, the mistress of a Mafia member. Besides shocking, he told me, he found it depressing to learn that the president of the United States and a Mafia leader shared a mistress. He noted that could never happen now, that society had changed so much. He mused that a president would be completely disgraced. Kennedy's recklessness troubled him deeply. It was something I could see he hadn't resolved in his own head, even after all these years. But since he couldn't come to terms with it, he just compartmentalized it.

President Kennedy's secret private life seemed like something out of an airport thriller. A cartoonish dashing president who puts the nation at risk with his foolhardy dalliances. Was

Ben sure that the affair had happened? This sounded like one of those stories that Ben deemed "too good to check."

He said he was sure and noted that one of the great Washington status symbols was to have access to private phone numbers of public people. Ben had them and so did Exner, in particular, the direct dial to Kennedy's secretary, Evelyn Lincoln.

This was one of those conversations that reminded me how much I loved my work. I was talking to a newspaperman who had been an intimate of perhaps our nation's most glamorous first couple. And witnessing Ben mentally time-travel back thirty years to the 1960s made the Kennedys all the more real.

"Were they in love?" I asked, referring to the president and First Lady.

Ben paused, reflecting. He thought despite all the womanizing that Jack did love Jackie. And Jackie, how did she feel about her husband? You could never really know what was in someone else's heart. But it seemed to him she was truly in love with who she *hoped* the president was. But also, it was obvious to Ben that she had taken to the First Lady role and she enjoyed the whole Camelot thing, right up to the end. "She did so well in the funeral. She was just extraordinary."

WHEN WE GOT TO THE 1970S AND WATERGATE, I felt more prepared than I had for earlier events. I had read Woodward's and Bernstein's books, seen the movie, and I had dug into Ben's files. I not only was familiar with the material, but I knew some of the players. The hard part was coming up with a question for Ben that he hadn't already been asked and answered or dodged a thousand times. This challenge illuminated for me something I've raised with my journalism students over the years: How do you find a new way to approach old news?

Even if readers weren't expecting Ben to divulge some previously withheld piece of information, they would rightfully be looking for his insights gained in the years following Watergate. So instead of questioning him about the *Post*'s reporting on the scandal, I prodded him to reflect on what it had all meant and how it had affected official Washington and the way the news is reported.

We had decided we would do these sessions in my airless little office because it was tucked away on another floor far from the newsroom with its distractions and curious onlookers. I'll never forget how odd Ben looked, with his broad shoulders and big persona, folded into the one small, uncomfortable chair I had for visitors. I was behind my desk, and it felt even odder with our roles, or at least the power balance, seemingly reversed.

So what to ask him about the Watergate years? Deep Throat as a topic was a nonstarter. Having worked for all three of these Watergate legends, I knew how seriously they all took the sanctity of the secret. (It would be another fifteen years until former FBI official Mark Felt revealed through a spokesperson in a 2005 *Vanity Fair* piece that he was Woodward's source dubbed "Deep Throat.")

But one day I did ask Ben: "Do you get sick of it, the Deep Throat part of it, people always asking you who it is?"

"I mean, they always sort of [ask] Who's Deep Throat,

that's sort of a standard. No, I can say this to you, there's a residual fear in my soul that that isn't quite straight."

My heart sank. I was both fascinated and disturbed. I thought about the Bill Casey deathbed scene and the flap that broke out when *Veil* was published. People cast doubt on whether it had actually happened, including Casey's own wife. But I had been there that day when Woodward came back from the interview; it was still fresh in my mind because that was just four years earlier. It was too much of a stretch for Woodward to have gone to the hospital, concocted the deathbed conversation, and then returned home and playacted his excitement over the "get." I didn't believe that Woodward would have embellished what happened with Casey or Deep Throat or anything else.

"And do you think that's partially because of the Janet Cooke thing?" I asked Ben.

The Janet Cooke debacle had been one of the few incidents in Ben's career that he hadn't been able to shake off. (Woodward, who was Metro editor at the time, also felt stained by the episode, publicly sharing responsibility for the false story having been published.) Cooke was a young and ambitious Metro reporter who had fabricated a story about "Jimmy," an eight-year-old heroin addict who had been turned on to the drug by his mother's boyfriend. The front-page story rocked the city of Washington as officials scrambled to find the boy and save him.

Well, the reason they couldn't find him was that he didn't exist. But this wasn't revealed until after the reporter won a Pulitzer and discrepancies in her bio began to surface. This took much longer to happen than it would in today's Internet world. For the paper riding high on the glory of Watergate, this was a disaster that happened under Ben's watch, one he never completely got over.

He brooded about it on the rare occasions he allowed his mind to go there. The brooding led to his fascination with deception. He immersed himself in the topic, carefully studying the work of Sissela Bok, a Harvard professor who studied liars and their motivations. People lying to you, your sources or your own reporters, was the one thing he didn't know how to guard against in any sort of foolproof way, and that gnawed at him. Sure, you could have a two-source rule, but what if two sources lied to you? Or what if the reporter lied to his editors about having two sources? I was used to hearing him muse along these lines, but this was the first time he had done so specifically in the context of the *Post*'s Watergate coverage.

"I mean, I know that you trust them, but do you think that that fear—" I asked. Alarmed, I was trying to get him to say that it was an irrational fear that prompted him to wonder about this stuff.

I was afraid this rare moment of introspection was about to pass, this uncharacteristic raw reflection was quickly dissipating. I wanted the honesty for the good of the book but at the same time, I was troubled by the honesty. "You can't argue with success. I mean, one way or another they were right. Whether they've embellished that or not," Ben said.

He was now talking more to himself than to me, noting that Woodward had promised to reveal the identity of his famously unnamed source after the mystery man died. When that happened, Ben speculated, it would set off a flurry of people trying to fact-check whether it was true.

While he was imagining a day in the future when Deep Throat died and his identity could then be revealed, my mind flashed on something else, something I had wondered about but never actually expressed aloud. Now was my chance: How did Ben feel about the Casey deathbed confession?

Ben said he had no doubts about whether Woodward had actually gained entry into Casey's hospital room.

I told Ben that Woodward had sent me there first, to locate Casey—who was checked in under an alias—and scope out the security situation. I admitted to Ben that I went but chickened out, that I felt nervous and uncomfortable and returned home empty-handed. I described how excited Woodward was when he returned from having found Casey.

"I have some doubts as to what Casey said," Ben told me.

I was stunned. Not that he thought this, but that he was saying it to me. I wasn't his wife. I wasn't Katharine Graham. I wasn't important. But maybe that was the point.

We talked about how sick Casey was, reportedly sedated and totally out of it from his recent brain surgery.

It wasn't that Ben thought that Woodward lied. He believed Casey said something. But whether or not it was coherent was the question. What Woodward was claiming, Ben said, was *so* dramatic. "There was no retreat from that story once it was out."

My heart sank.

After the interview I transcribed it, as I did all our sessions, threw the cassette tape in the filing cabinet with the others, and printed out the transcript for Ben. I sometimes underlined passages I thought he should include or expand upon. I didn't with this one: better to pretend it hadn't happened. If Ben uttered these doubts in public, he would be disloyal to Woodward. But if he stayed silent, was he honoring the best, most obtainable version of the truth? These two ideals were at odds with each other here in an irreconcilable way. An unintended lesson I learned in my role of amanuensis was that the lure of a compelling narrative can sometimes conflict with one's concept of loyalty. I was a friend before I was a journalist, an admirable quality or a professional failing, depending on your vantage point.

I felt uncomfortable and wished I could unknow what I had just heard and willed myself to forget the conversation after I transcribed it. Call it denial. Call it survival. Whatever you call it, it would be more than two decades before I would be asked to revisit that conversation.

FIVE

The Jewish Amy Tan

Fall down seven times, get up eight.
—VARIOUSLY ATTRIBUTED JAPANESE PROVERB

I continued to work with Ben while he wrote his autobiography, interviewing him, acting as a sounding board, and researching to fill in memory gaps and provide context. During that time, I also wrote occasionally for the *Post*, trying to keep my hand in the game.

One time I submitted an essay to the *Post*'s Sunday Outlook opinion section. It was about living in the nation's capital, a place whose culture and climate I was becoming less enamored of the longer I stayed. I had become restless and talked about leaving. I felt mismatched with a city obsessed with politics rather than art and literature. I blamed geography because it was easier than blaming myself. More to the point, I should have reflected on why I was still playing the role of assistant rather than focusing on my own work. Instead, I projected my dissatisfaction onto the muggy, steamy city.

Since I hadn't heard back whether the piece was accepted or rejected, after working with Ben one day, I stopped by the desk of an editor at Outlook. I knew him from my days at Style. He was an eccentric, gifted wordsmith who had a highly excitable affect that involved a lot of stammering and gesticulating.

"*You* wrote this?" he said, peering at me over his glasses, which were slipping down the bridge of his nose.

"Yes, of course I wrote it."

Though he meant no harm, I was crushed. He was merely struggling to reconcile his preconceived notion of me as a girl Friday, mystified by the outlandish notion that I was a writer in my own right. I'm sure it would have horrified him to know that the question he blurted out would become a memory with no expiration date. He ran my article the next Sunday.

"Gauguin did it," I'd written on the topic of fleeing. "Just picked up and left. I wonder what the pollen count is in Tahiti. I have lost my *joie de Washington*. I am languid at best, catatonic at worst. It is more than the humidity. It is a reaction to a place where people mark events in their lives as personal as deaths and weddings with phrases like 'before the election' or 'after the inauguration.' I want to live in a place where phrases like 'before the drought' or 'after the flood' carry more weight."

My family and friends laughed about the piece. I was the girl who cried wolf, always talking about leaving Washington and never following through. I was now in my early thirties and hadn't made any overtures to build a life elsewhere. A few readers wrote in, both those who agreed and those who didn't, one reader remarking that I had neglected to appreciate the beauty of the city, focusing only on negatives.

I thought I was profound and jaded, that I had seen it all. I had no idea what Washington still had in store for me.

BEN AND I WORKED at a relaxed but steady pace. He seemed to be in no hurry to get the book done, and I welcomed the contrast from the intensity of Woodward and the chaos of Bernstein. My days had a leisurely pace to them. During Ben's writing of the manuscript, he would sometimes send me to the *Post* library to check a fact or get more information about something. Once he was finished writing a chapter I would fact-check it and make suggestions when I thought he should make something more clear or fill in an anecdote or cut a scene that didn't work.

Sometimes he would get an idea for the *How to Read a Newspaper* book, and he would give me something to research, maybe an old article to dig up that would illustrate an idea he had. And he loved finding funny corrections in other newspapers. The longer and stranger a correction, the bigger the kick he got out of it.

When I felt antsy, I roamed the newsroom and found someone to chat with or stopped by Ben's office to hang out with his secretary, Carol Leggett, with whom I had become good friends.

This less demanding schedule meant I had enough time to pursue a master's degree in English at nearby Georgetown University, something I wanted to do because I was toying with the idea of teaching. My mother had taught high school

English, and my growing interest in teaching reflected my wanting to keep her close. I had enrolled in the fall of 1990, a year after her death. Georgetown's campus was walking distance from Ben and Sally's house, so I arranged my schedule to work there on the days I had early evening classes. Being in an academic environment, surrounded by people who loved books, compelled me to return to my own novel, incorporating it into my studies when I took a class in women's autobiography and the autobiographical novel.

After a few semesters at Georgetown, I finally finished my *Poor Girls Always Have Singles* manuscript, which I had retitled *Miss Fortune*. I thought that was an easier title to remember and that it might more easily catch the eye of an agent or editor. I still clung to my dream of becoming a novelist.

An aptly named *Post* colleague, Charlie Trueheart, offered to give the first hundred pages of my novel to his literary agent. About a week later, the agent called excitedly and proclaimed that this novel would make me "the Jewish Amy Tan."

I shared this news with a few friends, and one of them brought over a bottle of champagne, and giddily we emptied it while imagining a future filled with book tours, royalties, and reviews. But my hopes were quickly dashed when the agent called to say he felt the remaining two hundred pages "didn't deliver what the book initially promised."

The words stung terribly, but I decided I wasn't quite ready to give up. The agent had also said that I could rework those disappointing pages and then, if they were to his liking, he would try to sell the novel. I asked Ben for two weeks off without pay, and I feverishly edited and revised the manuscript, attempting to fix subplots and strengthen the overall story arc. At the end of the two weeks, I sent the manuscript to the agent, and again he wasn't impressed.

And so my dreams of being "the Jewish Amy Tan" dissolved, and I was still just the Jewish Barbara Feinman. Discouraged, I tabled the manuscript and told myself I would focus on Ben's book and finish getting my master's degree.

Around this time, in the late summer of 1992, the Georgetown English Department needed a journalist to teach undergraduates a section of Introduction to Journalism. At the last minute, the scheduled instructor, a *Post* reporter, had been awarded a Fulbright that would take her to Slovenia. Georgetown didn't have a journalism department or even a program, only one or two journalism courses each semester that were English electives. I had wanted to try my hand at teaching, and this was the perfect opportunity, so I signed on.

I also decided I wasn't ready to give up on getting *Miss Fortune* published, and so I found a new agent, this time a woman named Flip Brophy. She worked at Sterling Lord Literistic, a well-respected New York agency housed in a funky suite of offices across from Madison Square Park in the Flatiron District. When I visited for the first time, I was drawn to its lively, hip atmosphere. Books lined the crowded shelves and spilled out on any and all available flat surfaces.

Everyone who worked there, from the front desk receptionist to the rarely seen eponymous head of the agency, seemed impossibly cool. Washington media types, except for broadcast news on-air talent, didn't pay attention to the way they dressed, for the most part, and, as a motley tribe, they weren't very style conscious. New Yorkers seemed neurotically edgy and artsy whereas Washingtonians were coldly ambitious and myopically wonky. This literary agency, and New York City, gave me a sense of an alternative future.

Flip set to work shopping around my manuscript to several publishing houses. She was a fixture in the New York publishing scene and editors took her calls. She represented mostly journalists and politicians, counting among her clients Senator Gary Hart, Pulitzer Prize–winning journalist Richard Ben Cramer, writer James McBride, and a host of others, known, unknown, and those teetering between the two. Everyone loved Flip and she seemed to love everyone, thriving in the frenetic hothouse atmospheres of Washington media and New York literati. She had that rare quality of making you feel like you were a great secret she was about to share with the world.

The responses began to pour in. Editors liked the characters and the writing but, echoing the first agent's assessment, felt the plot didn't deliver. After a few weeks, it was clear that no one was going to make an offer. Crushed, I thanked Flip for her considerable efforts and retreated into a mental fetal position while the old internal audiotape of writerly doom played itself in my head: *Was I kidding myself? How would I know when it was time to give up? Was it time to give up?* I didn't want to be a quitter. Besides, writing was a compulsion. I always seemed to drift back to it even if I resolved to move on.

I took out a wrinkled, folded-up note from one of my writing professors at Berkeley. He was Leonard Michaels, whose first novel, *The Men's Club*, was published in 1981, a year before I was in his class. He had written my recommendation letter to the *Washington Post* ten years before. Attached to a copy of the letter on official university stationery, he had stapled a scrawled note from a memo pad. "Barbara, You're a good writer. A real one. Stay with it, become your own teacher soon . . . LM."

In the past his words had comforted me, but this time I wondered if he was just being nice, if it was a stock message worded to placate anxious student writers. He wasn't the type to be gratuitously kind, I countered. My memory of his style during writing workshop sessions was that he didn't suffer fools.

I had a new thought: Maybe he wasn't being kind; maybe he was just wrong. And what exactly did he mean by, "become your own teacher"? The advice was as cryptic as a fortune cookie message. I folded up the note and put it back in my box of keepsakes. And once again, I stowed away the manuscript in a file cabinet.

Though Flip couldn't sell *Miss Fortune*, she didn't give up on me. Not long after the rejections poured in, she phoned. "Don't worry about the novel. We'll go back to it at some point," she said, trotting out her brisk New York business-woman tone that she slipped into when she was discussing something unpleasant and was impatient to move on to a new topic. "How would you like to ghostwrite a book for a congresswoman?"

By this point, in early 1993, I had worked with Bob Woodward and Carl Bernstein, and I was still helping Ben. In addition, I had done research or editing on a handful of other books on a more limited basis. As I listened to Flip's description of the potential gig, I recognized a whole new level of editorial involvement. I would have about six months to write an entire book for a newly elected Democratic congress-woman from Pennsylvania, Marjorie Margolies-Mezvinsky.

The 1992 elections had ushered in more freshmen women to Congress than ever before. This congresswoman, Flip explained, had a deal with Crown to chronicle her first eight months in the House of Representatives during what was billed as the "Year of the Woman." Not only would I interview the congresswoman so I could tell her story, in her voice, but I would also talk to her female colleagues, as well as a few of the men, to include their perspectives.

It was a tempting offer. And it was new territory for me—I would be in the driver's seat, writing an entire book, even if it wasn't under my own name. But it would mean I would have to leave Ben. I had now been working with him going on three years. While we had gotten much of the first book done, we were moving slowly, and there was little mention of the second book. I didn't want to abandon Ben, but I also couldn't keep my professional life on hold indefinitely. I was still feeling restless, perhaps more so than ever.

The words of Harriet Fier, the formidable Style assignment editor, rang in my ears: *Don't let yourself get too fat and happy.* It was scary to think about leaving Ben and even scarier to sign on to write an entire book. My heart sank as I admitted that the fear was proof I should do it.

I summoned up my nerve and went to see Ben one morning. He was doing a crossword puzzle, and when I told him I had something to tell him, he peered at me over his reading glasses and put the folded newspaper down on his desk. I launched into a long explanation about my unsold novel and said that even though this wasn't fiction, it was an opportunity to actually write a book rather than merely research and edit one.

"Look," he said, "you need to do what you think is best. We've gotten a lot of this thing done. Just find me someone who can take over. And you will still be around. Sally won't let you escape," he said, laughing, picking up his crossword.

Relieved, I assured him I would find a replacement to take over the remaining research and get that person up to speed before I left. I enlisted the aid of a young friend at the *Post*, for whom this would be a great opportunity, and the transition was made smoothly. I hoped we would stay close, but it was time for me to move on.

Marjorie Margolies-Mezvinsky was a former Philadelphia NBC news reporter who had covered Congress. She understood the media better than most and knew how to take full advantage of this knowledge. A petite, energetic dynamo, she knew that a book about herself and her female colleagues as they came to power would position her as a sort of political pioneer. She had already become a public figure in her high-profile broadcast job but also as the wife of an Iowa Democratic congressman, Ed Mezvinsky, whom she had met on the job and who had lost his reelection bid after serving two terms.

Before her marriage Marjorie had also attracted a lot of attention as the first single American woman to adopt a child from another country; she testified before Congress in 1976 in a successful effort to influence legislation on adoption and immigration practices.

Her desire to tell the story of this particular group of women had a lot of potential, particularly because it spoke loudly to the largest book-buying demographic: middle-aged women. And Marjorie and I had much in common as we shared the same religion, politics, social class, and even our small stature. It was not that much of a stretch for me to appropriate her voice.

When someone as accomplished as Marjorie hires someone like me to write a book for them, someone invariably raises the question of why they don't have what it takes to write their own book. I got asked this constantly when I told people what I did for a living. The answer is that sometimes they do have the talent, but they don't have the time.

Say what you will about politicians, but the ones I have known keep grueling schedules and are run ragged between committee meetings and votes, constituent obligations, and fund-raising for the omnipresent next election—not to mention having to divide their time between Washington and their home state. It's a rare member of Congress who would be able to research, organize, and write a book while still in office, even if he or she had literary inclinations. The ones who are also parents are particularly challenged. Marjorie was the mother of a blended brood of eleven children (two adopted daughters, three adopted sons, two biological sons, and four stepdaughters). This role left her no time for book writing.

As it had with Ben, working for Marjorie entailed doing a lot of background research on events and issues to inform the interview sessions with her as well as with her colleagues and other people in her universe, transcribing the raw material, organizing it, and then shaping it all into a narrative. Interviewing dozens of members of Congress was a primer in both politics and American civics. Though I had been to the Hill on many occasions, it had been mostly for Style reporting. Now I would be getting a behind-the-scenes look at the legislative and political process.

Nearly all the women in Congress we approached for an interview agreed to participate. I was doing the work under Marjorie's auspices, and that gave me a level of access that reporters can only dream of, but what would ultimately make it into the book was completely Marjorie's decision. I had to remind myself time and again that I was on the inside of the rope line as an invitee, a ghost, and not as a reporter. I was excited to have inside access to such an impressive group of professional women. I wanted to get a sense of who they really were and what motivated them. My earlier jobs had let me observe up close extremely successful men, but this was an opportunity to study people more like me. Because I was representing Marjorie and her book project rather than my own article for a newspaper or magazine, I hoped my subjects would be more forthcoming than they might otherwise be, that I could glean something beyond what they had revealed publicly.

Unfortunately, my hopes were quickly dashed. As I went from interview to interview, I had the growing suspicion that everything they were saying to me and my tape recorder they had already said before in stump speeches and press interviews. The members' responses were carefully crafted and stripped of anything that could be used against them in future campaign ads.

This was pre-Internet and pre-Google so I had the time-consuming task of going back through the archives to see what each of them had said in the past and to whom. When I did, my worst fears were confirmed, that much of the material I was getting during the interviews was recycled pablum. I would have to ask better questions if I wanted usable material. Hearing that they were fighting for their constituents and that they had come to Washington to make a difference was admirable but predictable and uninteresting.

In addition to how guarded these professional politicians had been trained to be, they were usually more comfortable talking about policies than telling stories. Because they were professional problem solvers, their milieu was polling data and number-crunching. Narrative arc was a foreign concept. Answers to questions fell into two categories: safe, generic bromides or mind-numbing wonk-speak.

After one particularly eyes-glazing-over transcribing session, I came up with what I hoped would be some more compelling questions. One, in particular, proved effective. "If your life as a congresswoman were a movie, what's the defining moment?" Because I was asking them to imagine something, it played to a more relaxed and candid response. It was almost like a game. When I got any traction, I kept going. Sometimes they would stop themselves just as they began to say something interesting, becoming self-conscious. "Pretend I'm not here," I would say gently, prodding them to keep going.

Usually they would need more direction: "What's the opening scene of this movie that would introduce the point you want to make about this place and yourself?" Then I would move in for the specific, defining moment. Sometimes it wasn't a moment but a fact or a detail. In journalism this is called getting "the name of the dog," as in getting the name of the dog/horse/turtle of the porn star/embezzler/tech start-up CEO you're profiling.

"I want the positive moment and the negative moment," I would instruct. This approach helped knock loose some memories and anecdotes, and it helped me figure out which women wanted to be more open but either needed help in how to communicate in that way or wanted to size me up a bit more before revealing themselves. While some, no matter how I asked, nudged, or cajoled, would not give up anything beyond what you could find in their official bios, others did open up, one woman even explaining in depth the context of her suicide attempt, another talking about personal experiences informing a stance on abortion.

A book by a sitting congresswoman was not going to have the sort of revelations you would find in a political biography written by a historian or journalist. But getting these women to open up a bit to humanize them in my own mind enabled me to portray them as three-dimensional.

Around this time, as I made my way through the interview list, I began asking Marjorie to consider putting my name on the cover as a "with." In the parlance of publishing, whether you call yourself a writer, a collaborator, a book doctor, a midwife, or a ghost doesn't much matter in the scheme of things. What does matter is getting your name on the cover. By *matter* I don't mean it necessarily helps you get more work. These gigs are gotten mainly by word of mouth, in editor and agent publishing circles. It matters because it gives you more street cred with people outside of the business.

In the publishing world, it's a rarity when a "name" actually pens his own book; everyone from the receptionist to the CEO at every publishing house and literary agency knows that if you want to figure out who wrote the book, look no further than the sea of names on the acknowledgment page. So I made the case to Marjorie that it would help my career and it wouldn't hurt hers. It would be perceived as an act of generosity, one woman helping another. She readily agreed and instructed Crown to give me a "with." I don't know why she did it, but I was glad she did.

I spent that spring and summer researching, reporting, transcribing, and writing. The book was coming together, and Marjorie squeezed me into her schedule when she could, though sometimes it meant literally chasing after her in the halls of Congress or accompanying her on the train ride back to Philly or even on the private Capitol Hill underground subway system as she and her colleagues scurried to and from votes. The days were mostly filled with the tedium of the legislative process, congressional life not nearly as entertaining as *House of Cards* or *Veep* or *The West Wing* has portrayed.

But on August 5, 1993, a true drama played out on the floor of the House of Representatives, and Marjorie was a key player, though certainly not by choice. President Clinton found himself a single vote short to get his economic plan, his first budget, through the House. He had promised to take on the challenge of the country's deficit, and his strategy was to reprioritize the budget and introduce a stimulus package.

Marjorie had been the only freshman Democrat to vote against both facets of his plan in earlier iterations. Her district was the most Republican leaning of any Democrat's in Congress and she knew that if she changed her no vote to a yes in this next round, she would surely be voted out of office.

Jake Tapper, now of CNN, was then her press secretary. On that August day, he told her the president was on the line. Marjorie heard the president ask her what would it take? They talked for another minute or two, and then she agreed to switch her vote, supporting the president's plan. This was considered by some to be an act of political suicide and by others as one of party fealty. Seventeen years later, political reporter Karen Tumulty, writing for *Time*, would reflect on this moment, characterizing it as "one of the most extraordinary spectacles I have ever witnessed in the House Chamber. . . . The other side of the Chamber seemed to explode. Republicans pulled out their hankies and started waving them at her, chanting: 'Bye-bye, Margie.'"

This made for a lively scene in the book: though no one was physically pushed onto the subway tracks, Marjorie must have felt she had been thrown under the bus by the Democratic Party. It was obvious to all that she would lose her reelection campaign. Before that happened, she had a book to finish and some political favors to collect on.

Two months to the day after the historic vote that effectively ended Marjorie's congressional career, First Lady Hillary Clinton sat down with us to be interviewed for the book. While she wasn't a member of Congress, the First Lady had spent a lot of time dealing with Congress during her tenure as the head of the Clinton administration task force to overhaul health-care reform. Her policy role was unprecedented for a First Lady. Her participation in the book was obviously something the marketing department could promote in publicity materials. This was a good start, but I wondered what else the president and First Lady would do to repay Marjorie for the vote that everyone knew was going to cost her her seat. Marjorie, in the interim, had been traveling around her district and hearing from angry constituents.

I was along to assist Marjorie while Mrs. Clinton had one of her aides present. An official White House photo shows me wearing an ill-fitting suit, one I had bought specifically for that meeting, and my unruly hair was pulled back in a ponytail in a semisuccessful attempt to tame it. We had spent a lot of time preparing for the interview and had a list of questions prepared. I was awestruck by the White House. I had been there on several occasions in my role as freelance party reporter for the Style section, but I had never participated in a private meeting.

I dutifully took notes, obsessively checking the tape recorder to make sure it was working. I had brought along extra batteries, pens, reporter's notepads, and notes. Soon my nerves settled down when I saw that Marjorie and Mrs. Clinton were doing just fine without my input. Just to prove to myself I could put several words together in the right order and make them come out of my mouth audibly, I promised myself I would ask at least one question before the interview concluded.

The First Lady and the congresswoman discussed what it meant for more women than ever before to be in Congress, that women approached legislative work differently from their male counterparts. Women were more likely to use their life experiences to inform this work and were less concerned with wielding power.

Women in politics had to deal with a lot of bullshit and bad behavior on the part of men who were resisting this sharing of the stage. Issues like rape, violence, and reproductive health were now getting airtime. Maybe more women in Congress would really change things, and for the better, I thought. I was excited by the conversation; Mrs. Clinton's enthusiasm illuminated the room as she talked about how it made her feel to see so many women in office. I wondered how maddening it must be to have to wear the corset of First Ladydom when you have a law degree from Yale and are committed to issues such as global women's rights and affordable health care.

The interview was wrapping up and Marjorie looked at me. "Do you have anything you want to ask?"

"A real quick one," I said, nodding. I did have one question, an obvious one but something that I really thought should be addressed. "When do you think we'll have a woman president?" The second half of the question, the part I was too intimidated to actually ask, was "and would you be interested in being that woman?"

"Sometime in the next fifteen or twenty years," she said, smiling.

That was fall of 1993. Fifteen years before she would first run for the presidency. She came pretty close to her own prediction.

As the Republican House members had so coarsely predicted, Marjorie's constituents showed no mercy in town hall meetings and other public venues where she appeared on trips home; Marjorie and her staff watched as her chances of being reelected deteriorated from unlikely to grim. A few months after our White House interview, an otherwise cheerless holiday season was brightened by an invitation from the Clintons for Marjorie and her family to attend Renaissance Weekend at Hilton Head, South Carolina.

An exclusive annual retreat for top people to talk about public policy, Renaissance Weekend was described by the *New York Times* as a "festival of earnestness." It was also an opportunity for Marjorie to make useful connections for her post-Congress future. But the most valuable of these connections was one that neither she nor even the most calculating political operative could have engineered or even predicted: Marjorie's oldest son, Marc, and the Clintons' only child, Chelsea, would meet, starting a teenage friendship that would flourish when they both ended up attending Stanford University.

This friendship eventually evolved into an adult relationship that led to marriage in 2010, making Marjorie and the Clintons in-laws. This union, worthy of a Venn diagram illustrating the incestuous nature of political Washington, got the predictable amount of media attention, focusing on the scandals and setbacks of the couple's parents, rather than noting how much Marjorie had actually accomplished. I felt the press overlooked an equally meaningful aspect of the story.

The sheer perseverance and resilience it must have taken to live a life that included being the mother of eleven children, the recipient of five Emmys, author of three books, and stints as the head of the National Women's Business Council, the director, deputy chair of the U.S. delegation to the United Nations Fourth World Conference on Women, and executive director of the Women's Campaign Fund—that to me seems like something worth exploring. And the setbacks: Losing office. Bankruptcy. Convicted spouse. Divorce. (The marriage ended in 2007 after Ed Mezvinsky reportedly spiraled downward, culminating in his serving five years in prison after pleading guilty to dozens of felonies, receiving a diagnosis of bipolar disorder, and becoming entangled in various lawsuits. He had fallen prey to a variety of Nigerian scams and then engaged in some illegal activities to dig himself out of debt.) Marjorie's life is the living embodiment of that Japanese proverb: *Fall down seven times, get up eight.*

The complexity of challenges that Marjorie has encountered and dealt with in her life is pretty staggering and I'm not sure she's been given the respect she deserves just for the resilience she has demonstrated. Washington is a town where everything is measured in polls and fund-raising dollars. You're either up or you're down, you're in or you're out. You're good or you're bad. You're a conniving opportunist or a selfless do-gooder. You value yourself only by whether you are perceived as a player or not. I had fallen into that trap myself: estimating my own value using others' criteria, mistaking proximity to power as proof of my worthiness.

AFTER MARJORIE'S BOOK HIT THE BOOKSTORES in the early spring of 1994, it was again time to ask, "What next?" I had worked for Woodward, Bernstein, Bradlee, and now had a "with" on a book that received favorable reviews and some attention. I also had my master's and was teaching Introduction to Journalism on a regular basis at Georgetown. Unsolicited, book projects were now coming my way, and I was beginning to have the luxury of turning down work that wasn't appealing, either because the compensation wasn't enough or the client promised to be difficult. Saying no was hard at first because I was afraid the work would dry up. But it didn't.

Later that spring I received an unusual offer from a former *Washington Post* Food section editor who had relocated to Maine to run the *Bangor Daily News*. He invited me to come up to Maine for the summer and be a floating newsroom writing coach. I would make my way through the roster of reporters, stationed throughout the state in little one-person bureaus, and work with them on improving their writing. It wasn't exactly Gauguin taking off for Tahiti, but it would get me out of D.C. during its worst weather.

I was more than ready to trade in lobbyists and the White House for lobsters and lighthouses, at least for a summer. While I was proud of Marjorie's book, it wasn't mine. Like a surrogate mother leaving the baby behind at the hospital, I felt empty.

I packed up my apartment, put my stuff in storage, said good-bye to my friends, and headed north. When I arrived, I stayed with my new boss and his wife for a few days, and they helped me comb the classifieds for a place to live. I found a room for rent on a horse farm owned by a friendly, warm woman named Bunny. I loved horses, having ridden in college, and Bunny promised to give me lessons in addition to occasional hot meals. I settled in and began to get to know my way around the newsroom and town.

The local news business was a welcome change from what

I was used to. Conflicts of interest, for instance, were totally different. Instead of power couples like Andrea Mitchell and Alan Greenspan navigating overlapping realms of politics and journalism, here in Maine it was fishermen doubling as business reporters. Ethical dilemmas were quaint compared to those the Washington press corps faced: rather than worrying about whether you can use what you overhear as a soccer mom in the bleachers about the congressman's marriage, it was more along the lines of must you recuse yourself from reporting on the effect of a recent drought on the price of blueberries?

The New England lifestyle was just more fun. The car I was driving at the time was made for a summer in Maine, a little blue convertible Miata with a standard shift, which I chronicled in a quarterly column I wrote for *Miata Magazine* (yes, there is such a thing). An essay I had written for *Glamour* magazine about the sense of power that driving fast gave me had caught the editor's eye, and he called me up and invited me to be their "girl columnist." For a few years I wrote what amounted to a serial love letter to driving. It culminated in my attending Skip Barber Racing School, one of the best places to learn how to drive a racecar, something on my bucket list.

I flirted with the idea of staying in Bangor. I daydreamed about the newspaper hiring me on in a permanent editor position. Or, maybe Stephen King, who lived in town, needed an assistant. Never mind that I hated horror stories. I was thirty-four years old, time to settle down, and Maine seemed like a sane place. I pictured myself marrying a lobsterman and having children and living in a lighthouse. I hadn't actually met any lobstermen or anyone who lived in a lighthouse. Still. Maybe I could stay.

But then one day I got a phone call when I was in the newsroom working with one of the sports reporters. On the line was Bob Barnett, a D.C. book agent/lawyer to the stars. He was both Woodward's and Ben's agent. He was calling because he represented a woman named Hanan Ashrawi, who he explained was a well-known and well-respected spokesperson for the Palestinians in the Occupied Territories and a university professor. She had completed a draft of *This Side of Peace*, a memoir of her struggles as a Christian Arab woman in a Muslim, male-dominated world, having to navigate between the likes of Yassir Arafat and Shimon Peres. Alice Mayhew was the editor on the book, Barnett said, and they were hoping I was available to help out for a month, maybe five weeks.

It sounded like a good gig, but it meant returning to Washington. Which of course, having not met my lobsterman, I was inclined to do anyway, as my contract with the Bangor paper was just for the summer. We discussed the details a few more minutes, and then I asked about compensation.

He told me to come up with a figure. My mind went blank. My brother, David, a former government lawyer and now a junk bond trader, had taught me that the first rule of negotiating was never to name a number first. So I said I really didn't know, hoping that would force Barnett to float the first figure.

But he asked me again what I was looking for so I had to ask him if he would hold a sec, and I dialed my brother who answered by blurting his last name. I could hear guys screaming numbers in the background. I quickly told him what was going on.

"Okay, get back on the line and just tell him $40k." Then I heard a muffled sound, which must have been David's hand over the receiver. He was trading something, a gazillion of this, a thousand of that, shorting this, long on that.

"Forty thousand? For five weeks of work? Are you crazy?" I said when he came back on the line. "I can't ask for that." We lived in two different worlds. His was in a Michael Douglas movie, and mine was by Nora Ephron.

"Don't be a chump. If they want you enough, they will pay you what you're worth. Tell him it's inconvenient, it will mess up your vacation, blah blah blah." His hand went back over the receiver, and he was yelling numbers again. "Just go back to him and say $30k."

I pressed the blinking light and said, "Hi, Bob. Um, I was going to take a vacation after my job here ended. But I guess I could come back for this. But it's inconvenient. I guess I could do it for $20k."

"Twenty thousand dollars?" His tone was incredulous. He was practically sputtering. "Why, that's"—he paused to do the math—"an annual rate of $240k."

I asked him to hold again as I went back to David, who was yelling again, calling someone in the background a moron. I repeated what Barnett had said, about the annual rate.

"You got a pen?" His tone had gone from patronizing to impatient.

"Yes," I said dutifully.

"Okay, write this down so you don't screw it up. Then get back on the phone with this guy and read it word for word: 'Yes, your math is correct. What's your point?'"

Barnett agreed to the $20k, so a few weeks later I packed up my car, made my rounds at the newsroom, hugged Bunny and every single one of her horses good-bye, and headed south.

When I got back to Washington, Alice sent me the manuscript and asked me to look for places in the narrative where personal history could be woven into the author's role on the world stage of the Middle East peace process. Hanan would travel to Washington and spend a handful of days with me during which we were to work on making the manuscript more accessible to a wide audience.

After reading her manuscript, I was excited to meet Hanan. She was a woman of many accomplishments, someone who was an alluring mix of strength and warmth. The woman who wrote these pages was very wise, and I was humbled that anyone thought I could help make this good book even better.

I wasn't disappointed when I met her. She was the sort of person with whom you instantly feel a connection. She had an immediacy and an authenticity about her that elicited the same of those in her presence. Though serious and not one to mince words, she was also fun and loved chocolate and tobacco, both of which she encouraged me to share.

During one of these sugar and cigarette breaks, she inhaled deeply, looked me straight in the eye, and asked, "When are you going to start focusing on your own writing?"

Good question.

Taken aback by her interest in me, I just shrugged and mumbled. Less out of reluctance and more out of denial. I was touched by her interest. A strong role model for women and fierce supporter of women's rights, she was keeping with her core values in encouraging me. What she wrote in her acknowledgments section, like Professor Michaels's words, buoyed my spirits: "Barbara Feinman, craftswoman and friend, understood both structure and substance."

These two experiences, Marjorie putting my name on the cover of her book and Hanan challenging me to do my own work, helped move me toward bolstering myself to establish my own voice, to stake a claim as a writer with her own story to tell. I felt something shifting, as though I were at a crossroads with my writing, and that I still had a chance to change course.

But I had built up a solid reputation as a book doctor, and this town would never have a shortage of people who wanted to "author" books but who couldn't or didn't want to write them themselves. I had to make a living. It wasn't realistic to think I could do that by writing novels, even if I managed to get one published.

Was it time to make my peace with being a "craftswoman," as Hanan so kindly put it? What did it mean that I had gravitated to work that required—or allowed?—me to be silent, and invisible? Was it really so different from the fiction I longed to write? Was it time to give up on my fiction, even on my own voice, and be grateful for what I had: a steady stream of income and a comfortable life?

SIX

The Senator and His War

The universe is made of stories,
not of atoms.
—MURIEL RUKEYSER

After my summer in Maine, I relocated to the Eastern Shore of Maryland, where a few years back my siblings and I had bought a modest second home in Centreville, about an hour-and-forty-five-minute drive from Washington. The hundred-year-old house sat above a marsh, around the corner from the town public landing where you could launch a boat onto the Corsica River, a tributary of the Chesapeake Bay.

I decided I would rather live out there for a while than return to Washington. I wanted to see if living a couple of hours from Washington might be the solution I was looking for: close enough to sustain a writing career but far enough away to maintain my equilibrium. I already was paying my share of the mortgage on the house so my expenses would be minimal, and this way I wouldn't have to shell out rent money for an overpriced Washington apartment.

I also wouldn't be eating out with friends at expensive

Georgetown restaurants or drinking at trendy Adams Morgan bars. It would be a much more simple existence and I could focus on writing—both fiction for myself and editing gigs to pay the bills. I was eager to get settled, having first briefly stayed at my sister's house in Arlington, just outside of the city, while I worked on Hanan's book.

In addition to writing, I also planned to fit in a lot of ice-skating. There was a rink on the edge of Easton, about a half hour from our house, and shortly after I started going to morning public sessions, I was hired to teach little kids the basics like swizzles, t-stops, and crossovers. It was a solitary routine for the most part: I'd get up early, go to the rink, head home, fix lunch, and then sit at the computer for an afternoon of writing or editing.

The house was creaky and old, which meant that during the day, it was quaint and cozy. But at night, it felt kind of lonely, and, if I let my imagination get the best of me, it was even a little creepy. Luckily there were neighbors close enough that I didn't feel completely isolated.

With Hanan's manuscript finished, I turned my attention to my latest project: a book with Bob Kerrey, the former governor of Nebraska, now a Democratic senator. I was excited about it because rather than another political tome, Bob, a Vietnam veteran, wanted to write a personal memoir about war. We had tried to get some work done while I was in Maine and he was in Washington, but we hadn't made much progress. That's how he ended up coming out to my family's Eastern Shore getaway. I told him it would be a good place to write and reflect and we could hammer out a timeline and a to-do list for completing the project.

Right before Bob arrived, I had been away for a few weeks in California doing the reporting for a freelance magazine piece. I picked up Bob in the city and together we drove out to the country. I had described Centreville to him as a sleepy Maryland town on the water, a place where you wake up to the sound of wild Canada geese honking rather than that of car horns honking.

As soon as I opened the front door, it was obvious something was wrong. No one had been in the Maryland house during my absence, and now it was a scene out of Hitchcock. Bird poop everywhere, paintings askew, lamps knocked over, a couple of dead birds. I remembered that the chimney flue was broken, and my sister and brother-in-law had found a single dead bird in the living room the last time they had come for the weekend. But this time it looked like an entire flock of blackbirds had gained entry.

The worst discovery of all was up in my bedroom on the third floor, where I found two birds still alive. They were crazed, panicky, injured, and weak from starvation. I thought I was going to be sick when I found them. I yelled for the senator, who came running up the stairs and instantly went into Navy SEAL mode: no expression, no emotion, just *I'll deal with it*. He asked for a broom, gloves, and garbage bags and then told me to go outside.

When he finally appeared, I asked where the two surviving birds were. He said he had killed them.

Why? I thought. *How could you? Was that really your only option?*, etc.

He had to kill them. They were nearly dead; it was the humane thing to do. But somehow that was lost on me. All

I could focus on was the act's gruesomeness, and something had shifted, at least in my mind. I felt he had let me down, or I had let him down. It was unarticulated, but it was there. Sometimes it takes the lens of time to give you clarity. In that particular instance, it took two decades.

THE PROJECT WITH BOB KERREY had pretty much fallen into my lap. One evening the previous spring, shortly before I left on my Maine adventure, I went to a get-together at the home of my friend Martha Sherrill, then a staff writer for the *Post*'s Style section, who also wrote occasional celebrity profiles for *Esquire*. She lived in a tony Georgetown row house that accommodated the dinner parties she enjoyed hosting.

Flip Brophy, who was her agent as well as mine, was down from New York for a few days to meet with her various D.C. clients, and last minute, Martha decided to throw a dinner party for her. Martha had invited Nebraska senator Bob Kerrey, a decorated war hero who had run for the presidency in 1992. The only other thing I knew about Bob was that when he was governor, he had caused quite a stir when his actress girlfriend, Debra Winger, moved into the governor's mansion. He was divorced, and she was single, but the media couldn't resist obsessing over a politician and a sexy movie star cohabiting in the nation's heartland.

I had interviewed plenty of members of Congress, first during my party reporting years and then during the Marjorie Margolies-Mezvinsky project, but I wasn't in the habit of socializing with them and it wasn't something on my bucket list, given how stiff I found many of them. But I knew Bob

Kerrey was one of Flip's clients so that gave me hope he might not be the typical buttoned-up politician.

Reality surpassed expectations.

Sometime between salad and dessert, I learned that Bob (we were by this point on a first-name basis) was trying to write a war memoir. When I asked how much of the manuscript he had completed, Flip laughed. I guess you could say his enthusiasm, up to that point, had apparently exceeded his output. He had lots of reasons: It was hard to carve out the time. He wasn't getting much traction when he did sit down to write. There was crucial research to be done. He and I talked books for a while, and then the conversation drifted to other topics, laughter punctuating the chatter.

Martha is not just a gifted writer. She is also a masterful cook and that night, as always, the food was great and the wine was plenty. By the time we made our way to the candlelit dining room, we were all very relaxed. I guess I was particularly relaxed. There are mean drunks and happy drunks, and then there is me, a storyteller. Give me a glass, and I'll tell you an anecdote. Give me a bottle, and I turn into Scheherazade. Somehow I found myself telling my dinner companions about a date I had gone on the week before, one that Flip had set me up on while I was in New York City.

I explained that I thought the date went well but I hadn't heard from him. I wanted to know if they thought I should call him.

Bob asked where my date lived and I thought for a moment and then replied, "Brooklyn."

The table considered my options, gave me some advice, and then the topic turned elsewhere. Meanwhile, Bob had left the room, saying something about needing to call in about a vote. In the background we could hear him on the phone in Martha's kitchen.

Then he was back in the dining room, standing behind me, rattling off addresses he had written on the back of an envelope.

Slowly it dawned on me they were New York street addresses. I turned around, horrified, and saw Bob laughing and heading back to the phone, then dialing.

"You bastard!" I screamed. "Stop him! He's calling Michael Epstein!"

I ran after him, wrestled the phone from him, pleading with him. He gave up and returned to the table.

I never heard from Epstein but Bob did.

A year and a half later, Martha wrote a profile of Bob that *Esquire* published. In it, she recounted that anecdote and Epstein saw it. He wrote a tongue-in-cheek note to Bob at the Senate, telling him which address in directory assistance was his. And under his name, where a letter writer's title would go on a formal business letter, he had typed: "Hypnotic Television Producer." That was in reference to Martha's lead-in to the anecdote:

> One of the dinner guests, a Washington writer named
> Barbara Feinman, had told a long hypnotic story about
> a blind date she had been on in New York with a TV
> producer named Michael Epstein.

Note that Martha had written that *I* had told a "long, hypnotic story," not that Michael Epstein was "hypnotic."

Sheesh. Men.

Besides my less than successful love life ending up in a national magazine, the other thing to come out of that dinner was that Bob called me and asked if I would be interested in helping him with his book.

AFTER MEETING TO TALK LOGISTICS, I readily signed on to help Bob. I was excited about the project. The structure was going to prove to be a little tricky, complicated because he had two stories to tell: his own Vietnam War experiences as a Navy SEAL and his uncle John's (his father's brother) as a captured soldier in World War II. Much of the original impetus for writing the book was that Bob had promised his father on his deathbed that he would investigate the mysterious circumstances of Bob's uncle John's death. I intuited that while it was important to Bob to keep the promise he had made to his father, what was really compelling him was a need to unburden himself of something in his own past.

I had come to understand that the price of vulnerability—of presenting yourself as a real person in an age of Photoshop, branding campaigns, and crisis management teams—is too much to pay for politicians who are in perpetual campaign mode. I was intrigued by how the tension between a writer's urge to tell and a politician's instinct to obscure would play out in this project.

I sensed Bob might be willing to go to that place of truth telling that makes writing "come alive." When I had run into trouble with clients in the past, it was usually when I tried to hold up a mirror to what was really there rather than reflect back the image they wanted to project. I didn't think that would happen this time: I felt liberated by Bob's motivation to write a book; rather than further his political career or make money, his compulsion to tell this story grew out of a sense of unfinished business on a psychic level.

As I got to know him, I was struck, again and again, by Bob's creativity and unusual mix of prankster, tortured soul, poet, policy wonk, and businessman. In the same day, he could spend the early morning hours lost in the solitary activity of cutting up magazines and pasting images into montages that he created for his friends and himself. Then he would put on a suit and a tie and go vote on a bill or take to the Senate floor to debate some policy issue.

It was clear from that first evening that Bob was a complex man. Simultaneously approachable and inaccessible. He was charming and funny. He was a gold mine for the magazine political profiler because his quirkiness made for great copy. It was easy to forget that just a few years earlier he had been a presidential candidate, running against Bill Clinton in the 1992 Democratic primary.

Bob's candor was disarming and refreshing, an oasis of authenticity in a culture where character can be as malleable as Play-Doh. But that proclivity for being who he really was is what set his handlers on edge and sometimes led to him being his own worst opponent, like the time he told an off-color joke about lesbians to fellow candidate Bill Clinton with an open C-SPAN mike nearby. People loved his candor but that didn't necessarily mean they felt comfortable sending him to the White House. He dropped out shortly after finishing third in the New Hampshire primary. To become commander in chief, there could be no unscripted or unedited moment. That was a box that couldn't contain Bob.

I prodded him to write and helped him figure out where the story began—something that every memoirist or autobiographer must determine early in the process. Bowing to the sanctity of chronology, do you begin at the beginning and risk boring your readers with biographical material that comes decades before the main action or heart of the story? Or do you identify the reason you are writing the book and start with the touch point of that event? Or maybe a flashback or a flash-forward will work. The choices are numerous.

We also came up with a research plan to track down some elusive ghosts in his personal history and that of his uncle. Soon enough he was producing chapters. Periodically I would drive over the Bay Bridge back to Washington to work with him, and I tried to schedule these meetings with the evenings when I was teaching my weekly class at Georgetown. As Flip had predicted, Bob proved himself to be a strong and compelling writer who quickly found his narrative voice.

What we knew about Bob's uncle was this: that he had died somehow in the Philippines more than two years after the Bataan Death March of Allied prisoners across the Philippine Islands in the spring of 1942. Fifty years had passed, and I was skeptical we could find anything new. But I sensed that the lack of information regarding Bob's uncle's death was an obstacle to telling his own story. I'm not using the word *closure*, a word that really raises my hackles, overused by too many TV "experts" on hand every time a national tragedy unfolds.

Bob said his youngest sister, who lived on a farm in Nebraska, was the keeper of assorted family records, and he suggested we pay her a visit. Shortly thereafter, we flew out to the heartland to gather documents and memories from Bob's family. It was a fruitful visit. I learned that Bob's father had told Bob that before John had left for his overseas duty, he had a serious girlfriend named Evangeline, or "Vangie."

Among the documents his family shared were letters from Vangie to John's parents. Vangie worked for the OSS (Office of Strategic Services and predecessor to the CIA). The return address was in the Washington area. Fifty years had passed, but I still hoped she might be living in the area. Then a young woman in her twenties, now she would be in her seventies.

As soon as I returned to Centreville, I got out a Washington phone book and started dialing. I must have called at least a dozen people with Vangie's maiden name. She had probably married and changed her name, but I hoped I would stumble upon a relative who shared her maiden name. I left message after message on answering machines or talked to people who had never heard of Vangie. But when I got to the last name on the list, I hit pay dirt: a relative, who told me Vangie had died of cancer twenty years earlier in 1975. But her sister was alive, and she lived in Reston, Virginia, about forty minutes from downtown D.C.

Bob and I arranged for a visit with Georgia, Vangie's sister. She had letters that John had written to Vangie, and a particularly intimate one recalled an evening they shared at the Shoreham Hotel that included a dip in the pool. Not long after we got a copy of this letter, one evening Bob went to the Shoreham, got a drink, and sat by the pool, reflecting on the ghosts of Vangie and John. Refusing to be defeated by the passage of time, Bob tried to connect through proximity, searching for something. I didn't know what it was, and I'm not sure he knew either. Bob was especially dogged by the mystery of how John died.

We knew Bob's father believed John had died on October 17, 1944, in the Philippines. John had been stationed in Manila, at General MacArthur's headquarters. When Bataan fell, John's family feared that he was taken captive and had been forced to join the Bataan Death March. Bob's father tried to find out what had happened to John, but all he received was confirmation of his death from the army.

So we took up where Bob's dad left off. I had John's name and rank, deployment location, and date of death. After a few phone calls to government agencies, I established that if John's veteran service records still existed, they would be in the National Archives' facility in College Park, Maryland. I packed a bag with snacks, pens, paper, and sticky notes, knowing this was going to take some camping out among dusty, crumbling records. One of my students volunteered to help, and together we spent a few days poring over documents.

Just when I thought it was time to give up, we found a file with declassified documents—the debriefings of the three men who were with John when he died. These confirmed he had survived the death march, escaped his captivity, and, hoping to be rescued, survived for nearly three years as a guerrilla in the Philippines during the Japanese occupation, in a landlocked and densely forested area.

One day they got word that an American submarine would

meet them at Baler Bay, in the northeastern part of Luzon Island in the Philippines. The group could walk three hours through the mountains or take a quick boat trip to get to their destination. They chose the mountain walk while John and another man, a Filipino, took the boat. They hit bad weather, and the boat either capsized or was blown out to sea. The debriefing told a disjointed story in which suspicions were raised that perhaps the Filipino, who came ashore agitated and disoriented, had killed Bob's uncle. John had been a strong swimmer and it was unlikely he had drowned.

This information was bittersweet. It was painful to learn that John had come so close to being rescued and reunited with his family and Vangie. But we were relieved that at last we finally knew what had happened. Or at least we had a sense of what happened. Knowing is better than not knowing. That's something a journalist or a memoirist has to believe. And I think it gave Bob some comfort to know he had honored his father's wishes to get at the truth.

At least he had gotten to *that* truth. Getting at his own truth was somewhat more difficult. In a letter he wrote from Nebraska about a year after we started working together, he reflected, "I wonder about this book today; it's getting where I don't like the subject of the story. You may know the feeling."

UNBEKNOWNST TO BOB OR TO ME, soon after I was digging around in the National Archives trying to find out what happened to John so many years before, a reporter was digging through other records there investigating Bob's war record. The reporter, Gregory Vistica, was looking into a tip that claimed Bob had been a key figure in a My Lai–type massacre. The reporter had found army radio logs that noted "an old man from Thanh Phong presented himself to the district chief's headquarters with claims for retribution for alleged atrocities committed the night of Feb. 25 and 26 February 1969."

In 1969, Bob was a twenty-five-year-old Navy SEAL who led his team on a nighttime raid of a village in the Mekong Delta. They had intelligence that Viet Cong leaders were gathering to meet there, and they went looking for them. What they found and what happened next is at the center of the dispute. Bob remembered they were fired at and that they killed women and children who were in the line of fire, between the SEAL team and what they thought was an "armed cadre in the village."

In 2001, after four years of research, Vistica believed he had enough information for a *New York Times* Sunday magazine cover story. Soon after, he coproduced a *60 Minutes* segment, and finally in early 2003, he published a book on his investigation, which was titled *The Education of Lieutenant Kerrey*.

What ensued was ugly: Vistica's account implied that Bob was covering up war crimes. Three months before the cover story ran, Bob had retired from the Senate, taking the job of president of the New School in Manhattan. In one of his interviews with Vistica, he said that his decision to leave the Senate and not to challenge Al Gore in the 2000 presidential primary wasn't tied to what had happened in Vietnam.

Bob's book, *When I Was a Young Man*, had come out between the publication of the *New York Times* piece and Vistica's book. Bob did not try to erase from his memoir the raid that Vistica had labeled as a war crime. That raid permeated Bob's entire book in subtle and not so subtle ways. He described the context and events of the raid over eight very raw pages that were bookended by his feelings about the war and the subsequent incident in which his right leg was blown apart. Bob wrote that he remembered very little "of what happened in a clear and reliable way," but Vistica wasn't satisfied with fog-of-war memory explanations and interviewed others who were present.

Bob's war experiences informed every moment that came after and that's what his book was meant to document: how war affects warriors. Bearing witness to Bob's reckoning with his past and confronting his Vietnam memories was a discomfiting process I couldn't relate to or fully understand. He was a Medal of Honor recipient, but in the years I knew him I saw the actual medal only once, when I asked him to show it to me. I was insufficiently prepared to understand the ambivalence of those who served in a war as controversial as Vietnam. What did I know of war? I had never served. I did not come from a military family.

Although my father served in World War II, he didn't see combat, and the military wasn't a part of our family identity. He had teletype skills from working in a Chicago courier office before the war, qualifying him for a position in the army's Signal Corps when most of the men at the volunteer board went to the infantry. He set up his communication equipment in King Victor Emmanuel III's palace in Caserta, Italy, outside Naples. He spent the war in the throne room as Nazi warplanes strafed the Italian countryside. Many of those who volunteered alongside him didn't come home. My father did and, thanks to the GI bill, he attended the University of Illinois, where he met my mother.

So my father, who had come home mentally and physically unscathed, hadn't prepared me for this assignment. What I lacked in subject matter expertise, I tried to make up for with basic empathy.

Bob's time in Vietnam ended a few weeks after the deadly raid, when on a subsequent mission, he took enemy fire. Bob's leg had been amputated midcalf as a result of an exploding grenade. He wore a prosthetic, which he was known to joke about, but it also gave him a lot of pain—irritation where the stump met the prosthetic and phantom pain. He didn't talk about the pain. One day we took a drive along Rock Creek Parkway, which runs north-south through the city and ends at the Potomac River.

I had picked up Bob from the Capitol, midafternoon, as I had on other occasions, and I always felt like I was driving the getaway car from a jailbreak. Usually we ended up at a restaurant or a bar, but this time he asked if we could find a drugstore. I could tell something was bothering him because he wasn't his usual cheerful self. When he came out, I finally pressed him to tell me what was wrong, and he said the prosthetic was irritating his skin and he needed some sort of ointment or bandage—I can't remember which. He didn't want sympathy, and I let it go.

What the war had done to him at his core was hard to measure, especially because I met him so many years after he went to Vietnam; I don't know who he was before he served. But there was a toughness, a grittiness that was obscured by the passage of time and by what his present life required of him. Magazine articles focused on his quirkiness—the usual "this is not your average politician" anecdotes, and also on his sensitive side—his love of literature and poetry. The profiles usually mentioned that he liked to work out his frustrations and confusion in the weird collages he made for the various people in his life, including me. Though he was a gentle person and a loyal friend, I sensed he also had a calcified place in his soul, a secret refuge that people who have witnessed or even taken part in the worst that humanity has to offer keep hidden from plain sight.

Twenty years later, I got a retrospective glimpse into that secret place. A student of mine, a combat veteran who had served two tours in Afghanistan, in addition to being a talented journalist, was also a gifted fiction writer. He asked me to read a short story he had written and drafts went back and forth between us as he worked on it. It was about a young man who goes off to war and ultimately shoots and kills a young boy who reaches for a rifle and the effect it has on his soul. I thought the story was better if the main character didn't have to explicitly justify the shoot because any reasonable reader would know that while it was tragic, it was also justifiable. Other readers thought he should justify the shoot.

I became invested in the story, particularly in how he would ultimately end it. I could see he was wondering why a female with no ties to combat was having such a personal reaction to his story. I told him the story of the birds in my house and how Bob Kerrey had handled the situation.

My story, like my student's, was a good shoot/bad shoot thing. It dawned on me then that the Hitchcock scene at the

Maryland house had been a cosmic test, and I failed. Who are we as readers—as people—to judge a situation we've never been in? By being more compassionate to my student's main character, I was trying to give myself a second chance. Crazy, I know, but that's what fiction gives us, second chances.

I muddled on, same as before, trying to help Bob find the truest thread of his story. But without knowing what happened on that night in 1969, it was hard; he had alluded to something dark, but I didn't push, and he didn't offer. A passage from my diary at the time:

> BK came out to Centreville today. We drove out first
> to Conquest Beach, and beyond. I told him he needs to
> concentrate less on the story of his family and more on his
> interior story.
>
> He told me some story—a short story? A movie?—about
> a guy losing a finger and never running his hands across the
> water, swimming, fishing—with grace—that was the key—
> he had lost the grace.
>
> That was I guess what BK feels he lost when he lost his
> leg, he feels like he lost physical grace? The other moment—
> true moment of the day was when he said he could never go
> home at the end of the day and kick off his shoes.
>
> I said he must have found a different way and he said yes.
> And I said but it wasn't the same and he agreed.
>
> I have to help him tell the truth but it's not fair to force
> him to do something he's not inclined to do . . . But if he
> doesn't tell the truth then it's just another war book.

Though that passage makes it clear I sensed that something awful was eating at him, it wasn't my place to push too hard. Ghostwriters, book doctors, and editors often talk about feeling as though they are practicing psychotherapy or even sitting in moral judgment, a judge and jury who puts a person's past on trial. But we don't have a license to practice medicine or law.

I don't know whether Bob and his men broke the rules of war or morality—or even whether there is a difference between those two. And I don't know what I would do in a situation like that. What I do know is that Bob cared about the people of his state and of his country. He took every vote seriously, and he agonized over many of them.

In the same way he agonized over his Senate work, he agonized over his book, wanting to get it just right, not only the quality of the writing but the memoirist's balancing act between privacy and truth telling. The process of this sort of calibration was valuable to observe, for my work as both a literary midwife and as a writer myself.

Now, having contributed in various capacities to several high-profile books, I felt ready for a new challenge. What came next proved to be a challenge—but not the sort I imagined.

SEVEN

Ghost in the Machine

Did you know Japanese ghosts have
feet? They find it so strange that
ours don't.
—E-MAIL FROM A FRIEND ON A FELLOWSHIP
IN JAPAN

Ten years earlier, when I was still in my twenties, I found
myself standing on the side of the road in Lee, Massachusetts, a former mill town now billed as the "gateway" to the
Berkshires.

It was Labor Day weekend, and I was with a friend and
her boyfriend heading back to D.C. from her family's farm in
Vermont. The clutch had blown in their car, and they were
bickering about whose fault it was. Seeing as I'm naturally
conflict averse and had nothing to add to the conversation, I
drifted away, unnoticed, toward an old Victorian house with
a sign promising JUNK & ANTIQUES. Mercifully, it was open,
and I decided to go in.

I wasn't in the market for a silver snuffbox, an antique
compass, or any number of ship salvage pieces, such as a
mermaid masthead, which would be a cool though hardly
practical acquisition. But vintage jewelry always got my at-

tention, and soon enough I spotted a glass case containing cameos, lockets, and other trinkets.

As I took it all in, my gaze stopped on a tiny clothbound book with the word *Diary* embossed on its faded dark green cover. I asked the woman behind the counter if I could take a look, and she gingerly pulled it out for me.

The diary chronicled the year of 1872 in the life of a teenage girl named Elizabeth Morley. "Libbie," as she referred to herself, had lived in Lee, and she had siblings, parents, cousins, aunts, and uncles, all of whom she referred to in passing. Most of the entries were one or two sentences and were written in a delicate cursive with violet ink. The shopkeeper said she'd sell it to me for a dollar so I bought it, got change for the Coke machine outside, and found myself a shady tree to sit under and let myself be transported back in time.

While my friends were busy resolving our twentieth-century problem, I got lost in the nineteenth century. At first I was disappointed because so many of the entries were mundane observations, focusing on the weather (without central air-conditioning or heat, that was understandable) and various medical ailments of hers and those in her immediate circle (toothaches, headaches, and colds). But eventually a more compelling narrative began to emerge: I noticed that Libbie took pains to note every encounter she had with the family's pastor. A close reading of the diary revealed a fixation on him, and on her Christian faith as a means to connect with him.

I closed the diary when my friends came to say they had tracked down a mechanic who said he could replace the clutch the next day if he could get his hands on the right parts. So with no other viable options, we spent the night at a nearby motel.

The following afternoon we left the town of Lee behind us, but Libbie stayed with me. She occupied a place in my imagination as I wondered what happened to her in the years following the one she had chronicled. A year or two later, again on Labor Day weekend, the same friend and I stopped in Lee on our way back from Vermont and found Libbie's grave site in the town cemetery, high on a hill with a panoramic view of the town. I had found out that Lee was once a paper mill town, and it supplied newsprint for the *New York Times*. It was also known for its marble quarries.

The more I learned about the town and what life was like for a young girl in that era, the more I yearned to know what had become of Libbie. Some years later, I returned to Lee so I could spend time in the town hall records office, the same building where folk singer Arlo Guthrie appeared before a blind judge and his seeing-eye dog for a littering charge, an incident made famous in the song "Alice's Restaurant" and the movie that followed.

I would learn through death records that Libbie became a "carpet weaver" and that what she had written in her diary about one of her cousins was confirmed in the death records: the cousin had died because she was an "opium eater." There was a bleakness to her diary entries, both in what she said and what she didn't say. And that absence of information—what she chose to withhold—fueled my imagination with a certain velocity.

I created my own story of a girl, inspired by Libbie and sharing her name, who, after an inappropriate encounter with her pastor, seeks spiritual comfort in a non-Christian faith, the rising movement of spiritualism—a precursor to the women's movement. Spiritualism was often a young woman's ticket to freedom, a socially acceptable reason to leave home and travel to other towns, participating in séances that facilitated reunions with departed relatives. I set the story ten years earlier than the real Libbie's so that my narrative would coincide with the Civil War.

And this is where it gets weird: my fictional character Libbie ended up in the Lincoln White House, facilitating a séance for First Lady Mary Todd Lincoln, who, in her grief-stricken state over the recent death of her young son Willie, was desperate to commune with him.

I wrote that scene a few years before I would end up in the White House under circumstances oddly reminiscent of that.

EVERYTHING SEEMS TO START with a phone call, and this one was from an editorial assistant who told me to hang on. A moment later, Alice Mayhew came on the line. "We've got a very interesting project in Washington that needs a writer." She paused as though she were choosing her words carefully. "Very interesting. But I can't say who it is."

My heart beat faster. Alice wasn't prone to drama. If she said something was very interesting, that meant it was *very* interesting.

"I'm available," I blurted out, as though I had to respond quickly or I could lose to a higher bidder. My mind was a blur: *Am I really available?* I was still working on Bob Kerrey's war book, but that was part-time and piecemeal. I could work around that.

"Good, good," she said, sounding, as she always did, as though she were in a hurry, probably because she always was. "It's a very prominent woman. That's all I can share right now." My curiosity was increasing by the second. "Her people will contact you," Alice continued. "Is this the best number to reach you?"

Her people. She had "people." That meant she was big. Or at least not small. Since the project was based in Washington, it was likely someone in politics, government, or media. My mind was spinning as I thought about the women I had met during the Marjorie project. A representative or senator? Interesting, but I didn't think Alice would think they were *very* interesting. Sandra Day O'Connor? Ruth Bader Ginsburg? No, it wasn't likely that a sitting justice would write a book, at least not about the inner workings of the Supreme Court. Tipper Gore? *Very* interesting? Meh.

The next morning I left the house early to teach hockey stops and bunny hops to the tiny-tot skating class. Afterward I skipped my own workout, hurrying home to check my answering machine. But when I got home, the light wasn't blinking. I made myself a sandwich and sat down to eat it, staring out at the marsh. The silence, broken only by the clock over the mantel, became more than I could bear. I thought I might go mad waiting for Mystery Woman's "people" to call. I went outside and spent some time doing yard work even though it was still winter. I left the door slightly ajar so I could hear the phone, and finally it rang.

A young woman identified herself and said she was calling from the White House.

THE WHITE HOUSE!

She wanted to know if I was available later that day for an interview with the First Lady. And could I bring some writing samples and a résumé? I mumbled something that resembled an affirmative answer. Then I came to my senses and explained I was on the Eastern Shore of Maryland and would need several hours. She suggested a time, and I agreed, scribbling down which security gate I was to report to.

To say I wasn't dressed properly at the moment to have a meeting with Hillary Clinton was an understatement: I was wearing jeans with holes in the knees and literally had garden soil under my fingernails. But I rallied, transforming myself into a presentable professional. I printed out my résumé, rifled through my files, and gathered some bylines from the *Post*, throwing it all in a folder.

I jumped in my car, praying I had enough gas in the tank and that I wouldn't hit bridge traffic. I couldn't believe it. I had a chance to work with the First Lady of the United States.

That was a big deal, and if I got the gig, it would launch me into a whole other stratosphere professionally. But I also admired her, everything that she had done on behalf of families and children, and it would be an honor to work on her book.

A few hours later I was standing at the White House gate, feeling like an imposter when the guard asked me if I had an appointment. I replied, "The First Lady," my voice shaking a little. He looked at his clipboard and peered at a screen inside his little glass-encased booth. It appeared he couldn't find my name on the list and I was sure he was about to say I must be mistaken. And maybe I was. Maybe I had imagined it all.

But I also knew that people often misheard "Simon" for "Feinman" so I spelled my name slowly and loudly, over the sound of nearby protesters in Lafayette Park across Pennsylvania Avenue. His face registered recognition and he waved me in, the iron gate clicking open, the kingdom beckoning.

A young staffer met me at the door where the guard had indicated I should approach, and soon enough I was walking through the halls of the People's House, simultaneously trying to affect an air of nonchalance while taking in every single detail I could possibly register. I had been there before many times to cover state dinners for the Style section, and once for the meeting with Marjorie Margolies-Mezvinsky, but I had never been to the first family's residence, which is where my guide told me we were heading.

A few minutes later I found myself face-to-face with Hillary Clinton in a cozy sitting room, drinking coffee served by a White House usher. Though I had been ancillary to the interview Marjorie and I had conducted, at least I had a sense of what to expect; this time I couldn't get away with mostly just listening, however.

I had included in my writing samples a long essay I had done for the Style section that was really a love letter to the sport of figure skating. Mrs. Clinton had been a figure skater in her youth, and I saw her pull out that clip and her eyes light up. That led to an easy conversation that moved from skating to writing and the process of book writing.

My nerves calmed down after the first few minutes, and Mrs. Clinton was cordial and had a way about her that made you feel like she was really listening. In part it was her habit of nodding, which was oddly comforting. She looked at my

résumé, really just a list of the various books I had contributed to, and we talked briefly about Marjorie's book.

We ended the meeting with her telling me they would be
in touch with the people at Simon & Schuster once she made
a decision. Her people would call their people who would
call my people (my agent).

I waited and ruminated and brooded. Would I get the job?
Who else was in the running? I couldn't possibly get the job.
I would die if I didn't get the job. I wanted the job so much.
Until I got the job.

A few days later Flip called to say that Simon & Schuster
called, and that Mrs. Clinton had chosen me. I got the impression she hadn't interviewed a lot of people. That made
sense; the more people you told, the more likely the news of
the book deal would leak prematurely. Alice recommended
me and that carried a lot of weight, Flip explained.

As Flip was giving me the good news, all of a sudden I
began to wonder if I really wanted to become involved in
such a scandal-ridden administration. It was early 1995, and
during the two years that Bill Clinton had been president,
the press had swung from one Clinton scandal or PR disaster
to the next like a kid on monkey bars: Travelgate, Filegate,
Vince Foster, and Whitewater. Everyone who worked in the
White House those days seemed to end up getting served a
subpoena.

The president had put Hillary in charge of overhauling the
nation's health-care system, and the whole thing had been a
debacle, ending in defeat in September 1994. This had left
Mrs. Clinton tarnished, and whatever this book project was
purportedly about, it was really about her refashioning her

image. People in Washington rarely write books because the writing muse visits them; rather, they have a campaign to win, a cause to lobby for, a scandal to overcome, or an image to fix.

It's not enough money, I said to Flip. I can't remember what the first offer was. She went back to them, and they came back with a higher offer. She was negotiating with the publishing house because the money would be paid out directly from them to me, rather than the usual arrangement where the advance goes to the author and the author then pays the ghost. The First Lady would not be paid an advance, and any royalties would be donated to charity.

"Not enough," I told Flip.

Long pause. "Really? Is something else going on?" Flip was both a great negotiator and a wise observer of human nature. "If you don't want to do this, you don't have to," she said. "But you need to be honest with me and with yourself."

"I don't know. I do want to do this. I'm just . . ."

Flip got them up to an even higher fee, more than any I had landed so far. In the end, I accepted the job because it was a lot of money, too much money for a freelance writer to turn down. And having this on my résumé would elevate me into the first tier of ghostwriters, enabling me to permanently up my rates.

The other reason I took it was that nearly everyone around me said I'd be crazy not to. When I think back to that moment, I'm reminded of John Steinbeck's novella *The Pearl*. Based on a Mexican folktale, it's the story of a poor pearl diver in Mexico who finds an enormous pearl, "perfect as the moon," and the cascading disasters that happen in his life after he finds it. Like the difficulties of some modern-day lottery winners, his own actions as well as those of others who prey upon him make him wish he had never found the pearl.

I just couldn't shake the bad feeling that started in my gut and settled in my chest, somewhere between anxiety and dread. I'm not saying that I foresaw that this project would become my own "pearl," but just that I felt uneasy. Am I confusing hindsight with sensing regret? Or do I wish I had never gone down the ghostwriting path at all? I thought it was a practical application of my love of writing. When I graduated from Berkeley, I thought I was going to be a writer. As a "writer" I pictured myself writing novels in a garret and somehow magically that garret's rent would take care of itself.

My father, who wanted me to follow my siblings to law school, warned early and often that I would struggle to make a living as a writer. He had grown up during the Depression and, though I didn't find this out until years after I graduated from college, he wanted to be a journalist or an English professor but instead he became a salesman and eventually founded his own small company. His concern for me pursuing a career as a writer was really just his own fear projected.

When I told him the First Lady had chosen me (!) to write her book, I knew I was putting a period at the end of any sentence about law school or bad choices forevermore. He was in kvelling overdrive, bragging to everyone he met between Chicago and Miami.

During the past twenty-four years, I have counseled hundreds of students whose hearts were pulling them toward newsrooms or publishing houses and their parents were tugging them toward law school. Go to law school if you yearn to be a lawyer. Become a writer if you yearn to write. Note that the last sentence lacks parallelism. I said if you "yearn to write" not "yearn to become a writer." There's a difference.

If the romance of "being a writer" is what draws you, forget about it. Not to be a buzzkill but "being a writer" is as much about estimated taxes, paying your own health insurance, and getting rejected on a regular basis as it is about adoring audiences, bylines, and book tours. The students who have a compulsion to write are the ones who will figure out how to make a living doing it. So, yes, go try the writing thing, I tell the obsessed ones. With one caveat: Be a writer but marry a lawyer.

My students who are now successful writers and journalists thank me for that advice more than for anything else I've tried to impart in the classroom or during office hours. And I've had a few who have become lawyers or consultants and confided in me that they wished they had listened to me.

I knew right away that I would have to move back to the city. I needed to be available on the spur of the moment to work with the First Lady, and I also needed the resources of a big library. This was pre-Google so whatever I couldn't find in the files supplied by the White House, I would need to track down through LexisNexis or some other database.

I rented an apartment in Dupont Circle, around the corner from the Washington Hilton, where President Reagan had been shot, near shops and restaurants, just a mile and a half from the White House. My agent handled the details of my book contract, including when I would be paid and by whom, what expenses would be covered, and how I would be acknowledged in the book. The contract included a confidentiality clause.

I was quickly consumed by the task at hand: to make something out of nothing. There wasn't even a working title, much less an idea. The editor I would be working with was someone I didn't know, but we spoke on the phone and she sounded lovely. Shortly after that she came down from New York, and we had a few meetings at the White House with the First Lady to figure out a plan.

The book would showcase Mrs. Clinton's work on behalf of children and her commitment to various issues and policies concerning women and children. Her staff gave me copies of her speeches and other public documents so I could learn what the First Lady's position was on various issues, and I began poring over hundreds of pages. This was all helpful, but the book's shape, its narrative arc, and its overarching point—all that was still unresolved. We would figure all this out by my interviewing the First Lady about relevant topics—mainly what she had learned through the years in her various advocacy roles on behalf of policies related to children. I was to take what she told me, along with what I could find in her files of speeches and other written material, and cobble together first drafts. She would use those as a starting point to make it her own and then it would come back to me and then I would send it on to our editor.

I was reassured that her scheduler understood that this project was a priority and would try to fit me in accordingly so that we could make our deadline. It was February and Simon & Schuster wanted a completed manuscript by the end of the summer, if possible. Every book has its own way of coming into being and this one did not seem unusual except for the high-profile nature of its author. I knew that I needed to get down to business and not allow myself to become preoccupied by gossip and rumors.

One of the first things I wanted to do was come up with a title. Since the book didn't really have a direction or even a thesis, I thought that a title might help us get moving. Before I got this gig, I had begun some work on a magazine piece about successful businesswomen, and I had already scheduled an interview up in New York with the head of a record label. I didn't want to cancel the interview, even though I wasn't sure I was going to have time to bang out a feature piece while also writing a book. During my conversation with the recording executive, I asked her how she had been so successful professionally while dealing with a lot of personal challenges. "Well, you know there's this old African proverb, 'It takes a village to raise a child . . .'"

As soon as we finished the interview, I asked the record exec's assistant if I could use a phone. I couldn't wait to call the book editor. "I think I've got a great title," I said softly into the phone. The right title, as most writers know, can be vexingly elusive. The right title can brand a book, but even more valuably, it can chart its direction and define its thesis or focus.

I was anxious to get back to D.C. and go through Mrs. Clinton's speeches. If I could find an occasion in which she had actually used the phrase, it would indicate that the title was a good fit, that it was organically suited for Mrs. Clinton's book.

After an hour or two combing through binders of her speeches, I found an instance where Mrs. Clinton had used the phrase. When I had called our editor and test-drove the title, she loved it, as did the First Lady. That set in motion all the things that come with a title: the book jacket's design, promotional copy, and, most important, the book's actual framework. Before long we were producing chapters that fit into the "village" theme. Sometimes a title can do that—help to frame and clarify a book's overarching point. I felt like it was divine intervention—or desperation as the clock kept ticking: whatever it was, after we secured the title we were able to hammer out an outline and from there, we could figure out what direction our interviews and research should go in. Working on the book turned out to have three phases that involved me.

The first phase started in February, when I was hired, and lasted through May. During that time I would go over to the White House once or twice a week when the First Lady was in town. I would interview her for an hour or so, sometimes in the residence and sometimes in other areas of the White House, depending on what she was doing. After each interview, the tape was sent out to be transcribed and then I was given the transcript to flesh out early drafts of chapters.

I spent a fair amount of time with her during those interviews. Watching her in action over those first several months, I became fixated on her nodding habit—the thing I had found so comforting in our initial meeting when she interviewed me. I was now beginning to nod very slowly and frequently myself, much like she did. I began to wonder, as I started doing it myself, if the nodding was a way of keeping people at bay, of not letting them into her thought process. If you are listening, it means you aren't the one offering information. Again, a politician's instincts for self-preservation were at odds with an author's need to reveal. Though it was ostensibly a policy book, there were also expectations that there would be a through-line running directly from the First Lady's heart to what appeared on the page.

As I had on other book projects, I found the work to be alternatively stressful and isolating. The group of people whom a ghost has contact with is pretty limited: the subject, who is usually pretty busy and distracted with his or her own celebrity; the editor and her minions, who are usually overworked and hard to nail down; and whoever the ghost is tasked with interviewing or obtaining information from. So while this had sounded like a dream job to my friends and acquaintances, it was mostly like any other project, complete with deadlines and headaches.

There were of course some perks, like stealing White House stationery or getting to ride on *Air Force One* (actually referred to as *Executive One Foxtrot* when the First Lady was flying without her husband) to accompany Mrs. Clinton to an appearance on Oprah's show in Chicago on Tuesday, May 16, 1995, when she said that parents in particular, and society in general, needed to get more involved in child rearing.

My father, who still lived in Chicago, had remarried and was living downtown. When he heard the First Lady would be appearing on *Oprah*, he called and asked if I was coming to town with her, and could he and my stepmother meet her. I knew she had been very gracious to her staffers' families and so I asked if there was any possible way they could just stand outside the building and say hello as we were leaving the show. She said absolutely and stopped to meet them and take photographs with them. It was worth it to see my dad's face, beaming, and know he would never, ever again question my decision to become a writer and not do something more practical with my life.

A mosaic of memories is imprinted on my mind. It was such a busy, pressure cooker time in my life that much of it is a blur. But discrete moments stand out, like one that happened early on when our editor came down from New York to work on the book with us in the White House. Mrs. Clinton was busy with an event—her schedule was always jam-packed with what seemed like an endless parade of silly and time-wasting activities that were obligations hard to dodge.

The editor and I sneaked out on a balcony where we plotted to steal a moment to smoke. Neither of us were big smokers, but circumstances made the allure of a nicotine break hard to resist. We lit up, inhaled, and just as we were blowing out smoke, we looked up to see a Secret Service sharpshooter above us, on the White House roof, checking us out. We put out our cigarettes and retreated inside, nervously giggling.

The second phase of my work with the First Lady came toward the summer, when instead of going over to the White House just once or twice a week I went over several times a week. I worked in the first family's residence, in Mrs. Clinton's home office. I would start the day arriving in the ushers' office and either an usher would escort me up to the residence or they would call Capricia Marshall, who was a special assistant to the First Lady, to come get me. I liked Capricia. She was pleasant and friendly and always made me feel at home. I could see she was under a lot of pressure, but she was the type who would smile through it all.

The room I worked in was on the third floor of the residence. It was modest size with two desks and a sitting area. Sometimes Mrs. Clinton worked at the other desk, but often I was there alone. One evening when I was working late by myself, the phone rang.

I didn't usually answer it because no one would be calling me at the White House. In general, I tiptoed around the place, terrified of making a wrong move, committing some sort of a faux pas. But the phone kept ringing and ringing, and I thought I had better pick it up. I said hello, and the woman on the other end identified herself as a White House operator. She asked if I had seen the president.

"Um, no, I haven't," I said, waiting to hear what she would say next.

I remembered that when I first starting working at the White House, one of the young women on the First Lady's staff had given me an informal tour and pointed out an electronic box that tracked the president's movements by GPS. It struck me as a bit odd that the operator was trying to track him down the old-fashioned way.

"You haven't?" she said. Did she think I was harboring a sitting president?

"No, really, I haven't seen him," I insisted, and then, to underscore my statement, I added, "Ever."

It was true. By this time, I had been working in the White House for four or five months and, much to my disappointment, I had never set eyes on him.

I had begun to worry that I would come to the end of the book without having ever gotten to meet the president. I wanted to meet him because, well, he was the president, and

I had voted for him and also I was just plain curious about what he was like in person.

Soon after that exchange with the operator, I got my wish.

Mrs. Clinton and I were working in her office, and it was coming up on the dinner hour. I heard someone at the door and looked up from my screen and saw President Clinton there, smiling. Mrs. Clinton introduced me, and we exchanged a few pleasantries. Then he said he'd see her at dinner and disappeared. A few minutes later, she got up from her desk.

"Do you want to join us?" she asked.

"Join you?" Did she mean for dinner? And "us"—did she mean her and the president? Of the United States?

"For dinner. Would you like to join us?"

Dinner with the president of the United States and his wife. What an honor. And then I looked down and realized I was wearing sneakers. When we had first started working together, I had dressed up for the White House, but as the weeks wore on, I realized I was working mostly alone, and the days were long so I had begun to dress for comfort, seeing only an occasional aide or a researcher and the butlers who brought us lunch on a tray.

There they were. My New Balance sneakers. And they weren't that new. I couldn't possibly eat dinner with the president of the United States.

"I'm not really dressed for—"

"It's fine," she said, smiling warmly. "Please join us."

A few minutes later, I found myself seated at a small table in the solarium with President Clinton, Mrs. Clinton, and Kaki Hockersmith, an interior designer friend from Little

Rock who had done the Clinton White House private quarters redecoration in 1993. It reportedly cost close to four hundred thousand dollars. Like many White House decorating costs, it was criticized even though the funding had come from private sources.

The president asked how the book was going and then asked some general questions about the state of the publishing industry. I managed to string words into sentences and sentences into paragraphs. His responses seemed to indicate that I was making sense, but I can't swear to that.

Then Kaki presented the president with an early birthday present, a framed sketch of famous 1940s and 1950s Hollywood stars in silhouette, all mingling around a pool. We spent some time trying to determine who was who. This triggered the president to talk about his love for the movie *High Noon*.

During all this, our food was served. Though usually I have a healthy appetite, I couldn't possibly eat and instead pushed my food around the plate. When the butler was clearing our plates, as he took mine he winked at me.

"Sorry," I whispered. "I'm so nervous."

He leaned over and said, "Don't worry about it. Most people can't eat around the president, at least not the first time."

Afterward we walked down the hall, and I stopped at Mrs. Clinton's office, where I planned to keep working. The president said something about heading to the White House theater to watch a movie with "Steve." My memory is that he indicated he meant Spielberg (!). I figured the famous director, who was a big Democratic donor, was a guest at the White House but had had a dinner engagement in the city. Maybe I would run into him getting a late-night snack.

"Are you joining us?" President Clinton said politely as we approached the office.

"I need to get back to work, but thank you," I said quickly.

THE BOOK WAS DUE to Simon & Schuster by summer's end, and the pressure was mounting as our deadline approached because this was an incredibly tight production schedule, tighter than any I had ever been involved with. It looked like it was going to become necessary for me to accompany the Clintons on the seventeen-day family vacation to Jackson Hole, Wyoming, in August.

This sounds like a great trip, but I knew I would be stuck in some motel when I wasn't working with the First Lady on the book. What followed would be the final phase of my work on the book. There would be little to no downtime, and I would be thousands of miles away from my friends and family. And that's exactly what happened, and to make matters worse, I sprained my ankle a week before we were leaving. I was on crutches and not very adept at using them.

Mrs. Clinton saw me struggling to get to and from the White House, and she suggested I stay in one of the spare bedrooms in the residence. I slept there for three nights, in a room just down the hall from Mrs. Clinton's home office. It was very convenient, plus it gave me bragging rights.

My ankle was healing slowly, and I dreaded going to Wyoming. The first family would be staying at West Virginia senator John D. Rockefeller IV's eight-thousand-square-foot ranch in Grand Teton National Park. The hotel where the support staff and I stayed was not terribly far away, and someone got me a rental car so I could drive back and forth between the ranch and the hotel.

The White House staff was an insular bunch, and for the most part, they ignored me. I felt completely isolated and stressed out because of the pressure of trying to get the book finished in this insanely short amount of time. Mrs. Clinton spent much of her time working, and she was distant and preoccupied, worried about her upcoming trip to China. In addition to working on the book, she was also focused on the speech she was slated to deliver in Beijing at the United Nations Fourth World Conference on Women in early September.

She was meant to lead the American delegation, and it was an opportunity for her to showcase her commitment to the rights of women and children on a world stage. Her speech would be the first phase of her image makeover after the health-care debacle. Her image had not recovered, in part because the Senate Special Whitewater Committee hearings had begun that summer, during which her and her husband's business dealings would come under scrutiny once again, as would lingering questions regarding Deputy White House Counsel Vince Foster's suicide.

The book's publication would come just four months later. But the snag in this plan was a growing controversy about whether the First Lady should attend the conference because China was holding human rights advocate Harry Wu on espionage charges. Wu had spent nineteen years in Chinese labor camps, then come to the United States and become an American citizen, where he continued his human rights activism. Just a few months before, he had been detained during a visit back to China.

Mr. Wu was convicted and then, inexplicably, deported, so Mrs. Clinton's dilemma of whether or not to go became moot. Anyone who has studied the trajectory of her career would say that that speech was the beginning of becoming a politician in her own right and that her platform would be women's rights. Probably the most famous line from her speech is: "If there is one message that echoes forth from this conference, let it be that human rights are women's rights and women's rights are human rights, once and for all."

One day when I was staring out the window at the Rockefeller ranch, distracted by the natural beauty and wishing I was hiking or swimming, I received a package. The handwriting was familiar. I tore open the cardboard box and saw that Bob Kerrey had sent me a care package. We had talked on the phone the week before, and I must have sounded a bit down.

The box was filled with some small presents, mostly things to make me laugh, wacky collages he had made and gag gifts. But he had also included a letter, and its tone was somber, telling me about a friend who had just suffered the loss of a child.

"He will be thinking of death, now; wishing it would come to him, wondering why this had to happen," he wrote. "I don't have anything close to an answer. Sorry for the grief mixed with the gifts. I am afraid it's hard to find a day without both. I'll be happier when you finish the Village people."

So will I, I thought. *So will I.* Or so I thought.

EIGHT

Losing My Religion

To keep your secret is wisdom; but to
expect others to keep it is folly.
—SAMUEL JOHNSON

The stretch of Massachusetts Avenue NW that is referred to
as Embassy Row is home to some of the city's most prominent politicians and diplomats. It's also known for its magnificent old mansions and tree-lined sidewalks. And it's where
I found myself walking one mild, sunny October afternoon,
the sort of day that lulled me into ignoring my ambivalence
about living in Washington. I was even able to tell myself
that this swamp could be beautiful when the humidity wasn't
choking you every time you stepped out your door.

My walking companion this day was Bob Woodward, my
old boss and a resident of nearby Georgetown. Our afternoon
stroll had started from his home.

I had completed my work with Mrs. Clinton on *It Takes a
Village* just the week before, and I was now returning to my
"regular" life. I was in the process of trying to forget all the
First Lady's speech patterns and favorite turns of phrase and

various sensitivities. I wanted to reembody "Barbara," even though, by this point, I'd been involved with so many other people's voices, I wasn't exactly sure who "Barbara" was at times.

I knew the book's publication date was just three months away, in January 1996. With the manuscript in the hands of the publishing house and having been told it was going into production, I was given the all clear and had booked a ticket to Rome, where I planned to start a three-week tour of Italy, spending the first week with a friend, the latter two by myself.

I was looking forward to all of it, but particularly to the second leg of the trip when I'd take a train to Cinque Terre, the five small villages tossed along the Italian Riviera like a strand of perfect pearls swept ashore. I had last been to Italy after graduating from Berkeley, thirteen years earlier, and ever since then, I had missed Cinque Terre's little seaside cafés and sleepy rhythms. What better way to restart or at least unpause my real life than to spend a chunk of time in a place where no one knew me, where I could be exactly myself? This was my reasoning at the time, but I realize now that perhaps I hadn't thought it through.

Woodward had invited me over for coffee, "for a visit," he'd said on the phone. I'd been so busy during the eight months I worked on *Village* that I had neglected not only him, but pretty much everyone in my life. Eight years had passed since I'd worked for him on *Veil*, but we'd stayed in touch, I was invited to his and Elsa's wedding, and to occasional parties they threw, and every so often we would catch up over a meal. And, now that I was in my midthirties, I considered him a friend and a mentor, someone I still turned to for advice, both professional and personal. This is similar to the role he has played with other research assistants before and after me; we were an informal club of young people he had helped launch into the media world and continued to support and promote generously.

I had gone over to Woodward's house thinking we would catch up over coffee in his kitchen, but after a while he suggested we stretch our legs, take a stroll. During the four years I had worked for him and the subsequent eight I had known him, we had never taken a walk for the sake of walking, and in retrospect it's clear to me now that this should have been the tip-off that something was up.

I had accompanied him on plenty of interviews, to lots of places, out to lunch, even ice-skating with him and his young daughter, but we'd never gone for a leisurely walk. It was completely unexpected, which explains, in part, why I was wearing delicate black suede flats, with toe-shoe-like slippery satin laces that wouldn't stay tied. After they came undone for the umpteenth time, Woodward, out of impatience or kindness or both, kneeled down and tied them securely for me. The gesture was avuncular, but I was embarrassed by its intimacy.

After we dispensed with the personal catching up—how his daughter was doing in college, news about contemporaries of mine who had also helped him on books—Woodward asked me, as he had the few other times I'd seen him, what my impressions were of the First Lady, particularly now that my work on *Village* was complete and I could consider my time with her as a whole.

The year before, in 1994, Woodward had come out with *The Agenda*, a book about the Clinton administration's first hundred days. I knew he was working on another book about Clinton, but I didn't know what the book's focus was and I also knew him well enough not to ask. But it was logical he was picking up the narrative where *The Agenda* had left off.

Unsure what exactly Woodward was asking, I tried to answer in coolly general terms. I wanted to sound wise, as if I had some truly profound observations to share, as if the investigative training I'd received while working for him was alive and well in me and I could dissect Hillary Clinton with a cold and unsentimental eye. But I had signed a confidentiality agreement and didn't want to break the rules.

Woodward had been nothing but kind and generous to me for as long as I'd known him, and I admired him and valued his friendship. I also trusted him completely. This is what I'd always thought, what I'd always known to be true. The trustworthiness of Woodward, and of other people in my life with whom I had a similar relationship and past, was my religion, really. But I had told him early on that I had signed an agreement and he knew I was legally bound by the contract, so why was he pushing?

What was her mood, her state of mind, he wanted to know. Was she depressed? I'd come to work for Mrs. Clinton in early 1995, just months after her initiative on health care had been declared dead in September 1994. She was also dealing with the ongoing Whitewater mess. And before that, in 1993, she had suffered the personal loss of Vince Foster and had to endure the hateful and ridiculous rumors, gossip, and conspiracy theories surrounding his suicide. With these seemingly endless scandals that were stacking up like plates in a diner, who wouldn't be down?

It would be hard to imagine that anyone who had been through the experiences she'd had in recent years could come out the other side and not be a little battered. And it wasn't a state secret that she wasn't particularly carefree at this time in her life. *It Takes a Village*, obviously, was in large part meant to rehabilitate her image, to remind people that she had fought for the rights of women and children professionally as an attorney and advocate.

My stomach suddenly knotted up, and I knew. He was pressing me like a source. I'd read, transcribed, organized, and scrutinized hundreds of his interviews when I had worked for him at the *Post* and then as his researcher on *Veil*. I knew his interviewing techniques as well as I knew the name of the hospital where I'd been born or my mother's maiden name. I'd tried to use the techniques myself, to coax details and nuance and stories out of my ghostwriting clients. He knew I'd been in close proximity to the First Lady, a First Lady who had been more publicly acknowledged to be involved in policy making than any wife of the president in history.

I was all of a sudden aware that he was working on me in that moment, that he was using the convenience of our personal connection, the one I held so dear, to find out what I might know. The invitation to catch up, I now realized, had been a ruse because Woodward knew I was leaving town for nearly a month, and he intended to "empty my pockets" while my memory was still fresh.

I'd wanted to believe his interest in seeing me was personal, that our bond was still strong. And maybe it was. Maybe it wasn't an either/or calculus. Maybe he did care about me, but at the same time, he wanted to know what I knew. My value to him in that moment was as a commodity (knowledge) rather than as a friend. He must have thought—or felt—on some level that once a Woodward person, always a Woodward person, meaning a journalist who sucks up information. It was naive and magical thinking on my part to believe anything else was going on here.

Nothing, really? he said, with a mix of disbelief and disappointment in his eyes.

Not really, I answered, hesitating, thinking back to what had happened that spring day in the White House.

Woodward waited. We kept walking. The air between us felt heavy.

This, I had learned from observing the master, was the moment in the interview when it was critical for him not to spook his source by saying the wrong thing. This is when it's safest to stay quiet but maybe just cock your head to the side, expectantly. To calibrate the eye contact—not too much but not too little—so that candor is the only choice. When a child is on the brink of finally jumping from the edge of the pool into the deep end, if you nudge his back too soon, he might turn around and wrap himself around your shins and never let go. But if you stand there, quietly encouraging, he'll jump. Prod only when nothing else works. Hold out as long as possible to see if that's necessary. Which is what Woodward did, eyes full of restrained hope.

Finally, I gave in, I gave him the pearl, but not before spelling out all kinds of conditions that he couldn't use anything I told him. I told him this was just so he could understand the mood of the White House. I'm sure I was telling myself that that's why I was talking like this.

I won't, he said.

I believed him.

Have I asked myself why a thousand times? Ten thousand? Probably more. And the answers I come up with are never definitive, because how can I reconstruct what I was feeling in that one pivotal moment when I opened my mouth instead of keeping it closed? Why did I do it? Probably the main reason is because I trusted him not to use the material, which is what he promised. At least I trusted him not to use what I told him until the people involved were dead. Or I was dead. Also there's no question that I wanted to please him. To tell anyone a secret about something that went on in the White House is tempting, but to tell Bob "Watergate" Woodward, the maestro of knowing—it was irresistible.

And there's also my history of confusing the difference between wanting to trust someone and being able to trust someone. I fall for people. I fall too easily for them, whether it's a new fabulous friend, the best boss ever, or, back when I was single, for some great guy who turned out to be not so great. And though I embraced the anonymity of ghostwriting because it was unthreatening, it was also unsatisfying. I didn't recognize it then but now, twenty years later, I have to admit that this ambivalence played a part in my lapse in judgment.

The minute I started telling Woodward this story, I could almost see myself from a distance looking at the two of us walking down the beautiful street, and I could see the words coming out of my mouth.

In late March, just a few months after I'd started working with Mrs. Clinton on her book, she and fifteen-year-old Chelsea had gone on a tour of Egypt and five countries in South Asia. You may remember the photo ops of them riding camels in front of the pyramids and wearing safari hats atop elephants in Nepal. When they returned, I was called over to the White House for a "debriefing" of the trip.

By this time, Mrs. Clinton and I had written very little of the book, just a handful of scenes and sketches, and the title of course. The editors at Simon & Schuster were asking me for more pages, and in turn, I had been asking for more time on the First Lady's schedule. That was a large part of my job: to ask for more time, first politely, then more firmly but always apologetically.

I felt bad having to insist, especially because I could see that her scheduler, who was an extremely nice and funny person, was under a lot of pressure to fulfill all sorts of demands made on the First Lady's time, but this book couldn't be produced without Mrs. Clinton's attention. She wasn't the type of person to just slap her name on something someone else had written, which meant I had to generate pages that originated with her ideas and input and then went back to her for her to make her own. But that required time, lots of time.

I'd already steeped myself in the transcripts of speeches

she'd given and in videos of her public appearances, as well as anything published under her name. This was my routine. It was how I always worked. I began a project by pulling together all the available materials so I could engineer a believable, if not necessarily accurate, voice through which we could deliver the intended message. In some cases, for some clients, I was able to imagine, invent, and intuit what the client would say. I would then construct chapters that would come together as a complete manuscript, and the client would read them and make changes that then made it the client's own book.

But with someone as high profile and accomplished and closely observed as Hillary Clinton, I couldn't do that without more direct input from her. And the thing I was having trouble figuring out was what *was* the message of the book?

With *It Takes a Village*, though the stakes were higher than those I'd dealt with in the past, my struggles with it were the same ones I'd encountered before: authors expecting a book to materialize out of thin air, ordering up a finished book as if it were a bacon cheeseburger, but not realizing that a good book takes a lot of time, fresh material, and patience. I needed more time with Mrs. Clinton to get her ideas, her thoughts, her previous body of work summarized and into some semblance of a booklike product.

So when I was called to the White House for what they described as a "debriefing," I didn't know what to think because this hadn't been suggested before. I imagined my sitting in on a staff meeting during which the events of the trip would be reviewed and wise observations would be made about the First Lady and the First Daughter on their First

Camel Ride. I expected to go home yet again with an empty notebook.

But when I arrived that particular day at the White House for our meeting, I was taken to a sitting room I'd never been to during any of my previous visits. Soon two women, both in their mid- to late fifties, joined me. I didn't realize they were waiting for the same meeting until one of Mrs. Clinton's staffers arrived and made hasty introductions. One woman, the smaller of the two, was prim and professional and was introduced as Mary Catherine Bateson. The other, big boned and earthy looking with a rich mane of dark brown hair, was Jean Houston. Neither name meant anything to me.

The three of us followed our escort along the stately halls. We were headed for the first family's residence, where I'd been many times before, but then the aide said we'd be meeting in the solarium, a room well known for its southern exposure and panoramic view of the Washington Monument. If you imagine a typical photo of the White House's south face, the side with the semicircle of columns at its center, the solarium is the room sitting atop the semicircle.

This room's magnificent vantage point, with probably the best views in Washington, is accessible only to the privileged few who are invited. It is definitely not a stop on the daily White House tours. It served as a teen hangout for the Johnson girls, it was where Mamie Eisenhower held her bridge parties, where Nixon's son-in-law Ed Cox studied for the bar exam, and where, later, Nixon told his family he was resigning from the presidency. It was where Rosalynn Carter studied Spanish, where Nancy Reagan was told, just sixty-nine days into her husband's presidency, that he had been shot, and where the Gipper then recuperated from that assassination attempt. In other words, this was not just some room in the White House.

Its decor, unlike most of the mansion, had a lived-in, understated quality: comfy couches and chairs you could sink into and a few tables for dining or playing games. It was a place reserved for private life rather than photo opportunities. I sat down in a chair that faced the expansive view of the mall and tried not to stare at the two other women, while wondering what was going on.

It turns out that the two of them were just as interested in figuring out who I was. As we waited for the First Lady, Houston and Bateson tried to get a bead on me. They asked questions about my professional accomplishments. I felt like they were two cops working in tandem to get the suspect to reveal how she'd ended up at the scene of a crime. What other books have you worked on? they wanted to know. How did Hillary find you? Where did you go to school? When did you graduate? Their tone was gradually but noticeably shifting from curious to territorial. Then one of them asked if I considered myself religious.

I had been raised in a Reform Jewish household, but I was unreligious, really, agnostic at best. Religion just didn't resonate with me. But I had already taught at Georgetown for a couple of years, and it's a Jesuit university. So I was comfortable around religious-minded people, though I wasn't one myself. Even so, I hesitated when these two women asked me about my religion. Plus, I still had no idea who they were.

"Not religious in the traditional sense, necessarily," Houston said. "But spiritual, do you consider yourself spiritual?"

"Spiritual?" I said. "Sure, I guess."

"How so?"

"Well, I'm, uh, I'm a figure skater."

They looked at me with blank stares, as they should have, considering that I wasn't really sure where I was going with this.

"Skaters tend to be either jumpers or spinners," I began to explain slowly, allowing myself time to feel my way around, wanting to give these strangers some kind of answer, in part because I felt pressured, and also because their intrusiveness annoyed me and I thought it might be fun to mess with them. "And I'm a spinner. Definitely a spinner. And the practice of spinning," I went on, "it grounds me. The act of spinning is literally one of centering oneself. There's a beauty in going nowhere fast." I looked into their faces, and they were nodding. They appeared inclined to take themselves very seriously and perhaps that is what fueled my performance. "And in accepting this, you learn to focus not on the destination, but *on the journey.*"

Just then Mrs. Clinton entered the room and saved me from meandering further into my own nonsense. Finally, I thought, we were going to get down to the business at hand, whatever that business actually was. Because I was there solely to help the First Lady with her book project, I briefly wondered whether these women were being brought in on the book somehow.

Soon enough it became apparent what the spiritual inquisition had been about. Houston, I was piecing together from the conversation that followed, was some kind of spiritual or psychic guide and had, on other occasions, led a therapeutic exercise with the First Lady, one in which she would imagine she was addressing some historical figure.

I gathered next that the First Lady would then carry on a dialogue with that person. Apparently Houston and Bateson were here at the White House to facilitate another one of these role-playing activities. Nancy Reagan had her horoscopes and Mary Todd Lincoln had her séances. *Whatever gets you through the night*, I told myself.

Bateson remained a silent observer while Houston suggested the First Lady close her eyes and imagine she was talking to Eleanor Roosevelt. There they were together in the White House, the ghost of a former First Lady in conversation with the current First Lady, discussing the challenges of the job. Then Houston told her to switch roles and inhabit Mrs. Roosevelt's mind.

What was unfolding before me was oddly familiar, really just another iteration of method acting, what I engaged in to assume a ghostwriting role. I used it as a technique akin to literary ventriloquism, a means of appropriating authorial voice. As a writing tool it struck me as one of many useful ways to construct a voice. But this was not that: rather, what I was witness to felt like an act of desperation, not of creativity, and a deeply personal one at that. I wondered if everyone had forgotten I was there.

I'd gone to school in California and, although I'd never eaten magic mushrooms or taken LSD, I'd hung out with plenty of people who had and who had hallucinated all sorts of wacky stuff. So really, in the grand scheme of things, this wasn't such a big deal. Well, I guess that's true when it's happening with someone other than the wife of the leader of the free world. But watching Mrs. Clinton pretend to talk to Mahatma Gandhi and Eleanor Roosevelt spoke to her state of mind, I thought. If these two women were the people she chose to spend her time with, had she been brought to her knees by the Washington machine so forcibly that the only way up was through this silly exercise?

And so, while it wasn't exactly fodder for the type of book I was supposed to be birthing, it raised my curiosity, and I looked up Bateson and Houston as soon as I got home. Bateson, it turned out, was a cultural anthropologist and writer, having followed in the footsteps of her parents, the famous anthropologists Margaret Mead and Gregory Bateson. Houston was a New Agey author and motivational speaker who believed in various forms of psychic experience. A quick Google search now, twenty years after our meeting, brings up Houston's website, complete with the requisite "Dalai Lama and me" shot and a bio declaring that Houston, as a "scholar, philosopher and researcher in Human Capacities, is one of the foremost visionary thinkers and doers of our time. She is long regarded as one of the principal founders of the Human Potential Movement." She is also, apparently, the founder and sole teacher of something she refers to as the Mystery School.

But I didn't know any of this on that afternoon in 1995. All I knew was that Mrs. Clinton had summoned me to the White House to meet with a couple of women with whom she had some sort of ongoing relationship and who made me feel uneasy. No one seemed to think the afternoon's activities were out of the ordinary and so neither should I.

Nevertheless, as I left the White House that day, I felt unsettled about my standing. Mrs. Clinton's posse of handlers, schedulers, social secretaries, speechwriters, and other myriad helpers—the infamous "Hillaryland"—had always regarded me cordially but with little warmth and even less interest, and the vibe I had gotten from Houston and Bateson had felt downright frosty. People in Washington measured their own power by how closely they stood to the center. I was an outsider granted instant proximity. This gave me power, however temporary, and it may have threatened Hillaryland's power. But this was all abstract. I had a much more pressing and tangible concern: I didn't see how this session could possibly fit into the book we were supposed to be producing, and the afternoon I had just spent struck me as entirely fruitless. I didn't know what to think or how to proceed.

I RECOUNTED THE EVENTS of that afternoon that had occurred five months earlier as we made our way back to Woodward's house. A heavy, sickening feeling was growing in the pit of my stomach, but once I'd started talking and Woodward had started nodding his approval, the story just came out. He reassured me he would keep his promise not to tell anyone what I'd told him, that he'd protect me.

He wouldn't use the material I had given him. Not now, not ever. He had said he only wanted to understand Mrs. Clinton's general state of mind. This is what I wanted to hear and so I tried to silence the voice inside my head telling me I'd just made a huge mistake, both a tactical one and a moral one.

I went home, and with nothing else left to do before my

flight the next day, I cleaned up my apartment and made sure I'd paid all my bills before taking off for Italy. I like order in that specific way that a nervous person with an unquiet mind likes order. Before departing on a trip, I leave my home in an organized, tidy state.

Upon my return, I want to enter a home with a clean kitchen, a freshly made bed, and a bathroom that looks like it's had recent and vigorous contact with a sponge. I lived in a brownstone that featured a turret, a round open space that jutted off my living room with big windows that looked directly onto S Street with Florida and Connecticut Avenues in the distance. My sister's husband, the sculptor and furniture maker (who, you'll remember had been front-page news in the *Washington Post* back in the '80s, thanks to me), had built a desk for the space, a curved walnut surface with black metal legs and copper feet. I tidied the desk and dusted its surface, and filed away the stacks of papers that had accumulated over the months of *Village*.

As I was doing so I came across a microcassette tape. I held the tape in my hand and stared at the label, written in my inelegant scrawl: "Vince Foster."

Foster was a boyhood friend of Bill Clinton's and had hired Hillary Clinton at the Rose Law firm, which later became entangled in the Whitewater scandal. The president had appointed Foster White House deputy counsel. In May of 1993, just a few months after Foster began working in the Clinton administration, he got caught up in a Washington flap called Travelgate. Foster had become distraught over the possibility that in the coming weeks he'd be forced to testify before Congress regarding the Clintons' involvement.

In the summer of 1993, just six months after the Clintons moved into the White House, Foster was found dead of a self-inflicted gunshot in Fort Marcy Park, across the Potomac from northwest D.C., off George Washington Parkway. Later a torn-up, unsigned suicide note was discovered in Foster's briefcase, the last lines of which read, "I was not meant for the job or the spotlight of public life in Washington. Here ruining people is considered sport."

One of the themes of *It Takes a Village* was the resilience of children, and on the trip to Chicago for the *Oprah* show appearance, I'd finagled some face time with the First Lady and asked her about Vince Foster in the context of what children need in order to grow up to be resilient adults. I'd recorded her answer onto the tape that was now in my hand. Nothing even the slightest bit provocative was on it but, still, Foster's name was a lightning rod for conspiracy theorists who contended that the Clintons had had him murdered, so as I held it in my hand I felt uneasy, and I decided to put it away for safekeeping because it was too late in the day to arrange its return to the White House, which I was contractually obliged to do.

Since my desk didn't have any drawers I put it in my secretary, an old piece of furniture from my parents' house that had one of those fold-down writing surfaces. If you pulled down the desktop, it revealed a row of pigeonholes where you could line up bills to be paid or store envelopes or a letter opener. Or a tape from the White House you weren't really supposed to have retained.

That night I tossed and turned, fretting about flying but also about my conversation with Woodward. I'd known the man for a dozen years. I'd been to his wedding, his daughter's school plays. He had consoled me through my mother's illness and death. He wouldn't betray me. But what if he did? What if he somehow rationalized to himself that he wasn't betraying a source? Was there a Woodwardian loophole to the transaction that I wasn't considering? What if everything fell apart? What would I do if I didn't have my work writing books? It was too late to go to law school, like my father had wanted. I was in my midthirties, no spring chicken, as Ben Bradlee liked to point out as often as possible.

I put these thoughts on repeat and let them play over and over as I lay in bed and stared at the ceiling. Finally I told myself firmly that I just needed to get on the plane to Italy and embrace the whole *dolce far niente* thing: drink wine, stare out at the sea, and think about anything besides work. I always felt restless and tense after finishing a ghostwriting project, as if I'd been dropped off at a gas station on a lonely stretch of desert road and watched my fellow traveler drive off without me. I needed to get my bearings. I needed to get out of Washington.

FOR THREE WEEKS I traveled around Italy, first with a friend and then on my own, as planned. The friend was Deborah Needleman, now the editor of the *New York Times T Magazine*, and I'd known her since we became friends when we both worked at the *Post*. Deborah was obsessed with gardens and had arranged for us to tour several of Italy's most beautiful ones.

We were both total Italophiles, and we immersed ourselves in the scenery, the people, and the language. Spending time with her helped me begin to feel like myself again. This was before the Internet was as we know it now, so not only was I far away from Washington but I was also cut off from everyone I knew. With an ocean between us, I was able to push Mrs. Clinton and Woodward out of my mind, or at least hold them at bay.

After Rome we went to Florence, which is where Deborah and I separated, she to catch her flight back to New York, me to take the train to the Riviera. Soon enough I was stowed away at a little seaside hotel that was empty and affordable. No one knew where I was. No one even knew my name except the hotel receptionist because she had my passport locked in a safe. The anonymity of this, after the fishbowl of Washington, was intoxicating.

Each morning I spent a few hours writing fiction, and then I would go buy a sandwich and sit out by the sea for hours, just watching and listening to the waves crash against the shore. It was October so it was too cold to swim, and the beach was empty except for an occasional fisherman, with his cuttlefish haul, or a villager going for a stroll. I became fascinated by a young, beautiful nun who, each day, I saw taking a walk by the sea, dressed in a long gray-and-white habit, on the arm of an older woman I imagined to be her mother.

Every afternoon they took the same route at the same pace and never spoke. They had an air of stoic resignation about them and I decided the young nun was ill, probably with tuberculosis, and that the sea air had been prescribed by the local *dottore*. Or maybe she was lovesick, having forsaken man as her husband but finding marriage to the Lord personally unfulfilling. Maybe—fingers crossed—she had tragically fallen for an Italian priest.

I cycled through these various scenarios but never landed on a resolution. I hadn't left the frustrated novelist back at home. Wherever I went, there she was, trying to weave a dramatic plot point out of the mundane.

Is this the real me? I wondered. This curious, sometimes meddlesome thirtysomething who just wanted to *know*? Certainly that side of me had come in handy during my years of ghostwriting, but did that mean I liked it? That I should embrace it? It was embarrassing sometimes. More than once, at a party or with a client or even with a friend, I had asked just one more question and drawn a raised eyebrow or a sidelong look that said, *Why do you care? What's it to you?*

But really, what fascinated me more than what did happen—in the realm of journalism and to a certain extent, ghostwriting— was what *could* happen. So why was I spending so much of my time pursuing the former and not the latter? Was it as simple as what I told myself, that I had to make a living?

The sea air, the pasta, the potentially poignant Italian "characters" all around me—these were conditions ripe for self-reflection, but I knew I would be asking myself similar questions even if I were back in my apartment in D.C. I asked them every time I finished a project and was suddenly no longer required to focus on anyone other than myself. I felt like I'd been asking them for years. There I would be, on the brink of some breakthrough with the questions, and then another project would come along, and before I knew what had happened, I would be submerged in another person's life, their triumphs and troubles.

All too soon it was time to head to Milan, so I left behind the tragic nun and the *risotto al nero di seppia*. I took the train from Cinque Terre to Milan and spent a day sightseeing and visiting La Scala. After walking probably ten miles among the boutique-lined streets, I wore myself out and crawled into bed in a hotel room that was beyond my budget. My exhaustion had overruled my judgment.

On the flight home, I was agitated. The air was rough, bouncing us around. As we neared our destination, the plane dipped down through the clouds, and Washington was again visible, exactly as I had left it: The monuments of Jefferson, Lincoln, and Washington were arranged like step stones through a brilliant green lawn leading right up to the backyard of the White House. It was a beautiful city, I admitted, trying to talk myself into something. Maybe it would be good to be back, after all.

I SLID MY KEY into the lock and pushed open the door with my free hand. The Dupont Circle apartment I had moved into for the *Village* project was in an old brownstone with a working fireplace and an ornately carved wood mantel above it, and a congresswoman who lived beneath me. I loved the location, and the apartment was cozy, sunny, and full of character. It was a one-bedroom, considerably nicer and bigger than that first cockroach-filled studio in Foggy Bottom I'd lived in thirteen years earlier.

I pulled my suitcase over the threshold and into the foyer. Late-morning light flooded the living room through the turret windows. I was sleep deprived and starving for sugary or salty carbohydrates. I walked into the kitchen and stopped short, disoriented by what I saw there on the floor: blue-and-gray shards of something that looked familiar.

It took me a minute to understand the scene in front of me, but then I realized it was my beloved ceramic pie plate, a gift from my sister, who frequented craft fairs and had bought this for me as a housewarming gift when I'd moved into my first place. It had been on the shelf above the sink. Somehow it had become dislodged and shattered.

But that wasn't all. Inexplicably, a wine bottle, unopened, unbroken, was resting upside down on its thin top, leaning against the bottom of my refrigerator. It, too, had been on the shelf. How had it fallen a good six feet and not busted wide open? And even more incredible, how could it land upside down and remain standing? It made no sense.

I felt a little frightened and looked around, my mind replaying my movements of the last few minutes. The door had been locked when I slid the key in, hadn't it? When I put the key in the lock, I heard the deadbolt click open, hadn't I? Tentatively, I walked into the bedroom and then the bathroom and even the closet, looking everywhere, listening for anything. I reassured myself I was alone in the apartment and that nothing was missing.

My jewelry was untouched in its leather case, my graduation strand of pearls, my mother's diamond engagement watch, a pair of diamond stud earrings. None of it was exactly the Hope Diamond, but altogether there was probably five thousand dollars' worth of jewelry, a decent day's haul for a random burglar. But, no, it was all still there.

I went back to the living room and hit "play" on the answering machine. I don't know what I expected to hear: someone calling to say, *Hey, I broke in, smashed a ceramic dish, and left a wine bottle upside down on your kitchen floor. Hope you had a nice trip.* None of the messages was urgent. One friend had called to invite me to a dinner party scheduled for the next evening. I returned the call and said I'd love to come, that I'd just gotten back and that I'd be there with a bottle of wine and a story to go with it.

I succumbed to jet lag the next day, falling asleep for several hours, and woke up to darkness, nearly missing the dinner party. I took a shower, threw on some party clothes, and arrived midway through the main course. I presented the wine and told my dinner companions about it as the host uncorked it.

The consensus after several minutes of deliberation was that a truck or jackhammer must have caused a big vibration on the street, launching the pie plate and the bottle on their trajectories. That a bottle had landed and stayed balanced on its thin top was unlikely but not impossible, the crowd collectively concluded. We drank the wine and declared the case closed and I put it out of my mind.

The jet lag continued. I stumbled through the next few days, waking at weird hours, craving huevos rancheros at 2:00 A.M., watching *Cheers* reruns at 4:00 A.M., falling asleep at 11:00 A.M. On my fourth day home, I finally woke up at a normal hour and decided it was time to restore some semblance of a routine to my life. Since *Village* was done, I needed to find a new gig.

I looked at the to-do list I had started before my trip. Calling my agent was on the list, to check in about any new potential projects. I had a freelance story idea to write a pitch for. Then there were smaller tasks: call the dentist, get the chimney cleaned and order some wood, return the tape to the White House. Oh yeah, the tape. I walked over to the secretary and pulled down the movable door.

The tape wasn't where I'd left it, next to the letter opener. But the letter opener was there, alone, in the pigeonhole. My chest tightened as I remembered the broken pie plate and the oddly situated wine bottle.

I proceeded to tear the house apart, going from room to room, drawer by drawer. After many frantic minutes, panic mounting, I reached for the phone. I called Woodward.

Even after my work with Woodward ended, he was always the famous investigative reporter, and I was a researcher, collaborator, aspiring writer—a young woman trying to make it in a man's world, or at least a man's town. Despite the fact that I was upset with myself for telling him about what I witnessed in the solarium, I felt there was no one else to turn to in this situation. He would know what to do, I reassured myself. He always did.

When I called to tell him about the tape's existence and subsequent disappearance, he remained calm, which is what I expected. In general, Woodward never registered much range of emotion. In all the years I'd known him, I'd never seen him lose his cool, and he admired those with a similar temperament. He used to gently scold me, saying I should work on "emotional control." Now he asked me several questions in a flat, reportorial tone.

I could tell at first he thought I had just absentmindedly misplaced the tape. But when I explained that the tape was labeled "Vince Foster," he had grown quiet. He had me run through the events leading up to the tape's disappearance. When did I have it? For how long had I had it? Did anyone else have the key to my apartment? Why did I put it in the secretary? Was I absolutely sure that's where I put the tape? Yes, I said, I was sure. As we spoke, I grew more and more alarmed. It is the hotbed nature of Washington that, if it doesn't cause paranoia, it certainly provides the ideal breeding ground in which to flourish.

The cold truth is that, to this day, I don't know how the plate broke or what happened to the microcassette. No one knew about the tape. Not a soul. Because there was nothing to know. The only thing on it was an innocuous conversation, just something in passing in an effort to elicit book material. Yes, it was about Vince Foster but nothing about the circumstances of his death or anything specific about their friendship, just musing about the nature of resilience, why some people had it and others didn't.

If, in my absence while I was in Italy, Woodward, a world-famous investigative reporter, had gone nosing around the White House, asking thorny questions about a private meeting in which the First Lady participated in an unconventional talk-therapy session with New Agey overtones, it would be easy to follow the trail directly to me and make someone curious about what else I knew or had in my possession.

But that didn't occur to me then. It wouldn't occur to me for another ten months, when Woodward's book came out and made international headlines.

NINE

Village People

Son, this is a Washington, D.C., kind
of lie. It's when the other person knows
you're lying, and also knows you
know he knows.

—ALLEN DRURY, *ADVISE AND CONSENT*

I began to feel uneasy in my own apartment after I discovered the tape was missing. I wasn't really nervous that someone was coming back, but I felt a presence, almost like there was a low-level hum in the back of my brain, as if somebody left on the speakers after shutting off the stereo.

I would be in the kitchen, waiting for water to boil for pasta, and I would imagine someone taking my pie plate and smashing it. Did they do it purposefully to send a message? Or was it a slip of the hand as they searched the apartment? And the inexplicably positioned upside-down wine bottle? Why? Were these professionals who knew exactly how to mess with someone's head? "Mossad tactics, to unnerve you!" a newspaper friend who covers national security said later when I told him about the strange things that had happened. All I could do was roll my eyes.

I consoled myself by coming up with much less interesting but more plausible explanations. Washington is full of conspiracy theorists; it doesn't need another one, and my journalism training taught me to rely on evidence when evaluating things. So—where did that leave me?

POSSIBILITY #1: I misplaced the tape.

POSSIBILITY #2: While I was in Italy a big truck drove up my street, and the vibration of it shook the walls and made the pie plate fall from its place on the shelf and the wine bottle land upside down on its cork. Sure it did.

POSSIBILITY #3: It wasn't a truck that shook the walls, but a nearby jackhammer.

POSSIBILITY #4: A minor earthquake: they were not unheard of in the region, and never mind that there were no news reports of a minor quake while I was away or that anyone I knew remembered there being one.

Any of these explanations was possible, but I had no idea what the truth was, so I forced myself to put the whole thing out of my mind.

Not long after this, the phone rang, and I answered it to find a newsmagazine reporter on the line. She was calling to ask me if I had a comment about not being acknowledged in Mrs. Clinton's book. That was an interesting and surprising way to learn something I didn't know. Especially because my contract called for Mrs. Clinton to include me by name in the acknowledgments. This is the place in the book where the author thanks everyone from the UPS delivery guy to the ghostwriter. Not all authors include acknowledgments, but most of them do, and I had been thanked by all the authors I had worked with in the past. It was pretty standard stuff.

This reporter told me that early review copies were making the rounds, and she said the acknowledgments page included no names.

I got off the phone quickly, without revealing that what she was telling me was a surprise. I called my agent and told her what I had just learned. She said she would call Simon & Schuster and get back to me. A little insider baseball: Being acknowledged is a tad about ego, but it's mostly about earning capacity. Ghostwriters get their gigs through word of mouth; acknowledgments pages are one of the best ways to do that. And everyone in the business reads the acknowledgments pages like tea leaves. What isn't included is as telling as what is. I feared this was going to be a mess.

I was right: things quickly went from bad to worse. Flip called back to report that not only was the magazine writer correct about the lack of acknowledgment but that Simon & Schuster was withholding the final quarter of my fee. She reminded them that this payment was due when they signed off on the manuscript, which they had done a month earlier, before my trip. Now, suddenly, my agent was telling me the White House had instructed the publisher not to pay me.

This made no sense to me. Even if the First Lady had become unhappy with a manuscript she had worked on and approved herself, what reason would she have for telling Simon & Schuster not to pay me? It was their money, not hers; everyone involved had gone to great pains to make sure she had no financial interest in the book to protect her from the inevitable criticism if she accepted an advance or didn't promise to donate any future royalties. The way they were treating me was not only alarming, it was puzzling. By this time I had worked on more than a half-dozen high-profile books, most of them published by Simon & Schuster. The more I thought about it, the more I had to admit that in the food chain of Washington/New York literary/politico circles, a freelance ghost/editor is expendable if a sitting First Lady, soon to be a bestselling author, wants her expended. But still, it seemed pretty harsh.

When the publishing house wouldn't budge on the issue of the withheld payment, I called Woodward and Ben and Sally, each of whom had been published by Simon & Schuster. Woodward and Ben called the publisher. They didn't tell me what they said, and I didn't want to know. The whole thing was beyond mortifying.

The check arrived soon after that—which was a relief financially—but it didn't do anything to explain my fall from grace. I went over the events of the last eight months. The deadline pressure was substantial, but we had all worked hard—the editor, a researcher, the transcribers, myself, and, of course, the First Lady. If they didn't want me involved any longer, so be it. Given my résumé, I had been an odd choice in the first place. I assume there were plenty of people lining up in Hillaryland who wanted to leave their mark on this book. And if the First Lady felt the existing draft needed to go through another round of editing and rewriting, most books do and, besides, that was her prerogative. But this aggressive campaign to discredit my work struck me as grossly disproportionate and I racked my brain, going over the chronology of events that led me to this moment.

A few months after I was hired, now more than eight months earlier, the White House had issued a press release announcing the book project and acknowledging my involvement.

In reaction to that, the White House press corps wrote a spate of stories about the book project. The *New York Times* noted in April 1995: "The book will actually be written by Barbara Feinman, a journalism professor at Georgetown University in Washington. Ms. Feinman will conduct a series of interviews with Mrs. Clinton, who will help edit the resulting text."

With no input from me (or my agent or anyone connected to me), this story and others like it implicitly set up a narrative suggesting that Mrs. Clinton couldn't write her own book. The press release said I was hired to "prepare the manuscript," which journalists interpreted as "write the manuscript."

This was the middle of Whitewater and Mrs. Clinton's popularity was suffering big time, in part because of how the press portrayed her and in part because of the way she and the White House handled various situations. For whatever reasons, she had never fit into the Washington culture. There was the gaffe during the '92 campaign about her not standing by her man like Tammy Wynette and choosing not to stay home and bake cookies. Then the president put her in charge of a new health-care initiative, and it had not gone well. And there were allegations that she was involved in

Travelgate. And I'm sure there was an element of old guard Washington not ready to accept a First Lady who wanted to redefine the scope and influence of the position.

I'll leave it up to the historians and political scientists to sort out why she had become such a target. All I know is that when I arrived on the scene, she had an image problem, and as many political memoirs and manifestos are meant to do, this one was meant to recast her by highlighting the good work she'd done on behalf of families and children. That was a lot of pressure to put on a book and on the people charged with making it happen, namely me, our editor, our publisher, and Mrs. Clinton.

As I tried to figure out what had gone wrong I thought about how vague my original mandate was: to produce a book that would reflect the First Lady's track record and dedication to advocacy on children's issues. There was no title, no outline, no direction, no shape, no narrative. It was my job to figure out all of that, which is often how ghostwriting gigs go. But with so little time until our deadline and with the massive demands on the First Lady's schedule, it was inevitable that the manuscript would need more work after such a compressed timetable.

But none of this explained definitively why I wasn't included in the last round of edits and was suddenly regarded as persona non grata.

THE BOOK CAME OUT in early January 1996, and Mrs. Clinton embarked on a multicity promotional tour. I feared that, at least inside the Beltway, the book's reception would be doomed from the start. The "nattering nabobs of negativism" would be nibbling before long, and I knew that even if we had produced *War and Peace* meets the Bible, the reactions would still be a Rorschach test of how each person felt about the Clintons and how closely aligned each person was with them politically.

I assumed that the book's beautiful cover and lyrical title would entice admirers of the First Lady beyond the Beltway to line up to buy the book. But from where I was standing, sales seemed almost incidental.

Almost immediately Mrs. Clinton was hit with what was dubbed "ThankYouGate," a media flap about why she didn't she give credit to her ghostwriter. Me. As scandals go, it was a superficial one, a topic for pundits to have fun tossing around in an informal game of touch football. Nobody was saying that laws were broken or anything like that. But it still provided good political gossip.

Maureen Dowd wrote in her *New York Times* column on January 14, 1996:

> A donnybrook has erupted over Mrs. Clinton's
> odd decision not to give an acknowledgment to
> Barbara Feinman . . . and her friends feel she has
> been badly treated by the First Lady. Mrs. Clinton's
> "acknowledgments" page is, in fact, the perfect illustration
> of her problem. It must be the only acknowledgments
> page in existence that thanks nobody in particular. "I will
> not even attempt to acknowledge them individually," she
> writes. Those nine words are seven more than it would
> have taken to acknowledge Barbara Feinman.

The level of vitriol directed toward Mrs. Clinton surprised me. In addition to Dowd, everyone from Rush Limbaugh, who referred to me as something to the effect of "some poor journalism professor" to Don Imus—and countless others on the political spectrum in between—weighed in on it, illustrating the clichés that Washington enemies make strange bedfellows and that the enemy of my enemy is my friend.

The attention was overwhelming, and even though a lot of it was sympathetic to me, that wasn't much of a comfort. Another popular Washington cliché goes that all publicity is good publicity as long as they spell your name right (and even that proved not to matter). I guess that was true because people didn't seem to focus on what was being said about me but just that I was in the news.

The White House keeps a log of overnight guests, and at some point, it was released as part of the Whitewater investigation, and the *Washington Post*, among other publications, published it, and there was my name, though misspelled, listed alphabetically between Patricia Duff (who was briefly married to billionaire Ron Perelman and who, as a Clinton supporter, went around bragging that Bill Clinton was "one full-service president") and Jane Fonda.

Perversely, I was now getting more offers than ever to write people's books. I had become what Tom Wolfe called "a status detail," a telling possession or symbol that revealed a person's position in society. Having one's own ghostwriter in Washington was akin to driving a Ferrari Testarossa in Hollywood or owning a million-dollar parking place in Manhattan. Rising stock notwithstanding, it was mentally debilitating. It felt like I was a pawn in a game of everyone versus Hillary Clinton.

Even worse, all this sturm und drang about me not being acknowledged gave a lot of people the impression I was whining about it. And I most certainly wasn't. I wasn't saying anything. First of all, the fallout from me not being acknowledged by Mrs. Clinton had put me front and center, like taking out an ad in Times Square, so if attention had been what I wanted, not being acknowledged was the way to get it. I wasn't comfortable in the spotlight. Like most ghosts, real and imagined, I sought comfort in the shadows.

A particularly low moment was when a tabloid TV show camped out on my front lawn and kept ringing my buzzer, trying to get me to agree to an interview. Finally, when I couldn't stay inside any longer and called a friend to come rescue me, they filmed me coming out of the front door and hurrying across the front lawn to the street. Unfortunately, the grass was slippery with freshly fallen snow and, in a slapstick move worthy of Lucille Ball, I fell down on my butt.

As I was picking myself up, with cameras rolling, the reporter shoved a mic in my face and said, "Are you the First Lady's ghost?" The segment aired, but someone had mercy and didn't include the shot of me down for the count.

The media's attention stayed trained on the lack of acknowledgment instead of the actual book. It went on for a month, references ranging from oblique to specific.

Oblique: In a *New Yorker* piece, "Scenes from a Scandal: Why can't the children of Watergate get it right?," David Remnick imagined an Oliver Stone film in which the First Lady would be played by Meryl Streep, "her hair done up in a steely flip, roaming the crepuscular halls of the West Wing, swilling Chardonnay from the bottle and shrieking to the heavens. Careering down the halls, she shreds subpoenas and abuses ghostwriters . . ."

Specific: The *Washington Times* ran an editorial, "The Ghost and Mrs. Clinton; or, It Takes a Village to Write a Book." It outlined the timeline of my involvement, starting with the White House announcing that I would sit down with the First Lady to interview her and then write a draft, and so on. Then it chronicled Mrs. Clinton's statements that she had written the entire book in longhand (she had even invited reporters over to see the handwritten draft) and that I had been relegated to being an assistant.

"This is not to say that Ms. Feinman did all the work," the *Washington Times* wrote. "As could be expected of a project headlined by Mrs. Clinton, the research phase of the book was handled much like the dreaded Clinton Health Care Task Force, with hundreds of the Friends of Hillary in the kiddie-welfare establishment submitting anecdotes and policy prescriptions. It takes a village, indeed."

Yes, there were a lot of people involved. They got that right, and I was relieved someone said that, even if the editorial's point was to be snarky about the book's political agenda. There was a researcher and interns and transcribers in addition to our very hands-on editor, Mrs. Clinton, and me. And though her staff wasn't technically allowed to contribute to the book on company time—since their salaries were paid by taxpayers—they still gave advice and weighed in on various issues and offered ideas, anecdotes, and institutional knowledge.

I continued to keep my mouth shut, hoping the press attention would die down, but it did not. Which only agitated the White House more. Rumors started making their way back to me, whispers about my not getting along with the First Lady. I wondered about the origin of that because it was made up out of whole cloth; there had never been a single cross word spoken between us. But as the *Washington Post* noted in a piece about the authorship question, "Because Feinman signed a confidentiality statement, she declined to comment on this story. The White House, however, was eager to talk."

You must be wondering why I didn't simply get a copy of the book and compare it to the version of the manuscript I worked on.

I will tell you why. It comes down to one moment that is seared in my memory. I went over to Woodward's house at some point during the media shitstorm. I was preoccupied by one question: Why was the White House trashing me?

I was sitting at Woodward's kitchen table and he was standing. Maybe he was in the process of serving us coffee. All I remember is that he was standing and looking down at me, and he had a weird smile that I interpreted as meaning to be sympathetic but instead struck me as pleased, or relieved even. I remember thinking that what he was saying didn't track with his facial expression.

He was telling me that a political reporter we both knew, whom I don't want to name here, had told him that he had heard that the White House said I was "out of my league."

I was devastated because the way he said it was as though he, Woodward, believed that was the explanation for why they had not acknowledged me, per the contract, and why they tried to withhold my final payment and why they were minimizing my role.

If this respected political reporter was buying that, and Woodward was buying it, it must have been true, right?

So when Simon & Schuster didn't send me a complimentary copy of the book, I considered going to the bookstore to buy a copy but couldn't get myself to do it. And when my sister bought a copy and put it on her "Barbara" shelf in her living room, I never could bring myself to open the book and look at it, except for one Thanksgiving when everyone was in the family room after dinner. I had pulled the book down and flipped it open to the table of contents. I lost my nerve and returned it to its place before anyone caught me in the act.

If I had bought the book, or even borrowed it, I would have had to confront the truth. And the truth must have been what the White House was putting out about my work not being good enough to use in the final draft; otherwise, I couldn't imagine why Woodward would share with me what the political reporter had heard. So reading the book would be too painful. It would be too painful to see documentary evidence that nothing of my work, my heart, my intellect, or my humor made the final cut. Because even when you work on someone else's book, you still leave behind traces of yourself, scattered throughout random cells with your own literary DNA. It's a writer's way of saying, *I am here.*

What if my fears were right, that they hadn't used anything much of what I had contributed beyond the title? Or equally troubling, what if they *had* used my work and by retreating, I had allowed their false narrative to define me.

So in that moment the sense of failure and shame paralyzed me. And that moment turned into a day, which turned into a year, then five, then a decade. Then two decades. It was a classic case of confirmation bias. I had imposter syndrome and I had been discovered. And so I didn't look.

Until I was writing this book. My book. Writing it meant that I would ultimately have to do what I had refused to do twenty years ago. I had to be honest with myself in order to be honest with my readers. I couldn't avoid confronting the truth any longer.

I got in my car and drove to my sister's house and asked her if I could borrow the book, the book that had become radioactive in my mind and my life.

"What are you doing with it?" my sister said, her back to me as she reached up to the shelf where she kept the book. I couldn't see her face, but her tone was hesitant.

I held the book in my hands and marveled at how I had given over such power to such an innocuous little book with a lyrical jacket design displaying smiling children and a happy, hopeful title that was meant to evoke all that is possible in a world where children were treasured and respected. Finally, I looked at my sister. "I guess I'm going to read it. I've never gotten beyond the table of contents," I said, looking back down at the book. "I need to compare it to the draft I worked on."

"You mean you really never read this version?" She sounded incredulous. She had broached the topic a few times over the years and I had always responded vaguely, and then changed the subject.

I took the book home, made myself a pot of coffee, and sat down to confront the truth. I placed the published book and the manuscript side by side. The manuscript was musty and mildewed from twenty years of storage. The paper clips separating each chapter had rusted and orangish brown specks stained the tops of the first page of each chapter, rubbing off on my fingertips as I removed them.

I started out, going page by page. The opening was different, and my heart sank. I forced myself to keep going. And then I started to see sentences, then paragraphs, even whole pages that were identical, but for a bit of copyediting. Sometimes I would think I couldn't find a match and a few pages later I would find that a missing section had been moved forward. The process felt oddly familiar and I suddenly recalled playing a board game called Concentration in which you matched objects.

Overwhelmed after a few hours, I called my sister, who is a tax attorney and has an analytical mind, and asked her if she would help me finish matching text between the two versions and then quantify how much of my manuscript had made it into the published book.

The next morning my sister came over and suggested we download the Kindle version so that we could put in keywords when we came across a section in the manuscript that we couldn't find in the published book. We worked like that for five hours, putting yellow Post-it notes on every page of the manuscript whose contents had survived in the published book. Finally, we tallied up pages with identical or similar material.

Here is what we determined: at least 75 percent of the draft that I produced with Mrs. Clinton was used in the published version—some parts intact, other parts edited or moved around. The manuscript that I turned in and that was initially accepted met the 75,000 word length that my contract stipulated. Then, the new *Village* people churned out perhaps as much as an additional third of the book, summarizing various policies and programs to illustrate Mrs. Clinton's observations and findings. With the 25 percent that was not used of my version, and the new material that was added after I left, the published version ran about 90,000 words. As for the 25 percent of the manuscript that I worked on that wasn't included in the published version, after reviewing the unused material now, two decades later, I have to wonder if much of the trimming was driven by political calculations rather than literary concerns.

In a *Post* piece that dealt with ThankYouGate, the writer described how the White House invited journalists over to see Mrs. Clinton's longhand filling up hundreds of pages; the stunt was an orchestrated effort to leave the impression that my contribution was minimal. Even if that were true, which it wasn't, to dismiss my eight months of work—starting with coming up with a powerful title, to conducting interviews with her, to doing substantial research, to drafting chapters for her to make her own and help her focus on what she wanted to say—was dishonest.

The new material that was produced and added to the final draft must have been what was in longhand on the yellow legal pads that Mrs. Clinton had shown to members of the Washington press corps. In the stories that journalists wrote about the viewing, no one mentioned being offered an opportunity to compare manuscripts, nor did any reporter apparently think to request that. One of the media outlets that reported the event was *Time* magazine, running a side-bar to a story about Whitewater. "The Ghost and Mrs. Clinton" noted:

> Even before Hillary Clinton's new book, *It Takes a Village*, hit the stores, Washington heard the rumor: the book was ghosted. The charge so exasperated the White House that several journalists, including TIME correspondent James Carney, were invited to Mrs. Clinton's private study to check the manuscript, including legal pads covered with her handwriting. Says Carney: "There is no doubt Mrs. Clinton wrote great parts of the book."
>
> But as the White House acknowledged last week, there had been a collaborator. Barbara Feinman, a veteran book doctor, was hired by publisher Simon & Schuster to help organize the book and draft several chapters . . .

James "Jay" Carney, interestingly, covered the Clinton and Bush administrations until 2008 when he became Vice President Joe Biden's director of communications secretary and later replaced Robert Gibbs as President Obama's spokes-person, until 2014 when he went back to journalism briefly as a CNN political analyst. He's a top-level flack for Amazon now. His seamless transitions back and forth between journalist and spin doctor speak to his suitability to buy whole-sale the White House's narrative.

As for the published version, I found that many more studies were cited and some personal anecdotes had been deleted. In the version I worked on, I had tried to present her as knowledgeable, ruminative, compassionate, and sympathetic. This is what you hire a ghost to do—to channel the best and most compelling voice of the author. In the final version, I also noticed small but telling details that didn't take a literary forensic scholar to figure out the origins of. For instance, in a section that was in the book and not in the draft I worked on, Mrs. Clinton refers to a conversation she had in which "author and scholar Mary Catherine Bateson pointed out that when you juggle, eventually something gets dropped."

I guess they weren't talking about collaborators specifically, but still, it applies.

THE ISSUE OF AUTHORSHIP was not the only controversy surrounding the book.

The *Wall Street Journal* was interested in focusing on the financial arrangement: "Hillary Rodham Clinton's new book about children was supposed to divert attention from the ethics questions that have swirled around her. Instead the book itself is creating a bit of a flap." This article raised the issue of whether it was improper for the publisher to pay my fee instead of the First Lady, noting that some critics felt "the publisher's footing the bill for a writer amounts to a gift to the first family."

The piece provided the requisite Clintonian scandal context: "Questions about Mrs. Clinton's arrangements with the writer have arisen just as her friends, allies and the vast Clinton re-election apparatus are trying to lay in place an aggressive strategy to repair the First Lady's image."

The press scrutiny and criticism kept coming until the White House cried uncle, and I got a call from Maggie Williams, Mrs. Clinton's chief of staff. She told me they were going to issue a press release about my contribution to the book. Translation: The White House machine was going into damage-controlling backpedal mode. Maggie said they would fax over a draft, which she did a few minutes later. It was a cordial statement, in which Mrs. Clinton credited me with getting her started on early drafts and said I had helped for six months.

I didn't appreciate the dismissive and lawyerly tone, but I knew that if they took their gloves off, I would be the one who got knocked out. I felt cowed by their PR machine, however inept it was. My best plan was to retreat and hope this whole thing would all blow over. I knew the rhythms of the Washington news cycle. By next week, I would be eclipsed by something else.

But facts were facts. At the very least, I said when I called back, the timeline needed to be corrected. "I worked on the book for eight months," I told her.

And her response, just four words, was what finally drove home to me what I was dealing with.

"Would you take seven?"

"No, Maggie," I said, steeling myself. "I'll take eight. Because that's how long I worked on the book."

This haggling over the language and "facts" of that press release was a personal primer in how Washington works.

Looking back, I see that I didn't do a good enough job advocating for myself. I should have insisted on a face-to-face meeting. They wouldn't have told me anything and it probably wouldn't have done any good, but at least I would have felt like I wasn't complicit in my own erasure.

The White House press release didn't tamp down the criticism as they hoped. The media coverage of ThankYouGate continued.

EVERY TIME I THOUGHT my *Village* mess was over, it seemed to pop up again, like the arcade game Whac-A-Mole. In late January 1996, soon after the book was released, Mrs. Clinton was called to testify before a federal grand jury that was looking into the possibility of whether the White House had committed any obstructions of justice regarding the investigation into Mrs. Clinton's law firm's Whitewater-related work. After four hours of testimony, she emerged from the courthouse and told a crowd of Washington reporters, "I was glad to have the opportunity to tell the grand jury what I have been telling all of you. I do not know how the billing records came to be found where they were found, but I am pleased that they were found because they confirm what I have been saying."

Just as her appearance before the grand jury was making headlines, I learned that the Senate Whitewater Committee wanted to talk to people whose names showed up on the visitors' log for the White House residence between July 20 and August 15 of the previous year. It was during that time that White House aide Carolyn Huber noticed some computer printouts while straightening up "the book room," a small space used for storage of unsolicited gifts in the residence. I worked in a room that was close to the book room, which was also near the room I slept in when I stayed overnight at the residence in late July, which I did, you may remember, because I was on crutches and Mrs. Clinton invited me to stay at the White House.

Just my luck, the subpoenaed Rose Law Firm billing records, missing for two years, had turned up in the room next door to where I worked. According to press reports, Huber hadn't realized what she had found, and she packed the documents in a box and took it over to the East Wing, where they sat for months until she unpacked the box and realized what they were.

So, just as I had feared might happen, I got pulled into a serious Clinton scandal. The Senate Committee on Banking, Housing and Urban Affairs, colloquially referred to as the "Senate Whitewater hearings," "invited me" to come and be deposed. I was told that if I declined their invitation, I would receive a subpoena. *Subpoena* is one of those words that makes your heart beat faster, especially in this town. Washington lawyers cost anywhere from $300 to $1,000 an hour. I could quickly rack up a bill in the tens of thousands of dollars, even though I didn't know anything about Whitewater and had nothing to hide or share.

For a brief crazy moment, I considered showing up at the deposition without counsel, but I had also heard stories about people unwittingly perjuring themselves. So I hired a lawyer, a friend who had some experience in this particular brand of Washington silliness. He said it would be expensive, but that he would contact Simon & Schuster and remind them that were it not for my work on the book, I wouldn't be going before the committee. Ipso facto: My legal fees fell under the expenses clause in my contract. He was sure they would cover it.

He was right. The same people who months before had balked at paying me my full fee were falling over themselves to pay my legal bill. Apparently, the specter (pun intended) of the First Lady's ghostwriter being compelled to testify was a sobering thought for the White House. As for the publisher, I'm sure its executives just wanted this (and me) to go away.

A day or two before my scheduled deposition, Mrs. Clinton's lawyer, David Kendall, called me at home to ask me if I needed anything.

Suddenly, everyone seemed very concerned about me. I directed Mr. Kendall to my lawyer.

On February 12, 1996, my lawyer and I got in a cab and made our way down to the Dirksen Building on Capitol Hill. Dirksen is one of three Senate buildings, and it was built after World War II, complete with large hearing rooms to facilitate the emerging medium of television. I had spent plenty of time on the Hill, working on various political memoirs, but this was my first time being called there as a participant.

I was nervous about being deposed, because I was scared I might misspeak or misremember and get myself into legal trouble. And there was the possibility, my lawyer warned me, that the committee might want me to testify at the televised hearings. It was a maddening waste of everyone's time. I didn't know anything about Whitewater. I hadn't overheard anything or suspected anything. I had been focused on getting the book done and moving on; I didn't care about a failed land deal from a decade earlier.

It was a cold, drizzly, bleak Monday in February as the cab pulled up to the seven-story, marble-faced building. I asked my lawyer for the nine-hundredth time, "What could they possibly think that I know?"

He was a backslapping good ole boy from Texas. "Nothing, darlin'," he said, laughing as he paid the driver and held the door for me. "They know you know nothing. They just want to put the First Lady's ghost up there in front of the TV cameras. They want to embarrass her, not you."

That was little consolation to me as my mind flashed on the image of Anita Hill facing down all those crusty white male senators, a veritable firing squad of old farts.

We reported to room 534 Dirksen, the committee's headquarters, and were ushered into a big room where, seated at a long conference table, were two men in suits. One of them was Viet Dinh, the majority counsel, who would go on to become an assistant attorney general under George W. Bush and the chief architect of the Patriot Act.

The other was Glenn Ivey, the minority counsel, who two decades later would run for Maryland's Fourth District congressional seat (but lose in the primary). Introductions were made and Mr. Dinh smiled at me and invited us to take our seats. A woman sat in a corner typing every word that was uttered. I kept wanting to slow down and annunciate. *Did ya get that?* I thought.

I should probably confess something you may have already surmised: I'm not a very good grown-up. The more gravity a situation calls for, the more I want to misbehave, crack up, or make someone else crack up. Washington is a city full of people who take themselves too seriously, and this has had a perverse effect on me.

So my lawyer knew he had his work cut out for him in

terms of properly preparing and containing me. We'd already done deposition training 101: Be brief. The less you say, the less chance you have of screwing up. "Stick to yes or no whenever possible," he coached. It sounds easier than it is, especially for someone who makes her living telling stories. "Yes" or "no" doesn't make for great dialogue and does nothing for word count.

He also told me to tell the truth. Duh. Darn, I was planning on testifying that I caught Hillary shredding documents stamped "Whitewater: Don't Show Ken Starr."

He also told me not to speculate. Well, easier said than done. What if they asked me something I felt I should know? I was a people pleaser. Wasn't this like a test that I could pass or fail? "No, just tell them what you know. No more. No less," he said.

They started by having me state my name and address. Easy peasy. I can ace this test!

I used my best witness-being-deposed solemn voice. I figured if I drained any life from my tone, I had a fighting chance at staying out of jail and off camera.

"Be boring," my lawyer had implored. "You're not a guest on *Late Night.*"

I did great for the first few minutes. I followed all my lawyer's directions and heeded all his warnings. Then Mr. Dinh pulled out what was labeled, I kid you not, "Feinman exhibit A." It was a map of the White House residence. Exhibit A.

Wow. I have my own exhibit!

"Let me show you a sketch that we have of the third floor of the White House. And let me focus your attention in particular, north is facing down, so the top of the page is the south side—"

"Here's the thing, I don't do directions," I said.

My lawyer shot me a warning look and then jumped in before I could say anything else, pointing at the map. "There's the solarium, Washington Monument is over here." He was like a stage mom trying to direct me away from the stage pit. I was a first grader in a giant ladybug costume who was leaning too close to the edge of the stage.

Mr. Dinh echoed my lawyer: "The Washington Monument is at the top."

Everyone is so helpful! Mr. Dinh, the Republican, he was on my side!

My lawyer gave me a glare that said, *Remember why we are here.* This was about my relative value as a smoking gun. Nothing more. Nothing less.

We went on like this for several minutes, with them asking if I worked in this room or that room and if I ever heard any conversations about this person or that—all Whitewater-related names, the likes of which I'd heard on TV and read about in the newspapers.

They asked me every which way you could imagine. It began to sound like Dr. Seuss. *I do not like green eggs and ham . . . I did not hear any White House dirt, I did not see the President flirt. I did not meet a man named Jim. I heard no secrets regarding Susan McDougal or him.*

They were obsessed with "the book room," near Mrs. Clinton's home office, the room next to where we worked on the book. It was confusing because it was called the book room I guess because it had some books in it. It was here, apparently, that the mysteriously disappeared Rose Law Firm billing records were found. They wanted to figure out how subpoenaed records could just suddenly materialize.

"Did you on occasion stay overnight in the White House residence?"

"Toward the end of either—I think it was toward the end of July or beginning of August, I stayed over, I think, maybe four nights . . . because I was working late, and we just decided it would be easier for me and safer rather than going out late at night. And also, on July 30, I sprained my ankle and was hopping around and so it was just easier a couple of nights to stay over."

Then they asked me six different ways if I ever went in the book room when I was staying overnight. I kept telling them I only went in there twice, and when I did, I didn't notice anything. I went in there to speak to Mrs. Clinton who was exercising in a room beyond that room. Actually, I remember taking a wrong turn and ending up in a closet of the president's suits. I didn't mention that. Only I could get lost in a closet within a storage room.

"So you sprained your ankle on a Sunday?"

YES, I CONFESS, I'M CLUMSY. LOCK ME UP AND THROW AWAY THE KEY.

"Sunday night, I sprained it. Monday, I went to the doctor, and Mrs. Clinton told me to stay home and rest, and I would say that Tuesday and Wednesday someone came over and picked me up and drove me over to the White House."

"So this would be that one occasion on the Wednesday, right. And the record reflects that you had lunch at the White House. Is that consistent with your recollection?"

"Yeah, usually when I was working in Mrs. Clinton's office, one of the butlers would bring a sandwich up for me."

"A sandwich up," Mr. Dinh repeated, as though I had produced the smoking gun. "Would you take that sandwich in room 323?"

I CONFESS. I DID IT. I ATE MY SANDWICH IN ROOM 323!!! *Sheesh*, this was getting tedious.

"Most of the time you worked through lunch?"

"Yes."

"In room 323?"

"Yes."

"You'd make a good lawyer."

Why? Because I worked through lunch? Lawyers work through lunch? I thought they went to fancy steak joints and drank bourbon.

"My father wanted me to go to law school, and you can put that on the record."

"I think you found a better calling."

"I'll stipulate to that," my lawyer interjected to laughter. I sneered at him. Why can he make jokes, but I can't? I stole a glance at my lawyer while everyone laughed. We were all in this together, the mood seemed to suggest.

What was "this" exactly, though? Mr. Dinh, a conservative, must be out to get Mrs. Clinton. Mr. Ivey, working for the Democrats, must be charged with protecting her. I didn't want to get anybody, and I certainly didn't want to help the Republicans. I wasn't feeling real warm and fuzzy about my White House experience, but I didn't know anything, and above all else I wanted to *not* be called to testify for all the world, or at least those who tuned in to C-SPAN, to watch.

In the transcripts, we were already to page 43 and so far, our little comedy routine camaraderie aside, my testimony had been pretty unrevealing, certainly nothing worthy of putting me before a camera.

The mood modulated back and forth between lightheartedness and interrogation. The two investigators became serious as they homed in on the dinner I shared with the Clintons and Kaki the decorator from Arkansas. They wanted to know what we talked about. I told them it was hard to remember because I was so nervous eating dinner with the president. I mentioned the early birthday present Kaki had given him, the framed sketch of all the movie stars.

"Then the president spoke for a little bit about the movie *High Noon*."

"During this dinner, do you recall ever talking about Whitewater Development Corporation?"

"It never came up."

"What about Madison Guaranty Savings & Loan Association?"

"Never came up."

"Capital Management Services?"

"Never came up."

"Did you talk about Arkansas at all?"

"Not that I remember."

"Not even with Kaki Hockersmith and the president and First Lady?"

"I have no recollection of that. I'm pretty sure it didn't come up."

"Did you talk about the Whitewater hearings then progressing in the Senate Special Committee?"

"No."

"Now that I've got your attention focused on this particular date, do you recall if you went into any other room on the third floor besides 323 and the sunroom, and obviously your bedroom that night?"

"No. I went—after we ate dinner, everyone left, and I went back, straight back because I remember walking with Kaki and the president, and they went to the elevator, and I went back to our office to work."

"And the records indicate that that night you spent in the room next door, 324. Is that consistent with your recollection?"

"Yes."

"And I take it you did not use the exercise room that night?"

"No."

"And you did not get a video from the book room?"

"No. I didn't know there were videos in the book room."

"Well, next time you're at the White House—I understand there's no rental charges either."

"I'll keep that in mind."

"Although it could lead to another subpoena," joked Mr. Ivey. "You might want to try Blockbuster."

Hahahaha. Another subpoena! Those lawyers sure are a funny bunch.

"Let me direct your attention now to Saturday, August 5. I've placed in front of you a record labeled S 020020."

I looked at the document. "They have my name wrong on this. Feinstein, Iceberg, we're all the same."

My lawyer shot me a *knock off the Borscht Belt routine* look.

"What's the name on it?"

"Feinstein," I said, exasperated.

(Twenty years later, rereading the transcript of my testimony, I wonder why I was fixating on minor irritations, and yet I was unfazed that I was under oath talking about the president of the United States and his wife. People around the White House couldn't get either my name or my job right. I remembered one day I was called to the White House, and when I got to the gate I told the guard I should be on the list, that the First Lady was expecting me. "You're here to do her makeup?" the guard had asked, looking down at a clipboard. I laughed. In a sense I was a makeup artist.)

"Let me direct your attention to the entry labeled '8:30.' Do you recall having breakfast with Kaki Hockersmith that morning?"

"Yes."

"That indeed was you who is identified here as Barbara Feinstein?"

"Yes."

"And let me ask you specifically regarding that breakfast, did you and Ms. Hockersmith have any discussions of White-water Development Corporation?"

"No."

"Capital Management?"

"No."

"Have you ever heard of a person named Seth Ward?"

"Only in the last week from news accounts."

"So I take it that Mr. Ward did not come up as a topic of conversation, then, either?"

Well, actually, I said to Kaki, the Clintons' decorator, Please pass the croissants and do you think Seth Ward, one of the Arkansas businessmen caught up the Whitewater scandal, is guilty??

"No."

It went on like this for a while, running through the same questions about a trip our editor made down to D.C. We went through the logs that documented both of us staying overnight at the White House, eating various meals, being taken out on the balcony by Carolyn Huber to watch the helicopter departure, et cetera. *No, no, a thousand times no, I never heard anyone ever talk about Whitewater, and I never saw anything suspicious ever.*

"Have you ever had any discussions that you can recall of Rose Law Firm billing records?"

"Do you mean with my sister? What we saw on the news last night?"

"Let me just start with a specific. In the White House."

"No."

"At any time while you were in the White House?"

"Let me think for a minute to make sure because I believe the answer is no."

The transcript notes a "pause." I was probably thinking, *This is when they start waterboarding me. I better come up with something.* Except maybe waterboarding wasn't even a thing yet.

"I never had any discussions about any billing records in the White House. There was one occasion where the construction workers, who were there the entire summer making a lot of noise, broke through some plaster, and I believe Capricia [Marshall] came and unlocked a closet in the office where we were working, Mrs. Clinton and I were working, and I think there was some plaster or something, and Capricia was annoyed, and she relocked the door. And I have a vague recollection of somebody telling me that that was the closet in the office in which there were some records that had been publicized, that someone had put back in there or something. I don't remember the details . . ."

While I was recounting this last part, all three men's expressions changed. Everyone sat up straighter, and both of the committee lawyers started scribbling wildly, their eyes widening.

Uh-oh.

My lawyer, on the other hand, became expressionless, but his eyes told me what he was thinking: *Oh, darlin', you just won an all-expenses-paid trip to the televised Whitewater hearings.*

We spent what would reap another ten pages of transcript talking about the closet-and-falling-plaster scene.

"So somebody told you before Ms. Marshall came in the room, opened up the closet, and walked back out that it was the closet in which some things were put in there and removed?"

"Right."

"And by this general 'thing' some files had been put in and removed and publicized, do you remember whether it was the box of personal files from White House deputy counsel Vince Foster's office on the night of his death?"

The press had been very interested in the fact that Maggie Williams, the First Lady's chief of staff, had been in Foster's office the night of his suicide. A veteran Secret Service agent swore he saw her leave Foster's office carrying two handfuls of folders. She swore that she wasn't carrying any files and even took a lie detector test to prove it. I could see why Mr. Dinh was excited about my locked closet story. I just wasn't willing to connect dots that I couldn't verify should be connected.

"I just don't remember what it was."

"You just heard there were some records that were put in there and then removed and this had been publicized?"

"Right?"

"So the comment that somebody told you, this is the famous closet or something to that effect?"

"Yeah, something like that."

"Or infamous, depending on one's perspective."

IT WENT ON A BIT LONGER, and then they dismissed us. My lawyer predicted I would get a callback. If only it were an audition for a Broadway show.

The committee called my lawyer and said they wanted me to be a witness at the televised hearings. Shit. Shit. Shit.

It didn't matter that I didn't know anything juicy and hadn't done anything wrong. They just wanted to put me on camera and ask the First Lady's ghostwriter about locked closets, falling plaster, and missing documents.

Witnesses were judged for their composure, their appearance, their political currency. Women were judged particularly harshly. Anita Hill and Fawn Hall were both portrayed two-dimensionally and cartoonishly in the name of political expediency.

"I can't do this," I told my lawyer. "Think of a way out," I pleaded.

"It won't be so bad, darlin'." I imagined he was already strategizing about which power suit and tie to wear. All he needed to do was look polished and powerful, sitting behind me, nodding knowingly or shaking his head disapprovingly, then leaning over to whisper wise counsel in my ear.

"I can't do this," I muttered to no one in particular several times a day. On the day of the scheduled hearing, we got back in a cab and returned to the Hill. When we arrived at the Senate Green Room, my teeth began to chatter I was so nervous. I practiced saying, "No, sir." "Yes, sir." "I don't recall, sir."

We sat there all day. Eight hours. My lawyer repeated the same instructions to me whenever I asked him what I should do when I was called to testify. He gave me a piece of paper from his legal pad and suggested I write down a few key things to remember. We had been over it a hundred times. We both knew he was suggesting this exercise just to give me something to do. Say yes not yeah. No sound bites— don't be a wiseass. Eye contact with whoever is talking. Short answers. Poker face. Forthcoming. No attitude (underlined twice). Be boring. No sarcasm. When in doubt say, *May I consult with my counsel?*

I also scribbled on another piece of paper the following: *I don't have a statement. I believe that my counsel sent a letter to your committee yesterday, which I would appreciate having entered into the record.* Then, under that, was a little directional diagram with the words *east executive* running lengthwise and north/south/east/west noted in relationship. This, I am sure, was to calm my nerves regarding how I would answer questions that might reveal my poor navigational skills.

As the hours ticked by, my imagination was conjuring up all sorts of crazy headlines in the next day's papers: WHITE HOUSE GHOST NEEDS COMPASS TO FIND HER WAY OUT OF MESS.

Finally, the dinner hour came and went. I had worn myself out worrying. I begged my lawyer to try one more time to get them to change their minds. He took out a legal pad and wrote a long note, folded it in half.

He got up and talked to one of the Senate aides, who took the note. A few minutes later the aide came back and said we could go.

That was it. I don't remember what he wrote in the note. Perhaps that his client really did not know anything, and that it would be very detrimental to her career to have to speak publicly about her work in the White House.

Maybe that worked.

Maybe the senators were tired and were dreaming of steaks and bourbon by then. I was just relieved I made it over one more Washington hurdle and was still alive to tell the story. A story I hoped was now over. The end.

I was sadly mistaken.

TEN

Giving Up the Ghost

Writers are always selling
somebody out.

JOAN DIDION, *SLOUCHING TOWARDS BETHLEHEM*

Every September, as reliable as the autumnal equinox, at least one student—usually named Ashley or Elizabeth, from Greenwich, Connecticut, or Long Island—comes into my office, throws down her Birkin, and positions her Voss bottle on the edge of my desk (leaving a water ring), sinks into the cushy well-worn armchair, looks deeply and earnestly into my eyes, and says, "I want to be in *The New Yorker.*"

"Me too," I usually reply, my drollness wasted on youth.

The magazine was a fixture in my childhood home, and I grew up in a literate and literary household. My mom was a high school English teacher, and my dad was a Shakespeare scholar turned businessman. They each held up the magazine as *the* pinnacle of literary success.

I've carried on the tradition and am a loyal subscriber. Our house is filled with past issues in various states of engagement. My husband leaves them opened in different spots: on his nightstand means he's deeply involved in a story, and no one should touch the magazine; on the living room radiator means he's in the middle of a story, but I can read it too as long as I mark the page he is on; on the coffee table in the family room means there's something he hasn't gotten to yet, and he may not get to it, but he isn't ready to surrender it; on the Chinese decorative tray in the living room means he's totally done with it, and I can give it to my sister.

So, yes, the magazine is everywhere throughout our home, there to remind me of an article it published in February 1996, shortly after my Whitewater deposition, that I am desperate to forget. It's my Proustian madeleine with a side of food poisoning.

The piece was written by cultural critic and Harvard professor Henry Louis Gates Jr., and it was headlined HATING HILLARY, with "Hillary Clinton has been trashed right and left—but what's really fueling the furies?" as its subhead. The article contained a long section on *It Takes a Village*.

"Hillary's latest bouts of bad press do suggest someone whose sense of public relations is less than finely honed," Gates wrote. "Take the miscalculation that led to what Katha Pollitt has dubbed 'Thankyougate.' It started with the decision to hire Barbara Feinman to help out with the research for and writing of *It Takes a Village* (and not since Clark Clifford's memoirs has the publication of a book had such exquisitely bad timing). Feinman was a journalism instructor at Georgetown who had previously worked on books by Ben Bradlee and Bob Woodward, among others; but although her involvement in the project was announced publicly last spring, Hillary Clinton decided not to name her—or anyone else—in the book's acknowledgments. Sally Quinn says, 'All she expected was "Many thanks to Barbara Feinman, whose tireless efforts were greatly appreciated."' She would have died and gone to heaven."

Let me stop here and do what my literature professor colleagues call "a close reading," because there are so many reasons why I simply wanted to die when I read this back in 1996. First, how pathetic do I sound, the notion that a morsel of kind words would delight me?

I was upset about the lack of acknowledgment because it signaled there was a problem that I was completely unaware of, not because I was desperate for a word of gratitude. Of course, humiliating me was absolutely not Sally's goal. She wanted to underscore how stingy the First Lady was with thank-yous. She was trying to illustrate something about Mrs. Clinton's character through her actions.

"The manuscript's original due date was Labor Day," Gates went on. "At that point, about eight or nine chapters—which Feinman helped to organize, draft and edit—were submitted to the publisher."

Mr. Gates was wrong—we submitted chapters 1 through 10 and an introductory chapter that ran twenty-eight pages, as well as a three-page "interlude" to go between the introduction and the first chapter. So we submitted more than eleven chapters. And in addition to the wrong number of chapters, his implication was that somehow this was an incomplete manuscript. We submitted a complete manuscript—and it was one worked on by the whole village. And the publisher accepted that manuscript.

"According to Feinman, she was told that her work was

satisfactory . . ." Wait, wait, wait. Mr. Gates never made an effort to talk to me. So according to me according to whom? *Where's your attribution here, Dr. Gates?*

". . . and she subsequently left for a three-week vacation in Italy." True, and I was wishing I had stayed in Italy.

"A White House aide says that Hillary was appreciative of Feinman's efforts but was not fully satisfied with the direction of the book." Wait a minute again. Why are they relying on an anonymous source? Is this a matter of national security? They don't even call for a comment from me, and yet some "White House aide" gets to be anonymous. "Appreciative of Feinman's efforts"—sounds like I brought home a handprint in watercolors from kindergarten and Mommy said, "Good work!" Please. Appreciation in the book business is traditionally expressed on the acknowledgments page, especially when that is stipulated in the contract, which it was.

From what I was told and was able to piece together, Mrs. Clinton and our editor were satisfied with the book.

". . . and the bulk of the writing, revising, and editing took place after Labor Day—that is after Feinman's involvement with the project had largely ceased." Well, I worked on it through September, but we're not in a deposition (been there . . .) so let's not quibble. "Then matters got a lot stickier. There were discussions between Simon & Schuster and Feinman's agent about whether Feinman would be paid in full." Okay, we already went over that. The publisher had every intention of paying me until they were told not to.

Sally continued her defense of me. "'She was absolutely distraught,' Sally Quinn says. 'For one thing, she is planning to adopt a baby by herself, because she's thirty-six.'"

Okay, here we go! *Mega mega* mortification! Yes, I was considering adopting a baby. But I hadn't planned on publishing a baby announcement in the middle of a *New Yorker* profile about Hillary Clinton. Particularly because, um, I hadn't shared this news yet with everyone, like, for instance, my father.

"'So she's saving up all this money to go to China and adopt a baby girl. That was part of this little nest egg that she had.'"

OMG. Cue Sarah McLachlan singing a sad song over footage of me in a cage, looking mournfully at the camera, the starving ghostwriter who can't adopt her baby girl. I was far from destitute. Plenty of work was streaming my way: This town is full of people who want the First Lady's ghost to pen their memoirs and manifestos. And my involvement in this flap made me even more sought after. Welcome to Washington, the town of just-spell-my-name-right-on-the-subpoena.

Then Gates felt obliged to point out that: "(Other associates of Feinman reject any suggestion of financial extremity.)" "Associates"? What does he think I am, a law firm? It was just me in my apartment. Oops, I'm giving away the next part.

". . . it's hard to argue when Sally Quinn says, 'Hillary versus Barbara Feinman is a big loser, P.R.-wise.' She goes on, 'Barbara's a single woman, who lives alone in a one-bedroom apartment off Dupont Circle.'" Suddenly I'm picturing Sara Crewe in *The Little Princess* who ends up living as a pauper in an attic when it is believed she has been orphaned by her soldier father who is MIA. The truth is, I lived in a beautiful apartment in one of the priciest zip codes in the nation's capital. The neighbor below me was a congresswoman. Embassies were down the street.

"'Not only that but she has been a researcher at the *Washington Post*, and all her best friends are journalists. Everyone loves her'"—they like me, they really like me!—"'and she knows every journalist in town.'"

Let's unpack that, as the pundits like to say. Yes, I was a researcher at the *Post*. So I knew a lot of journalists. So does everyone who works in any newsroom. I knew the normal number of media people and politicos that someone who has worked in media for, by then, fourteen years would know.

My proximity to power was because the books I had worked on made me reasonably well connected using the metrics that informed Sally's criteria (*WashPo* journalists and New York publishing people). I understand that it must have been irresistible to her to defend me, someone whom she seemed to genuinely care for, and trash the First Lady, whom she had publicly criticized on several occasions and with whom she was engaging in some sort of weird power struggle.

Mercifully, she was almost done: "'This is what I'm saying about Hillary being book-smart and street-stupid.'" And then Gates continued, amplifying Sally's point: "Indeed, out of all the writers and researchers for hire in this world, why choose one who is closer friends with your critics than with you? Was the choice meant, in fact, to be a conciliatory gesture, a peace offering—giving a plum and profitable assignment to a favorite of the *Post*'s illuminati?"

That strikes me as way too strategic for that White House. Only someone in an ivory tower in another big city, who doesn't really understand Washington, would think the Clinton White House would feel the need to please the "*Post*'s

illuminati." The truth is much more prosaic. I was hired because I had worked on other Washington books published
by the same publisher producing Mrs. Clinton's book. I was
convenient.

In any case, I was so utterly mortified by this that I hid
under my bed for a week. Then, when I came out, miracle
of miracles, I discovered that only a few people had noticed.
The ones who had, sounding really impressed, said they saw
my name in *The New Yorker,* though they couldn't remember
why. A few more congratulated me on my impending motherhood. Close friends plied me with liquor and made jokes,
relentlessly. And then, as though etched in sand, the story
was washed away by the reliable tide of the news cycle.

FOUR MONTHS LATER, in late June 1996 on a Saturday afternoon, I got the call. It was four months after my Whitewater
deposition, five months after the *Village* book came out, and
eight months after I had returned from Italy to find things
broken and missing in my apartment.

"I need to give you a heads-up," Woodward began. My
heart started pounding so loudly I could barely hear his voice.

"About what?"

"An excerpt of my book is running in the paper tomorrow."
He paused while I gasped. Although I couldn't anticipate what
he was about to say, I knew it was going to be extremely upset-
ting. In words I can't remember precisely because I went into a
state of shock, he admitted that even though he promised not
to, he had taken what I told him in confidence and gone to the
other participants to confirm the story.

Sometimes it is permissible to take information gathered from a source and pursue it through other sources. But only if the original source's identity will not be compromised and if the source agrees to the reporter confirming the information elsewhere for the purposes of publication. I didn't want him to pursue this line of reporting and I had made that clear. These were the conditions under which I had told Woodward what I told him. And which he failed to honor. Later, I would cycle through many emotions, but in that moment I had just two reactions, in equal measure: panic and fury.

I began to sputter out variations of "How could you?" while my tone oscillated back and forth from stunned to distressed. His tone, though calm, belied a hint of nervousness, as he tried to assure me he didn't use my name and that he had reported out the story through other sources, other eyewitnesses. Which I interpreted as meaning he went to Jean Houston and Mary Catherine Bateson and the White House staffer who witnessed what I had and from them he gathered more information. He said he protected me by not naming me in what he wrote.

I was dumbfounded. Not naming me was worse, in a way, I pointed out. There were just five people in the room, and the other four knew I was there. It was obvious who the leak was. "How could you? How could you?" I asked him over and over.

The betrayal was devastating. It was even worse that it had been committed by someone I looked up to, by someone who had mentored me, who had sat across the dinner table from me a thousand times, who had helped me through bad times and cheered me on through the good. It was a breathtaking betrayal. And by "breathtaking" I mean literally that it took my breath away. As I type these words twenty years later, I feel my throat tighten.

And, yes, I am embarrassed to be *that* person, the sort who can't let go of old wounds. And I have allowed this wound, self-inflicted by my own bad judgment, to remain uncauterized, settling into permanent self-recrimination: I should not have shared that information and so I got what I deserved.

If that's so, why now, twenty years later, am I writing about this? More to the point, why am I exposing what I think Bob Woodward did to me? Because I can't expose myself without exposing him. Writing, when committed honestly, is an act of exposing. *Exposition.* Think about that word. It comes from the Latin *exponere,* defined as "to explain or to put forth."

I want to explain, to tell my story, having run out of enthusiasm for telling the stories of others. Woodward is just collateral damage in my quest to set the record straight, just as I suppose he tells himself I was collateral damage in his reporting out what he considered an important news story.

Set the record straight. Oh, how I recoil from those words even as I type them. Setting the record straight is the Washington cliché of all clichés, a peculiar compulsion and construction that allows people, usually via memoirs or op-eds or speeches, to say what's on their minds. What makes so many people here, myself included, believe they need to write their own "rough draft of history"? In part, it's because loyalty in this town can be bought, sold, and traded like crude oil or copper. And also because it is unbearable to accept that versions of oneself can only be authored by others whose own self-interest will live in Google searches until the end of time.

I don't remember how the phone call ended, just that I was in tears and he tried to reassure me that it wouldn't be a problem for me. He sounded slightly sheepish but at the same time he didn't seem to regret what he had done. He seemed focused on the big splash he was about to make. A splash in the same pool in which I was drowning.

The next day, June 23, 1996, along with millions of other Washingtonians, I read the 154-column-inch excerpt from Woodward's new book, *The Choice*, on the front page of the *Washington Post*. That's when I was able to fill in the missing pieces of a puzzle that had been the last eight months of my life.

It's true that Woodward's account had gone far beyond what I had told him. His reporting traced the beginning of the First Lady's relationship with Jean Houston and Mary Catherine Bateson back to a weekend at Camp David in late December 1994, several months before I met them. In addition to these women, other guests included self-help guru Marianne Williamson, Anthony Robbins, and Stephen R. Covey. It was a retreat of sharing and introspection, a weekend of healing.

Woodward made it clear in his usual stark and bloodless tone that he had contempt for this sort of navel-gazing. At least it was clear to me. But his tone was irrelevant; it was the facts he had gathered, in his typical vacuum-cleaner suck-it-all-up style, that enlightened me: "Jean Houston and Mary Catherine Bateson had followed up their weekend at Camp David with a series of letters, proposals and ideas on defining her role as First Lady and rising above the criticism and attacks. Houston had strongly encouraged Hillary to write a book, and Hillary had begun one, on children."

This helped me understand why Houston and Bateson appeared a bit disconcerted and annoyed when we met. Houston had previously told the First Lady she should write a book. And there I was, an unknown writer, someone outside the tribe, who seemed to appear out of thin air. I hadn't shared their communion at Camp David. I wasn't famous. I was nobody, an interloper.

As I read Woodward's excerpt, I was fascinated by all the details he had collected and the chronology he had constructed, complete with context and history. But what his account didn't include was a timeline of his reporting. He most likely began the moment my plane took off for Italy. The phrase about scales falling from one's eyes, from the biblical passage about Saul regaining his sight, comes to mind. The farther I read, following the breadcrumbs of his reporting, the more I was able to complete the picture of his betrayal. He must have contacted Houston and Bateson with questions, as well as Lissa Muscatine, Mrs. Clinton's speechwriter, who had been a *Washington Post* reporter and editor. Early on in my time at the White House, she had taken me under her wing and had even talked to me about staying on there to become a junior speechwriter, to help with a weekly newspaper column the First Lady was going to be writing.

Of course, I also flashed on the series of events that had unfolded in the last several months: the weird scene I discovered in my apartment when I got back from Italy; the press phone calls about the acknowledgments flap; my final payment being withheld. Could any of that have been caused by Woodward chasing the lead I gave him? His requests for interviews as he followed the story must have tipped off the

White House that I had told Woodward about the meeting between Mrs. Clinton and Houston and Bateson.

Predictably, the national news media ran with the story from Woodward's book. Ghosts, spirits, and psychics in the White House makes for a great news story, one that is perennially compelling. From the widely known Mary Todd Lincoln spiritualist séances to Florence Harding's fortune-tellers to Nancy Reagan's astrologer, the intersection of the occult and first ladies has always been a national obsession. In Mrs. Clinton's case, a therapeutic exercise was turned into a spooky, kooky séance that made for some pretty dramatic headlines: BOOK SAYS HILLARY TALKS TO DEAD; "SPIRITUAL EVENT" IS DENIED—HILLARY CLINTON SAYS SHE WAS BRAIN-STORMING FOR A BOOK; WHITE HOUSE: MRS. CLINTON NOT INTO SÉANCES: NEW AGE SESSIONS "BRAINSTORMING"; and FUSS OVER FIRST LADY'S "GURU" WIDE, NOT DEEP—HILLARY CLINTON CALLS IT "BRAINSTORMING"—POLITICAL STRATEGISTS RELUCTANT TO ATTACK.

I was terrified that someone in the press would connect the dots to me. That it eventually came from the *Washington Post* was particularly painful. The paper's grande dame of political writing, Mary McGrory, wrote:

> Unfortunately for Clinton, the proceedings of the gathering—which was attended by Houston's colleague, Mary Catherine Bateson, several Clinton staffers, and Barbara Feinman, Woodward's former researcher—were taped. Tape? You ask unbelievingly, with a member of the Nixon impeachment staff the principal figure? Yes, but for the benefit of Feinman, a writer-researcher who was at

the time helping Clinton with her book, the subsequent bestseller, *It Takes a Village*. No one asked the obvious question: "How would we like to see this on the front page of The Post?"—which is of course where it ended up.

I reached the end of her column, completely shamed by her innuendo, but also sick with wonder about the existence of a tape. It was never in my possession, nor did I even think one way or another that we were being taped. Most conversations for the book were taped so that we could capture any usable material. It was a White House tape recorder, operated by someone else, and if a transcript was made of that meeting, it wasn't shared with me, nor was I ever told that the afternoon's activities were fodder for the book.

In retrospect, it's likely that the meeting originated as simply a visit with Houston and Bateson, and I was included as an afterthought because I had been gently lobbying for more face time with the First Lady, becoming increasingly desperate to get material for the book. Merging the two meetings was probably viewed by a busy scheduler as a way of killing two birds with one stone.

Had someone broken into my apartment because they thought I had *that* tape? I couldn't really put together a plausible connection. Break-ins, missing tapes, these are the things of Washington thrillers, not real life. (In 2014, ten years after McGrory's death, John Norris wrote a long, fascinating story in *Politico* about her that said she had been on a list of media people whom Nixon had instructed the IRS to go after. "The plan to audit McGrory that year backfired," the article said. "She got a larger refund because she had under-reported her considerable charitable giving. And it certainly did not soften her coverage of the Nixon White House . . . McGrory's apartment was also broken into a number of times during this period. She had her theory on the unsolved crimes, saying she had been 'fooled completely' into thinking that the break-ins had been the work of 'honest thieves' rather than administration henchmen.")

On June 25, 1996, the same day McGrory's column ran, another *Post* columnist, Richard Cohen, weighed in, though he didn't dwell on the "séance" revelation:

> Just as interesting to me is a nugget in the Woodward book that has nothing to do with the dead and everything to do with the living. It is that both of Hillary Clinton's New Age Nudniks, Jean Houston and Mary Catherine Bateson, helped in the writing of *It Takes a Village: And Other Lessons Children Teach Us*, the First Lady's best-selling book. "So in October and November [1995], Houston virtually moved into the White House residence for several days at a time to help," Woodward writes. "Bateson came to help, too, at the end."

Cohen described my reported involvement in writing the book and listed a few of Mrs. Clinton's aides who had also, according to Woodward, helped write it. What Cohen found telling was that the White House was attempting to suggest that Mrs. Clinton had written the book without any help when "most public figures get professional help to write the books they do not have time, interest or ability to write."

"Who wants to acknowledge the help of two New Age specialists (What is that, anyway?) which will only produce controversy and, as we all can now see, some ridicule? (Houston once claimed to have dissolved an orange-sized lump in her right breast by going into a trance.) In the end, Mrs. Clinton acknowledged no one . . . ."

No acknowledgments page has ever been such a briar patch.

And then Robert Sam Anson, in the *New York Observer*, wrote that I had told Woodward about the "séance" to get even when I wasn't thanked in Mrs. Clinton's acknowledgments. He got the chronology all wrong and he made assumptions that weren't supported by the truth. In fact, he had it totally backward. I told Woodward about the "séance" because I had a big mouth and because I stupidly trusted him not to use the material. This was well before I knew anything about the lack of acknowledgment. Anson wrote: "In *The Choice*, Mr. Woodward notes the presence of the recorder, but doesn't reveal to whom the device belonged. If, however, one and one still add up to two, then both Mr. Woodward and Ms. Feinman have cause to feel ashamed."

He was right that I should feel ashamed, but as a journalist he still had an obligation to get his facts straight. The "device" belonged to the White House. I didn't tape the session or even realize it had been taped until I read Woodward's book.

Life goes on. New book projects came along, my personal life changed dramatically in the year that followed, and things happened that eclipsed and pushed to the margins the memories of that year of misery. When memories did intrude, I tried to forgive Woodward and myself. We rarely talked. I couldn't get past the betrayal, and I suspect he was happier not to have to think of it. Out of sight, out of mind. A few years later I showed up at an Easter party he threw, a family thing, out at his vacation home near Annapolis. He smiled and was gracious, and we pretended like the whole thing had never happened. I looked for signs of remorse, and all I detected was discomfort.

No one died, I would remind myself, and few remembered the details except for me. It didn't matter to anyone else. Being betrayed was an occupational hazard of moving in these circles. The news cycle kept spinning, rendering my little footnote to history old news, and then finally it washed down the drain of Washington dirty laundry, as though it had never happened.

But I couldn't truly forget. Protecting sources is a sacred cow in Washington, and Woodward was the high priest of espousing the importance of anonymous sources. Ten years after the "séance" mishegas, in 2005, Judith Miller, then a reporter for the *New York Times*, went to jail for eighty-five days rather than testify before a grand jury about her source in the Valerie Plame affair. Woodward was one of Miller's most vocal and prominent supporters, dramatically offering to serve a portion of her jail time during an appearance on *Larry King Live*.

"If the judge would permit it," he said, "I would go serve some of her jail time because I think the principle is that important, and it should be underscored. It's not a casual idea that we have confidential sources. It is absolutely vital."

AFTER THE "SÉANCE" FLAP RECEDED from Washington's fickle consciousness, I vowed to leave the city, this time for good. My friends saw me as the ghost who cried wolf because I had said I was doing this on at least a few other occasions. But this time I really meant it.

I figured I could live for a while on my savings while looking for a different sort of writing or editing gig somewhere, anywhere else. The Florida Keys randomly appealed to me. The weather was balmy and everything I associated with it—Hemingway, six-toed cats, hurricanes, key lime pie—seemed so very un-Washington. I gave my landlord thirty days' notice and began the dismantling of my Washington life. Then one morning, as I was sitting on the floor packing up my mother's Wedgewood, the phone rang.

I heard a friendly, familiar voice on the other end. "Hi, Barbara, it's Michael Lewis."

Michael was the author of *Liar's Poker*, and later *Moneyball*, *The Blind Side*, and a bunch of other bestsellers. He was a friend whose success was so stratospheric it was hard to be jealous of him. He was calling, he explained, because he had a potential writing gig for me. It was July 1996, and Bill Clinton was running against Bob Dole for a second term in office. For several months, Michael had been writing a campaign journal for *The New Republic*. He had started with the primaries and had chronicled the vast field of Republican contenders including Pat Buchanan, Lamar Alexander, Steve Forbes, Alan Keyes, and Morry Taylor.

I know. Morry who? That's exactly what I wondered when Michael told me Morry Taylor was looking for someone to write his political manifesto. Morry was the CEO of a tire company in Michigan, and he had entered the race when one of his factory workers challenged him to put his money where his mouth was. He had garnered .14 percent of the popular primary vote. Yes, that was *point* one four. He had served as great comedic relief for Michael, who wrote that his incentive for getting out of bed each morning was that every three days, he allowed himself to spend a day with "someone who was not Bob Dole."

While I listened to Michael tell me why I should sign on to write a manifesto by some Republican I had never heard of, I looked at the moving boxes filling my living room. I wanted to say "no thanks," but Michael is one of the most charming people I've ever met in my life. Some reporters bulldoze their way to information, but Michael does it through seduction. He has a charm that is enhanced by the southern tones of his Louisiana upbringing. "If he can't find a publisher, he'll just self-publish. He's willing to pay a lot of money. Maybe 150k."

"Could he afford that?" I asked, sitting up.

"He just paid $7 million of his own money to run for president," Michael said. "His company has about 80 percent of the North American construction equipment wheel market and 90 percent of the farm-equipment wheel market. A hundred fifty grand would be chump change to Morry."

I told him I had to think about it. I had promised myself I was giving up the ghost. I wanted to get out of Washington and away from politics. But that kind of money for four or five months' work would buy me a lot of freedom. I could get settled in the Keys and leisurely look for work, or even put that off and take time to work on writing fiction.

A few days later, I told Michael I would do it. I called my

landlord and asked if I could stay. I unpacked the boxes. A week later, I was headed to Detroit, sitting next to Michael, getting a crash course in all things Morry Taylor.

As we flew toward the Midwest and I listened to Michael's enthusiasm, it was dawning on me that I had signed on not only to be Morry's ghost but also to be a character in the *New Republic* campaign journal that would serve as the basis for Michael's book, *Trail Fever: Spin Doctors, Rented Strangers, Thumb Wrestlers, Toe Suckers, Grizzly Bears, and Other Creatures on the Road to the White House.* This was meta. Instead of writing about Washington characters, I was becoming one.

We went straight from the airport to Morry's house, and I met the great man himself. Morry was a compact, fast-talking, energetic man in his early fifties with strong opinions and a man-of-the-people style. "The Grizz," as Morry had been dubbed by Wall Street and encouraged everyone to refer to him, was refreshingly politically incorrect and unplugged. He had pulled out of the race a few months earlier, in March, after trying to position himself as a "poor man's Ross Perot."

I seriously did not share Morry's politics. After having ghosted primarily for Democrats, I wasn't sure how I was going to make the ideological leap. The trick was going to be balancing his style with his outrage. Michael, in his campaign journal, would later allude to my challenge: "She insists that the book must be written in the first-person singular, so that the reader experiences the full force of Morry's personality. 'It's easier for me to remember what Morry is trying to say if I'm channeling him through me,' she says. 'That's a frightening thought, channeling Morry,' I say. 'I've channeled worse,' she says."

To paraphrase Morry would be to drain his message of its power. His style was his substance: "The Census Bureau, they count you every ten years. What do they do the other nine years?" To someone who had just gotten burned by Washington, his outsider persona was something of a relief.

Dave Barry described Morry this way: "The Grizz has a very direct style of speech. He sounds a little like a Quentin Tarantino movie gangster who has somehow developed an intense interest in the U.S. trade deficit," and he summed up Morry's campaign message as two basic points: "1. The problem with this country is that the government is run by lawyers. 2. And these are stupid lawyers."

The whole first meeting is documented in Michael's book, Morry's and my interaction serving as a welcome departure from the usual political fodder that campaigns manufacture like so much raw sewage:

> By midafternoon Barbara is sitting in front of a big-screen TV clutching a Grizz T-shirt, drinking a Grizz bear (brewed by Morry in New Hampshire during the primary), and watching Morry—in a pink shirt with a cigar dangling from his mouth—fast-forwarding through a videotape of his various performances. He speeds right past his triumphant speech to the People, his various debates in Iowa and New Hampshire, his concession speech. At length he arrives at his new commercial for Titan Wheel—the one I watched him create merely a month ago. "Here," he says. "This is the best part." On the screen Morry morphs into a grizzly bear, and as he does he emits a roar even more menacing

than the one I recall. "That's my roar," he shouts with glee. "My real-life roar. They just slowed it down."

I remember that moment vividly. It was Michael watching me watching Morry watching me watching him watching himself on TV. And I remember exactly what I was thinking. I was wondering what the heck Michael had gotten me into and how the heck was I going to make a book materialize out of this. After all, "I'm a beautician, not a magician."

At some point during the afternoon, Michael slipped away, saying he had some work to do. I looked at him pleadingly. *Don't abandon me,* my eyes said. But Michael just smiled reassuringly and left. What I didn't know until much later when I read Michael's published account was that he was just outside the door, taking notes for what would become a hilarious scene in his campaign book in which Morry lectured me on the world according to Morry.

Michael left and I stayed on to bond with Morry and to interview him as much as possible in as short a time as possible so that I could start to write his manifesto. Given his hatred of lawyers, it occurred to me that a natural title for his book was *Kill All the Lawyers, and Other Ways to Fix the Government.*

Working with Morry proved to be the antidote to my *Village* woes. After having been caught in and chewed up by the White House machine, I loved the zaniness of Morry's world. I loved his *eff you* to political correctness, and I began to regain my sense of humor after a few days around him. He always seemed to be doing radio interviews, even though he had conceded the race months earlier, and he started mentioning the book on air. And then he started mentioning me, describing me as a "nice little Jewish girl who was mistreated by Hillary Clinton." At first I cringed, and then I just laughed. Even if I wanted to, there was no way to stop Morry from saying whatever flew into his head at any given moment. He couldn't be handled.

Eventually I returned to Washington and got to work. When I ran out of ideas, I went back to the Midwest and followed Morry around for a few days, asking him to expound on everything from flag burning to campaign finance reform. I taped him, transcribed him, and then translated him into what I hoped would be an engaging narrative that he felt adequately reflected his positions. His interest in the manifesto ebbed and flowed, and I was trying to be around for the flow parts.

One day Morry called and said I should come visit because he wanted me to attend the taping of a commercial he had scheduled for his tire company. He had rented a pair of trained grizzly bears; the female was six hundred pounds and the male one thousand pounds. Morry brought me along to the football field where the commercial was being filmed. He seated me fifty yards away because I was afraid of the bears even though he kept telling me they were trained. When Morry went to kick a field goal over the outstretched paws of one of the bears, she was stung by a horsefly and rose high up in the air, roaring so loudly it sent me running off the field.

Morry didn't blink.

In a way, I thought it was a shame he didn't get further along in the campaign. Morry wasn't ready for the Oval

Office, but he had intestinal fortitude and heart, two qualities in short supply in Washington.

We finished the book, he was happy with it, and when we couldn't find a publisher, he ended up self-publishing it. He handed it out at events around the country, often mentioning the nice Jewish girl who wrote the book, pointing at my name on the cover and declaring I deserved all the credit.

ELEVEN

Haunted

*After all . . . what is the past but what
we choose to remember?*
—AMY TAN, *THE BONESETTER'S DAUGHTER*

Writing other people's lives is a bit silly, like playing dress-up, clomping around in your mother's pumps that don't quite fit, but it also lets you have a momentary sense of what it's like to be someone else. That's what I told myself I was doing: rehearsing for my real life. But meanwhile, inhabiting the minds and lives of other people for a decade had afforded me a comfortable lifestyle: I could rent a nice place in one of the most expensive cities in the world; I didn't have any debt and I could take vacations and still save for the future. The money had been a great excuse to put off being fully present in my own interior life, which for a writer pretty much *is* your life.

By this time I had reached my midthirties, and I had to face the fact that this had become my real life, whether or not I had gotten here accidentally rather than purposefully. I could no longer hide under the guise of ingénue or mentee.

My youth and its promise had long since exceeded their expiration date. Time to grow up. We all define "growing up" a little differently. But before I could make room for myself and my own memories, I had to exorcise the ghosts of others. Growing up also meant getting married and having kids, two things that had eluded me. Washington is not an easy town for relationships. People work long hours and put their jobs first, and I had been guilty of both.

Though my book business kept me plenty busy, it was mainly a solitary endeavor, and I appreciated the human interaction that part-time teaching provided. By 1996, I had been teaching Introduction to Journalism at Georgetown University for four years, every Monday evening on the second floor of White-Gravenor, a decaying Gothic building. My classroom was below some sort of science lab that periodically oozed an unknown liquid through its floor onto my classroom's ceiling.

Because I taught in the evenings, I had minimal interaction with the regular full-time faculty in the English Department, but that fall semester after working with Morry, I did meet and get to know a colleague, an eighteenth-century-literature scholar, Dennis Todd, whose classes were scheduled during the daytime. One day Dennis mistakenly got a piece of mail advertising a journalism event. He brought it to me and we began talking. That led to a drink down by the Potomac that turned into dinner at an Italian restaurant across town.

Then, unexpectedly, he offered to wash my car. I realize that sounds vaguely obscene, but it was nothing more than a kind gesture when he noticed my car was splattered with mud. The car washing won my heart, and that led to him inviting me to stay for enchiladas, and the Mexican food stole my stomach. Twenty years later, he's still making me enchiladas (the car washing, not so much). We moved in together, married, and had a daughter just fourteen months after meeting.

I love being married and having a family and sometimes wonder what took me so long to settle down. Was it something about me? Or was it something about Washington? Why was it so hard to make a connection in a city whose currency is connections?

This is something that bothered me for quite a while: Before I met my husband, while I was working with Mrs. Clinton on her book, I began to despair that I was spending my days (and nights) involved in, entrenched even, in others' lives both professionally (ghosting memoirs and manifestos) and personally (I loved children and since I didn't have my own, I found ways to have them in my life: I volunteered at Children's Hospital; took care of friends' children; taught children how to ice-skate; and, most importantly, devoted myself to my niece and nephews).

But these surrogates weren't enough, so I found a shrink, signed on for weekly appointments, and committed to jump-starting my personal life. The irony of paying someone to listen to me narrate my own story was not lost on me. And the therapist, being a creature of Washington, seemed fascinated by the stories I told because—let's face it—there were good characters in these stories, even if I knew they weren't *my* stories. Listen to the one about Bob Woodward! Hillary Clinton! The senator who committed an indiscretion! The war hero who ran for president! Everyone else's story was easier to tell than my own. If I kept this up, I could spend forever without ever having to face my own demons.

After several months, I began to run out of material and decided that these sessions weren't helping, and so I pulled the plug. End of that story? Nope. Not in *this town*. Flash forward two years, and I'm married with an infant. I get a letter from the shrink, addressed to me at Georgetown's English Department, something to the effect of "I can't find you. Your phone number has changed. Could you please get in touch with me?" I speculated it must be something about the final bill. But why did she wait this long to contact me? Nervously, I dialed her number.

I should have guessed what she wanted. She wanted to write a book, and she wanted to *hire* me to help her. The violation of boundaries in this proposition was stunning and immediately obvious, at least to me. But this was Washington. A city with no borders: The personal is the professional, the private the public, and vice versa.

So why didn't I tell her no or even point out the ethical implications of working with someone who could catalog my secrets, phobias, and failures like they were butterflies? I dunno. Maybe I need a different shrink to answer that. Maybe it's as simple as I needed a gig, and she offered me one.

I was on hiatus from another book project, a sinking ship of a manuscript by a senator who shall remain nameless. Suffice it to say he had a female problem, though I know that doesn't really narrow things down much, does it? His wife didn't approve of his book project, and she seemed to resent my presence in their home. The files and I were exiled to the basement of the basement, which felt like taking a day hike through Stalin's gulag. This basement banishment seemed to underscore a shame that went along with this profession. Ghosts were to be spirited away, ignored, treated with disdain. A magazine piece I had read years before about celebrity memoirs quoted a book editor as noting that ghostwriters were "basically typists." That one had stung.

I secretly agreed with the senator's wife that the project was a bad idea. They had worked through their problems, or maybe around them; in any event, they seemed to be in a good place. So why revisit an unfortunate past? I believe he was compelled by an overarching sense that he was misunderstood and that his transgression had been exaggerated by the media and that it unfairly eclipsed a lifetime of public service.

At one point, I found myself standing outside their senatorial house in the August heat—when I was seven months pregnant, round and squat as a pumpkin, and sweating like a Sumo wrestler—listening to the wife threaten me that if this book had anything in it to hurt her husband, she would . . . I kept silent though I wanted to note that her husband's secrets were safe with me. After my Woodward experience, I was now the Fort Knox of collaborators.

As the months went by it became clear that the senator was destined not to finish his memoir, and that was just as well. I now had a baby to care for and had taken the semester off from teaching. So when the shrink with no boundaries came along, I was in need of a new gig. She would compensate me well. I told myself it would be a temporary and convenient solution.

Except it didn't feel temporary, and it was anything but convenient.

Almost immediately, she started calling several times a day, starting as early as 7:00 A.M. Her reliance on me quickly became suffocating. She knew I wasn't working on anything else, but I had told her that that could change. She expressed concern about whether I would continue to have enough time to work with her but quickly added she didn't resent the time that my daughter required. It struck me as an odd thing to say.

One day she brought over a gift for my daughter that one of her patients had made. It was a clown doll, its torso and limbs pieces of Styrofoam covered in cloth; its nose, eyes, and mouth were plastic buttons attached with straight pins. Talk about a choking hazard. Even worse, it had that creepy horror movie clown thing going on.

Dennis took one look and said, "This is getting really weird." Then he picked it up and, holding it at arm's length, took it out to the trash. After that, I gently began to push back against her ever-encroaching insertion into my life, but she pushed back even harder. Psychologically, of course, she had the advantage. As her patient I had shared with her my demons and my weaknesses—relevant here, my people-pleasing tendencies. The situation felt claustrophobic. And then, as happens too rarely in life, opportunity knocked on our door.

ONE EVENING, Dennis came home with a letter on official Georgetown University stationery. "We are pleased to inform you that you have been selected to be the professor-in-residence for the academic year 1999–2000," it said.

The chaos of our first year of parenthood had caused us to forget that Dennis had applied for the Villa program in Italy. I had studied Italian in college and lived there for the summer after graduating from Berkeley. My 1995 post-*Village* trip had renewed my determination to return someday and stay for a long time. This sojourn wasn't decided on a whim but rather was the end point of a slow-burning and ever-mounting desire that we shared to live in Italy and that I had to escape from Washington. And now we were going to do just that. Nine glorious months in Italy.

Like Henry Adams's *Democracy* character Madeleine Lightfoot Lee, who said she dreamed of running off to Egypt, I, too, was disillusioned with Washington. "Democracy has shaken my nerves to pieces," Adams's character proclaimed. "Oh, what rest it would be to live in the Great Pyramid and look out for ever at the polar star!"

The Georgetown compound wasn't just any villa; a Rockefeller had bequeathed it to Georgetown University. It was blissfully located in Fiesole, an ancient hill town that sits just above Florence: Villa Le Balze. *Le Balze* means "The Cliffs." Let that roll off your tongue and automatically the shoulders relax and exhaling becomes a natural and involuntary activity, something you no longer need to remind yourself to do.

Dolce far niente. Sweet to do nothing. Sweet to get the hell out of Washington.

We gave our landlord notice, put our belongings in a storage unit, stowed our car in Ben Bradlee's country home barn, and fled to Italy with our twenty-month-old daughter.

After a long flight, then a car ride through Florence and up a long, winding one-lane road to the town of Fiesole, we arrived at the Villa Le Balze. We were shown to the *villino* (little villa), a two-story apartment in a separate building across a garden from the main villa. From nearly any vantage point on the grounds, there was a truly breathtaking vista of Florence below, overlooking the river Arno. And just a short but heart-stopping walk up to the top of the hill stood Fiesole, a village with Etruscan ruins, a Roman amphitheater and temple, an eleventh-century cathedral, and numerous structures dating to the Renaissance.

The villa grounds included an internationally recognized maze of gardens and an active olive grove from which came the best olive oil I've ever tasted. Two amazing cooks were on duty to make lunch and dinner for the students and faculty, as well as housekeepers and gardeners to keep everything tidy and beautiful. The villa had survived being bombed during World War II, and it was still elegant with its high ceilings and big windows with panoramic views. The library had a piano and spectacular old bookshelves. It was the perfect place to sip a glass of red wine and curl up with E. M. Forster's *A Room with a View*.

We didn't know much about how Georgetown had ended up with the villa. We had heard through the university grapevine that a Rockefeller had left it to Georgetown so she wouldn't have to leave it to her children. The truth, as it so often does, turned out to be more complicated. According to Dominick Dunne, in a splashy *Vanity Fair* piece, the fabulously wealthy granddaughter of John D. Rockefeller, Margaret Rockefeller Strong, at age seventy-seven married her second husband, Raymundo de Larrain, who, thirty-three years her junior, convinced her to rewrite her will and leave her assets to him rather than her two children from her first marriage. A lawsuit ensued. The *New York Times* reported that the children's lawyer "argued that Mr. de Larrain had deliberately isolated their mother from her servants and from the Rockefeller family, then manipulated her into changing her will. In her final will, signed in Florida, the children were disinherited."

But at age eighty-two, Margaret had signed away the villa to the university in 1979, a year before she rewrote her will, and six years before her death. Did her husband convince her to do that? Did Georgetown? The truth was more complicated than the rumors we had heard. Her obituary notes that during the spring before the winter she died, she and her husband were awarded honorary degrees from Georgetown for their work on behalf of "culture, peace and world harmony" (the lack of familial harmony notwithstanding, apparently). Why she turned over the villa to Georgetown and not her children or her husband may be unknowable.

Uncontestable was how spectacular the gardens were. Her father, Charles Augustus Strong, a philosopher and author, had retreated there after his wife, the daughter of John D. Rockefeller, died. Though he owned the land, there was no existing home.

But Fiesole was a lovely, peaceful place for a widowed father of a nine-year-old girl to set down roots, so he hired two well-known English architects to design and build the villa. Here, Margaret could play among the olive groves and garden statues, and Charles could host other philosophers, among them his old friend and Harvard classmate George Santayana. It was a setting that appealed to young and old, to anyone who appreciated beauty and tranquility.

Just below Le Balze, to the east, literally across the road, was the Villa Medici, considered to be the first true Renaissance villa, which in 1458 had been the summer retreat of Cosimo the Elder and was now where the Argentine soccer star Gabriel Batistuta lived. To the north is the Villa San Girolamo, the setting for Michael Ondaatje's bestselling novel *The English Patient.*

Though we are not related to the Rockefellers or anyone else remotely rich or fancy, we were treated like royalty from the moment we arrived. My husband was addressed by one and all as *Professore,* and I was *Signora.* Our daughter, walking but barely talking, was called a variety of endearments including *carina, bambina, bella.*

Sasha had been an easy baby and she was an easy toddler. She slept through the night, took naps (the entire country took naps!), rarely fell ill, and had a happy, sunny disposition. In equal measure, she loved pasta and the attention of our students; there were about two dozen of them living at the villa for the semester. And for peer companionship, Sasha made friends with one of the cooks' small children, whose farm we regularly visited for playdates. I would marvel at my good fortune as I wended my way through Tuscan hills illuminated by the Italian sun, and I didn't miss driving through suburban Washington among its cranky commuters.

We quickly settled into a routine, with Dennis focused on teaching while I cared for Sasha. For the first time in eighteen years, I had time on my hands. I wasn't expected to teach. I didn't have a publisher breathing down my neck. I was there, gratefully, in the role of faculty spouse, with no other obligations than to mind our daughter. I could write, drink wine, and reflect on my life. Or just drink wine. I didn't feel like writing. I was having too much fun. We felt so incredibly welcomed in Italy. Wherever we went, people fawned over Sasha. Bakers, maître d's, shopkeepers, merry-go-round operators—everyone had at least a smile and usually a *dolce* for her.

More than anyone else, the Italian director of the program, Marcelo, and his wife, Cinzia, made us feel at home. Their daughter was exactly the same age as Sasha and, though they didn't share a language, they did share their toys, which is all that matters when you're two years old. And so it was to Marcelo we turned when we learned that for every Christmas holiday, the university muckety-mucks (wealthy alums and donors) took over the villino, and we would have to temporarily vacate the premises for three weeks.

Marcelo suggested we spend the first week, leading up to and including Christmas day, in Orvieto, a town in the region of Umbria. He arranged for us to borrow the villa's vehicle, and we drove there, first staying at a nunnery that took in boarders to help with the bills. The village was a magical place, particularly at this time of year, all lit up with holiday lights, fresh snow blanketing the cobblestone streets, and the smell of warm bread wafting out of the many bakeries as we strolled around, stopping for coffee, sweets, and vino whenever the spirit moved us.

Most of that week, I was able to live only in the moment, a state of being that usually eludes me. But when I did think of our future, it was about the house we would buy and the home wc would make when our Italian days came to their conclusion. Though I wasn't eager to return to Washington, I was excited to think about putting down roots. Before getting married, I had moved almost every two years, leading the typical young, single person's nomadic life. Moving so frequently had lost its appeal, and I looked forward to staying put in one place. It was in Orvieto that I found a brass door knocker for the house that Sasha would grow up in and leave from for college. I decided that one of Dennis's first household chores in our future home would be to affix that knocker to the front door so that each time we entered the housc we would remember our time in Italy.

Marcelo had suggested that after Umbria we travel to Tuscany, where his parents were caretakers on a farm. He said there was a converted barn for guests where we could write and make nice dinners amid the rolling hills. It sounded heavenly, and we readily agreed. So after Christmas, as the rest of the world braced for Y2K, we made our way from Umbria to Tuscany, following Marcelo's handwritten directions along a dirt road to where Marcelo's parents eagerly awaited us.

If the prognosticators were right and the modern world really did come to a standstill at Y2K, we wouldn't even notice as we were surrounded by vineyards and olive groves. The world could sort out its technological issues while we drank the local Chianti and hunted for black truffles.

The first night we ate dinner at Marcelo's parents' table, my bad Italian serving as the only means of communication between our hosts and us. The second day Marcelo's mother brought us an armful of leeks and taught Dennis, through pantomime, how to make leek risotto, a recipe he has made countless times over the last sixteen years for friends and family. The third day I asked for directions to the local butcher because I wanted to buy a chicken (mainly because it's one of the few things I could remember how to say: *Per favore, vorrei comprare un pollo.*)

Instead of directions, Marcelo's mother briefly disappeared and then presented us with a chicken she had just slaughtered, just for us. I'll leave out the details here. It tasted great but nearly rendered me a vegetarian.

It was here, without the Internet or a television or even a radio, that I was finally alone with my thoughts. I would look out the window of our rustic cottage, an old barn converted for the modern comforts that tourists expected, and see nothing but vineyards for miles and miles. Dennis would take Sasha out to give me some space, accompanying Marcelo's father as he hunted boar (okay, just pretending with a two-year-old along) or observed a herd of goats in the road and had a tour of the vineyards and learned about harvesting grapes. Dennis speaks no Italian, and Marcelo's father no English so, again, pantomime was the primary mode of communication.

One morning, coffee cup in hand, I sat at the desk in front of the window, gazing at the rows of grapevines. It felt like something was waiting to be written. I didn't know what. Out poured a several-thousand-word piece on ghostwriting in which I reflected on it as both a craft and a commercial endeavor. It also took shape as a declaration to give up the ghost. But first I had to explore why I had stuck with it for so many years.

If it was a detour, why hadn't I renavigated by now? What was the appeal of ghostwriting? I asked myself. Why had I been drawn to it, or at least not recoiled from it when I fell into it accidentally? It was alluring because it allowed me into worlds I wouldn't gain entry to otherwise. But that access did not give me the license to use what I observed, unlike a reporter's ability to use most of the material he or she gathers. So the trouble I was having was reconciling the tension between access and authority.

Also the proximity to power was fun. Being needed by someone who has a story the world wants to hear can be irresistible. But with that proximity comes dependency, sometimes in the form of codependency. Take for example one of my favorite ghostwriter stories of all time, that of baseball great Ty Cobb, who employed a journalist named Al Stump to write his autobiography. Things went bad quickly, mainly because Cobb was reportedly a miserable human being who made everyone in his orbit miserable. According to author Ben Yagoda, "Stump quit the project twice and was fired once. But he always came back. He was living out a ghostwriter's weird version of Stockholm syndrome."

Stockholm syndrome! Brilliant. It sounds hyperbolic, but any writer who has spent a lot of time with her subject can relate. Whether the subject is someone you've met or a fictional or historical character, research breeds a psychological intimacy. I can understand how it happens. The techniques of ghostwriting or character development foster sympathy that inevitably grows into empathy. To evoke characters—whether they are fictional or real—you first have to understand them before you share them. What are their motivations? Can you, the writer, find something in your own interior life that helps you empathize with your character's inner life?

No trait is more important for a ghost than empathy, something that is typically encouraged more in girls than in boys. As a ghost I had to convince myself that I was, for a time, another person. There were tangible things I did to achieve this: study the rhythm and cadence of the other's speech patterns and vocabulary preferences, writing style, politics, sensibilities, and philosophies. I looked at family photo albums, reviewed footage of TV appearances and other available material.

One of the things that helped me most in constructing a voice was employing my version of the Stanislavski method, a "grammar of acting," which instructs an actor through a series of techniques involving the concept of emotional memory, the internal triggering of emotions to become one with a character. Whether you're up on a stage or in front of a keyboard, you connect with your own memories to express someone else's feelings. I may not have cheated on my wife, but I can dig into the reservoir of crappy things I've done and come up with something to feel bad about.

I may not know what it's like to live in the shadow of a famous relative, but I have certainly felt jealousy about others who are more talented and successful. And a funny thing happens when you not only walk in someone else's shoes but also actually take up residence in their past: you blur the line between their lives and yours. Not in any sort of real or psycho way, but in a more deeply personal interior way.

Besides trying to get inside someone else's skin emotionally, I also needed to sound like my subject, or at least sound the way I think others would expect the person to sound. This takes what Vassar professor Donald Foster calls "literary forensics." If Foster's name sounds familiar, it's because he was plucked from Ivy Tower obscurity when a novel called *Primary Colors*, based on Bill Clinton's first presidential primary, identified its author as "anonymous," setting off a flurry of speculation as to who really wrote the roman à clef. Finally, *New York* magazine cracked the case when they consulted with Professor Foster, an expert in authenticating Shakespeare manuscripts. He ran *Primary Colors* through his computer software, studying all sorts of language markers such as sentence and paragraph length, vocabulary and punctuation patterns. Voilà! He determined that Joe Klein was the author.

The FBI then got the idea to use Foster for cases involving the written word such as the Unabomber's manifesto and the JonBenét Ramsey kidnapping ransom note. Foster's batting average turned out to be mixed but, for my purposes, there were techniques to be appropriated for my own work. Does your subject have favorite words? Phrases? Anecdotes? Themes? Does she speak and think in fully formed perfect paragraphs or does she interrupt herself a lot, digress? Does he use humor? Is he someone who pays attention to the details of language? Would he know how to properly use a semicolon? Is his style more folksy or wonky? If you're using old speeches to refashion into autobiography, how does the language need to be massaged to work for the eye rather than the ear?

Joe Queenan wrote a hilarious *New York Times* essay on

ghostwriting gone wrong and noted what happens when you hew a bit too closely to your subject's oratory: "Hillary Rodham Clinton put her name on a vast, unprecedentedly uninteresting autobiography, waiting until page 529 before disclosing that her speechwriter was responsible for many of the words in the book, which, coincidentally, read like the world's longest speech."

Sometimes it's not just typing, though you couldn't tell that from the mail I get, often from people who want to become ghosts themselves: "I'm unpublished, uneducated, and inexperienced in the field . . . the idea of ghostwriting appealed to me . . . HOW does one become a ghostwriter? I can't imagine I could put out an ad for politicians in hot water or aging Olympians."

I also get a lot of inquiries from strangers who want me to write their books on spec, meaning no money up front, but they are sure they have a bestseller on their hands and that the story will practically tell itself. These include associates of "celebrities" who want to tell the truth about Hollywood or Wall Street or an elite enclave, claiming that their story, if shared with the public, will blow the lid open on "wealthy industrialists" and "high-priced ruthless attorneys" and even "save lives."

Sometimes it's their own life they want to save, writing from a correctional facility. One such letter was from a convicted bank robber with multiple personalities. *No thanks*, I thought, *it's hard enough capturing one voice.* Another from a misunderstood embezzler. Then there are those who appealed to my ego, one writer claiming that because I had been "denounced," my "boldness" prompted her to want me as a collaborator.

And, finally, I get a lot of inquiries from journalists writing about my experiences with Hillary Clinton: one noting "lots of inconsistent reporting about it floating around," another asking about the role of ego in the process: "Does it ever creep up, when the praise is coming in and people are talking about the book you wrote but are not credited for publicly, do you ever mutter darkly into your whiskey 'you jerks don't even know'?"

As vexing as I ultimately found the whole business of midwifing others' books, it gave me the opportunity to go places emotionally that I never would have gone on my own. The fiction writer, the ghostwriter, and the thespian all get to test-drive personas in the safety of the creative process. Looking back, it unsettles me how seamlessly I took on the role of an emotional chameleon. I want to believe that the gravitational pull between me and ghosting was empathy, but it was more likely a defense mechanism. It was much less of a risk to work on other people's books—or so I thought—than to pursue my own projects. This work was a safe haven from my own fear of failure. I didn't articulate this to myself then, but I must have intuited it deep within.

WE RETURNED TO THE VILLA IN JANUARY and stayed there into the blissful spring, friends and family visiting us and accompanying us on weekend trips to Tuscan wineries and seaside villages. Another six months passed before we returned to Washington and another year before I tried to find a home for the article I wrote. I was ambivalent about lifting the veil (or the sheet; these ghost allusions are tedious but nearly automatic by now).

Finally, I submitted it to the Association of Writing Programs' magazine, the *Writer's Chronicle*, a well-regarded literary and academic publication that was not on the radar of the Washington press. It was exactly the sort of low-key venue I was comfortable with. I still didn't want to be noticed, but so much had been written about me without my input that I wanted to document a few basic facts about my work as a ghost.

I had hoped this personal essay would put an end to this for me.

Wishful thinking.

TWELVE

Learning to Vanish

I'm a beautician, not a magician.
—BUMPER STICKER SEEN ON THE PACIFIC COAST
HIGHWAY

We bought a modest Cape Cod house on a tree-lined cul-de-sac in Arlington, Virginia, just off the George Washington Parkway, a stone's throw from Key Bridge. Our neighborhood, Woodmont, was three miles from Georgetown's main campus. A favorite selling point for local real estate agents was that Woodmont was "one stoplight from the District."

That was true: Dennis and I could walk or bike to work except during the worst days of the winter. Still our house felt far removed from the hustle and bustle of urban living and the craziness of political Washington. *Here,* I thought, *we can raise our little girl in peace.* From our quiet suburban neighborhood you could see Washington off in the distance—the best vantage point from which to admire its beauty.

The harried pace of our Washington lives eclipsed our recent Italian bliss. We quickly settled into our new community and too easily slipped back into our teaching routines.

The habit of leisurely pasta lunches, drinking Chianti in Chianti, and long afternoon naps receded, too soon becoming faraway and another-lifetime sort of memories.

Our daughter made friends with children in the neighborhood, and we with their parents, hanging out at the bus stop or on the playground, chatting about our kids, our jobs, and our plans. When asked, I told people I was a journalism professor. Unless someone did some online sleuthing, my adventures in ghostwriting didn't come up.

Our commute was the most relaxing part of the day. I never grew tired of walking across Key Bridge, which connects northern Virginia to Georgetown. To the east lay the Kennedy Center, Roosevelt Island, the Watergate, and the Washington Monument and to the west, the beautiful banks of the Potomac and the trio of tiny islands called the Three Sisters. I love the myth of how this island cluster got its name: three young Algonquian sisters drowned during an attempt to rescue their brothers, who had been kidnapped by a rival tribe. The girls then turned into islands.

Some people say the islands emit a slow chiming, moaning sound when another victim is about to lose his or her life to the river's dangerous undercurrent. I'm not alone in finding the Three Sisters a compelling topic. They appear in a handful of novels, including Breena Clarke's *River, Cross My Heart*, in which the narrator ominously noted: "Legends abound that the Potomac River is a widowmaker, a childtaker, and a woman-swallower. According to the most famous tale, the river has already swallowed three sisters, three Catholic nuns. Yet it did not swallow them, only drowned them and belched them back up in the form of three small islands . . .

Nobody in his right mind goes swimming near the Three Sisters. The river has hands for sure at this spot. Maybe even the three nuns themselves, beneath the water's surface, are grabbing at ankles to pull down some company."

The weird mythology around the Three Sisters feeds this town's appetite for both conspiracy theories and for the supernatural. Moaning apparitions, revengeful spirits—as much as I tried, I couldn't get away from all things ghostly. Not only are they in abundance in this town, they feed into my belief that there is more here than meets the eye.

Regardless of whether three women actually died in the Potomac, the cluster of islands is more than just a source of mythmaking. There is a long history of people and organizations that have tried to incorporate a bridge involving the Three Sisters into a greater transportation project. Grandiose plans involving the Three Sisters began with Pierre L'Enfant in 1791, the architect charged by President Washington with laying our "Federal City," and more recently in the 1960s, those plans were revisited when a freeway and six-lane bridge were proposed by a group of legislators until the Foxhall Community Association, on the D.C. side, among others, killed the project. That particular plan had the Three Sisters Bridge ending just at Spout Run Parkway, the exit on George Washington Parkway that leads right to Woodmont.

The bridge separated us from the city, and though it was easy to cross, it provided a comforting psychological barrier. It not only separated suburb from city, but me from my past. After my ghost essay was published in 2002, I retreated into teaching. The essay had been my Dear John letter, and with its publication I vowed to turn down all ghostwriting offers, no matter how lucrative. It was just too draining, emotionally and mentally, both on the page and in the flesh. I wanted to live my own life, and I wanted that life to be calm, even placid.

I lulled myself into believing that bad memories and the aspects of the city associated with them were far away. But now and then I still ran headfirst into my past.

One of those times was on a snowy day in 2005, as my sister and I were making our way to our car in a synagogue parking lot. We had just attended a friend's daughter's bat mitzvah. A man approached us and said his battery was dead and that AAA said it would take hours to come help. Did we happen to have jumper cables?

We did, we said, and readily agreed to help. As I retrieved the cables from the trunk, I remarked that he looked awfully familiar but that I couldn't place him. "I think I've seen you on TV," I said, a common enough statement in Washington. He smiled and replied, "For a time I was on TV quite often. I was Mrs. Clinton's attorney." He held out his hand, and I took it. My face flushed as I realized who he was.

"Nice to meet you, Mr. Kendall. We're actually old friends," I joked. "I'm Barbara Feinman."

"Only in Washington," I muttered to my sister as I got back in the car. She couldn't hear me over the sound of her own laughter.

TEACHING PROVED TO BE a much better complement to family life than ghostwriting, though it came with its own set of frustrations. Georgetown didn't have any other full-time journalism professors, or even a formal journalism program, and I don't have a Ph.D., so there was no precedent for an outsider like me securing tenure. With no hope of attaining this academic rite of passage, I was rendered invisible.

In a system preoccupied with rank and tenure, being an adjunct, a lecturer, an instructor, or even a "visiting professor" (faculty are known to "visit" campuses for a decade or more) was tantamount to being a stowaway on an ocean liner. As long as you stayed belowdecks and out of sight, they usually wouldn't throw you overboard.

But Georgetown does have another class of adjuncts. While they enter the university as academic outsiders, they are instantly considered insiders because of their capital city brand of celebrity. Membership in Official Washington trumps any sort of academia insiderness. So though they may not have the academic credentials their scholarly colleagues do, Big Names instantly get fancy titles and red carpet treatment.

Another way to move from outsider to insider at Georgetown is to closely identify with one's Catholic roots. As a secular Jew, that was obviously a nonstarter for me at a Jesuit university. Nonetheless, I did truly come to love the Jesuit mission, and I unabashedly believed our own promotional material. I would find myself occasionally talking to prospective students about *cura personalis*, the Jesuit ideal of caring for the whole person, and when someone would shoot me that *Wait, aren't you Jewish?* look, I would stumble through my self-deprecating comedy act about being the honorary head of Jews for Jesuits.

One's rank in the academic caste system is of no interest to students; they focus only on how you can serve them, be it writing letters of recommendation, dispensing career counseling, or quelling their anxieties about grades. When one of our students asks for something in a particularly soul-sucking way (a letter of recommendation request on Thanksgiving Day, for instance), a colleague of mine invariably quotes Gabrielle Burton, the author of two books inspired by Tamsen Donner, the mother who stayed behind with her husband when her daughters were rescued from the infamous Donner Party expedition. Burton, a mother of five daughters, wrote: "The nicest husbands and children will eat you up alive if you offer yourself on the plate, and they'll ask for seconds." Motherhood, teaching, ghostwriting—they all are a giving away of oneself that can have great rewards but also leave one feeling diminished.

Despite being exiled to the realm of adjuncts, I was luckier than most, tenured or untenured. I was teaching journalism in the English Department so I was left to my own devices. English literature and theory scholars regarded journalism as an unworthy academic discipline, and they paid it no attention. That autonomy was a gift that I cherished. Eventually I was able to create and build two programs, one at the graduate level and one undergraduate. I was content to do my own thing, in spite of or even because of my low profile. Particularly after the turmoil of my ghostwriting years, I welcomed the refuge Georgetown provided me.

Most of the time I could distract myself with the tasks associated with teaching and running a program, but occasionally I was reminded that Georgetown wasn't just any university in any campus town. One evening my husband and I went to a surprise dinner party for a friend and English Department colleague, an accomplished poet turning sixty. We didn't know the hosts. They were the next-door neighbors of our poet friend and his wife, also our colleague. They lived in Georgetown in one of the smart brownstones typical of the exclusive neighborhood, just blocks from the university where we all teach.

Instructed to arrive by 7:00 P.M. in order to elude detection, we knocked on the door shortly before our deadline and scurried inside. As she collected our coats and drink orders, the hostess told us apologetically that her husband had slipped on ice and was marooned upstairs in bed with a broken ankle. Throughout the night his absence provoked my curiosity. I kept picturing Jimmy Stewart in *Rear Window.*

At about 7:45 P.M., well into our second cocktail, along with two dozen other guests, we were shepherded into the library, a book-lined, wood-paneled room with leather furniture and tasteful art. Our hostess asked us to quiet down so that David, the guest of honor, wouldn't hear us as he approached the front door. But where *was* David? He had been invited over ostensibly for a drink and a bedside visit with the bedridden host, but it was now nearly a half hour beyond the appointed arrival time.

His wife, who had gone to check on him, returned, explaining that when David had opened their front door, he noticed someone lying on the ground across the street. He ran over and found it was a teenager in the throes of a medical emergency. Another neighbor, walking her dog, rushed to the scene and instructed David not to finish the emergency call he'd begun to make. Instead, she fished around in the young man's pockets, found his phone, went to his contacts,

and called his parents. He was the son of a high-level administration official, she explained.

It had begun to rain so David ran back into the house to get
something to cover the young man. He grabbed his own teenage son's baby blanket, a sentimental worn piece of cloth that
held more memories than warmth at this point. He rushed back
and covered the rain-soaked young man. Within moments, a
caravan of Secret Service agents arrived with the worried parents, who were dressed in black tie, along with a private ambulance. They loaded up the patient and hurried off.

David then crossed the street and knocked on the door.
He entered to shouts and cries of "Surprise!" He looked
stunned, trying to make sense of his university colleagues
standing alongside his college roommate and the dozens
of friends he'd made in between. Surprise parties can be a
dicey endeavor, but it turned out he truly was surprised and
genuinely touched.

The party got into full swing, a catered affair with a buffet
boasting a row of shiny stainless steel tureens filled with
amazing Indian dishes and a well-known chef who beamed
as his culinary skills were lauded by one and all. Toasts and
speeches followed, and a cake. And it was all quite fun, but I
felt myself slipping away, preoccupied by the scene that had
just unfolded on the street and the fact that I would probably
never know in totality what happened: it was just the middle
of a story with an unknowable beginning and ending.

The birthday boy, who was making the rounds during dessert, came and sat beside me, which I took as an opportunity
to interrogate him. What did he think had happened? What
did the man say? What did his wife say? What did the Secret

Service say? Trained as a journalist I needed all the blanks filled in, but the novelist in me wanted to know what happened merely as a means to an end: I longed to imagine what *could have* happened. The stuff that lands on the front page or the home page no longer interested me as much as what makes a novel memorable.

David told us what little he had gleaned.

"It's the beginning of a thriller," I said, reaching for my merlot. My husband tried not to roll his eyes. I could read him as though there was a ticker running across his forehead. *She thinks everything that happens is the beginning of a thriller. A Washington thriller. A thriller she would write the first three chapters of and then abandon.*

"Openings are easy, it's the rest of the plot that is hard," Dennis countered. "What happens next?"

"I don't know," I said, "but you've got the son of [the name of whom I don't want to reveal here because the kid didn't choose to be in the public eye; some clichés deserve to persist] having some sort of medical emergency around the corner from Bob Woodward, the preeminent investigative reporter in the world, just outside the front door of a famous poet."

"Not to mention Nancy Reagan's scheduler in the house behind this one," David chimed in.

Dennis shot him a *don't encourage her* look, which I ignored.

"Doesn't that sound—" I began.

"Like a typical Washington occurrence," Dennis interrupted, his fork poised above his slice of birthday cake. I could see he was sizing up the icing he was about to eat and that he was merely humoring me by staying in the conversation when all he really wanted to do was become lost in the buttercream.

Dennis is much more interested in good food than powerful people; his culinary-oriented priorities are one of the many reasons I married him. "So they both live in Georgetown," he said. "Lots of powerful people do. Half the people in Georgetown are famous or powerful, and the other half live there because they want to live near them."

Dennis was right, of course, and I immediately thought of poor Viola Drath, the ninety-one-year-old socialite who had been murdered in her own house in 2011 just two blocks from here, on Woodward's street. Upon sentencing, her husband, forty years her junior, was described by the U.S. attorney: "Albrecht Muth has pretended to be an Iraqi general, a Count, and an East German spy, but in truth he is a cold-blooded killer who strangled his elderly wife to death."

It was a crazy story that was crazy in a specifically Washington way. It featured an unscrupulous younger man and a sad, wealthy older woman and their very weird marriage—that part of it isn't geographically specific. But what drove him to marry a woman four decades older was not just money but power, a certain brand of Washington power that is more about your résumé than your bank account. Muth nursed such an obsessive desire to penetrate the inner circle of the Washington elite that he took extreme measures to try to impress, making up a dossier that was part Graham Greene and part Monty Python.

"He often wore an eye patch, and said he had lost the eye while fighting as a mercenary in South America, but he later stopped wearing the patch," reported the *Washington Post*.

"He had a military uniform—which prosecutors say he ordered online—and wore it on the streets of Georgetown, telling neighbors he was an Iraqi general."

Henry Allen, former *Washington Post* reporter and keen observer of this city's inhabitants, wrote in 1999 that there is "a sense that none of us quite belong here, that we're all obituaries waiting to happen; while at the same time the city of Washington feels like a conspiracy we're all in together, and nobody else in America quite understands, even though they pay for it."

Of course, most people don't go to such lengths to belong as Viola Drath's husband, but after thirty years in this town, I feel like I've run into more than a few Albrecht Muths. It's a town full of posers, pretenders, inflaters, imposters, takers, and fakers. There are many facets of any city, of course, and I don't mean to reduce Washington to a sum of its clichés. I'm talking specifically about federal Washington, political Washington, the Washington where I've made my life, and the Washington I'm still trying to make sense of after three decades.

I woke up the next morning after the surprise party with a mild hangover and a nutty fixation on the whereabouts of our friends' son's missing baby blanket. It probably looked like an old tattered *schmata* to anyone else, but to David and Joy I knew it had great sentimental value. Surely they were mourning its loss. I thought of our daughter's baby blanket, safely stowed in the back of my closet.

But this was Washington and six degrees of separation is less a pop culture meme and more a way of doing business: one of the poet's guests had connections to an administration connection and so it took just two phone calls through the top people network to get a message to the administration official's Secret Service detail, "The good Samaritans in Georgetown would appreciate the baby blanket being returned."

The next day came an officious knock—*rap rap rap*—on the heavy wood front door. David opened it to find the high-level administration official, his son, and a couple of Secret Service agents on his doorstep, baby blanket in tow. The town, for all its pomp and circumstance, was just a small village, really. It was hard to get lost in the crowd, or forgotten. As I would soon enough be reminded once again.

THIRTEEN

Torches Lit

Be again, be again. (Pause.)
All that old misery. (Pause.)
Once wasn't enough for you.
—SAMUEL BECKETT, *KRAPP'S LAST TAPE*

"I found something in your old interviews with Ben."

I was on the phone with Jeff Himmelman. Like me, he was a former researcher for both Bob Woodward and Ben Bradlee. It was March 2011, and Jeff was writing his own book—a biography of Ben.

When I first learned about Jeff's project a year earlier, I had fretted a bit. I wasn't concerned that the book wouldn't be good—Jeff is a masterful writer and reporter—but I was concerned that he might disturb the delicate ecosystem of the *Washington Post* legacy. Giving a journalist license to forage for material among Ben's paper trail of the Pentagon Papers and Watergate was bound to shake loose some fact or anecdote that didn't jibe with the mythology that had grown up around the newspaper's rise. Though the biography wasn't "authorized"—meaning that Ben had no veto power over what Jeff wrote—Ben had given him complete access to his private papers and encouraged others to cooperate.

Still it seemed a tricky proposition for Jeff to write a book about someone he deeply loved and respected. Ben had been married three times, fathered and raised four children, and raised an additional four stepchildren. And as a journalist, he had also been front and center for some of the most important stories of the last fifty years. It had been a "good life," as the title of his autobiography said, but it had also been big, complicated, and, at times, messy. Although I didn't have anything specific in mind, I had wondered if Jeff might find something that would pit a biographer's integrity against a friend's personal loyalty.

During our weekly sessions, I had on a few occasions witnessed Ben reflecting on his role during some key moments of his career. But it had been up to him what he included in his book, and very little of that survived to the written page, particularly in the sections describing the reporting of the Watergate story that secured his place in history. This did not escape Jeff's attention as he went through the transcripts of my interviews with Ben.

So when Jeff said he'd found something, I sat forward in my chair, listening intently as he read what Ben had said to me twenty-one years earlier: "You know I have a little problem with Deep Throat. Did that potted [plant] incident ever happen? . . . and meeting in some garage. One meeting in the garage? Fifty meetings in the garage? I don't know how many meetings in the garage . . . There's a residual fear in my soul that that isn't quite straight."

I gulped.

Jeff was silent, waiting for me to process what he had said, waiting while I mentally traveled back two decades. Waiting is something a reporter must become good at. We both knew the reporter's interview trick of saying something and letting it dangle. Eventually your subject will find the silence so uncomfortable they will say something, anything. We had learned this from the same person.

Finally, I gave in. "What are you asking, Jeff?"

"I guess I want to know if you remember Ben saying that. It's not in *A Good Life*. So do you remember if you talked about including it in the book?"

What I remembered was an image frozen in time, and the sense that I had consciously willed myself to forget it.

It was Ben's face. That amazing, rugged, beautiful face, a face etched with lines that told a story, so many stories. With those warm, hazel brown eyes, which then, in this memory, were not quite seventy and still lit up like those of a much younger man, a man who could still electrify the object of his gaze. But in that moment, the look had not been electrifying. The look was somewhere between guilt and fear: guilt for thinking such a sacrilegious thought and fear that even a single detail of the Watergate story was embellished.

I had seen that look just a few times during our interviews, usually when he was saying something very raw, something we both knew wasn't going to make it into his autobiography. The-larger-than-life, fill-up-the-room confidence was eclipsed by a flash of vulnerability at the self-realization that he might not fully embrace every single aspect of the Watergate lore. This was not offered as a confession but rather as a statement for the record.

I would like to say I have some skill at getting famous, powerful people to reveal things they otherwise wouldn't, but I don't. I'm just a competent interviewer who isn't scary, who doesn't intimidate, and who knows when to get out of the way and let it happen. I am reminded of something CIA director Bill Casey told Woodward: *Everyone always says more than they are supposed to.*

People want to talk. It's the lifeblood of journalism. They may not want to talk about what you want to talk about, at least not initially, but they want to talk. And Ben wanted to talk that day. To the tape recorder. Sometimes journalists believe, or at least they hope, a source will forget that a tape recorder is running. But someone with Ben's experience and sophistication would never—could never—forget about a tape recorder. Sources are wary of tape recorders; they are concerned about what happens to their words once technology has captured them. Technology doesn't edit on behalf of legacy or loyalty. Technology preserves. Be it a harmless truth or a dangerous truth.

I unexpectedly found myself in the uncomfortable position of hearing something from one living legend about another living legend, and I felt an almost familial loyalty to both of them. I heard Ben say what he said, but we never revisited it, and the moment passed. After I transcribed the session, I pushed it to the back of my mind, where it stayed for two decades, until Jeff yanked it back to the forefront.

It wasn't my place to tell Jeff to use the reflection or not, just as it hadn't been my place with Ben. Its absence in Ben's autobiography was not a lie. It was, after all, just a thought Ben had had. He, like all of us, had millions of thoughts. Perhaps when he read the transcript I prepared of our exchange, he decided he didn't even agree with what he'd said.

But Jeff had found this, and because of Ben's role in the Watergate story and because of Watergate's importance in the nation's collective consciousness, plenty of people were going to talk about and evaluate whether Ben's reflection, more than twenty years later, mattered. Ben cared deeply about the truth, finding it, protecting it, and preserving it. Wasn't that, after all, what the Watergate story represented? That throwing a little sunshine on Nixon's White House revealed what was really going on there?

Ben's agreement to give Jeff access to his papers was his way of giving the whole truth another chance. Ben recognized that Jason Robards's portrayal of him cemented his role in the public's mind for generations to come. But with that attention also came an uneasiness about Hollywood's version of him and Watergate: he never wanted it to eclipse the truth, which he trusted was extraordinary enough.

If Washington were a person, it would be diagnosed with narcissistic personality disorder, a town that has fallen in love with itself and its own myths. This was never more true than when considering Watergate's role in this town's self-reverence. For the fortieth anniversary of the Watergate break-in, *Washington Post* reporter Marc Fisher wrote: "As the years slip by, the Watergate story—the tale of a criminal conspiracy to cover up misdeeds by a president and his top advisers—drifts toward myth, losing some of its nuance. Fact and fiction blur. Hollywood's rendition takes up more bandwidth than the original investigative journalism."

After Jeff asked me if I remembered this moment in my

interviews with Ben, he said he was going to talk to Ben and to Woodward, and he would probably call me back to follow up.

And a few days later, he did call back to say he had spoken to both men separately. One of the things Woodward wanted to know, according to Jeff, was whether Jeff had talked to me, and, if so, what I had to say about the transcribed exchange.

Woodward was very concerned about Jeff including the transcribed conversation in his book, Jeff said, explaining what had happened since our previous conversation. After a few days of tense exchanges between Jeff and Woodward, they arranged a meeting at Ben's house.

Woodward had continued to question whether Jeff had accurately characterized the conversation that occurred more than two decades earlier. I didn't know what else I could tell Jeff. "I stand by my interviewing and by my transcribing. I personally transcribed all those interviews."

But then the obvious occurred to me. My recollection didn't matter. All the tapes were preserved; it should be easy enough to find the tape and let the past speak for itself.

"Why don't you just listen to the tape yourself?"

"That's the weird thing," Jeff said. "All the tapes of all your interviews are there, in a box. Except that one."

There was no explanation for that. Even a conspiracy theorist would have a hard time explaining how someone could have gotten his hands on that particular tape or even could have known it existed. It had been stored on the seventh floor of the *Post* building, locked away in a room. My mind flashed on the other missing tape, the one from my interview with Hillary Clinton.

"I just want to stay out of it," I said finally. I told Jeff I didn't remember that specific exchange but that it sounded like Ben. I did remember talking about Watergate and feeling upset by what Ben said. It was slowly coming back to me in bits and pieces. Meanwhile, around this time, Ben's memory had begun to fail. I was the only one who could reliably cast doubt on the transcript's accuracy or bolster the account with additional information. I felt pressured and wanted to distance myself.

I didn't want to be a footnote to a footnote in another Washington story.

The material involving the transcript remained in Jeff's book. It was another year and a half before *Yours in Truth* went on sale and was excerpted in *New York* magazine, which led to a quintessential Washington flap: the intersection of a tempest in a teapot and insider baseball. Woodward denounced Jeff, and it played out, among other places, in *Politico*'s "Playbook," which was billed as "Mike Allen's must-read briefing on what's driving the day in Washington." On April 12, 2012, Allen ran parts of an e-mail Woodward sent to him.

Woodward accused Jeff of a "journalistic felony" because though Jeff's book included it, the *New York* magazine excerpt left out a contemporary quote of Ben's that Woodward said "undercut the premise of the piece": "'if you would ask me, do I think he (Woodward) embellished, I would say no.' Ben went on to say about me, 'He did nothing to play down the drama of all of this.' About [Mark] Felt ['Deep Throat'], Ben said, 'was (there) anything that I knew about him from Bob that didn't ring true, and I don't know of anything.'"

This was Woodward's way, methodically offering up facts. But then, in a departure from his usual manner, Woodward noted sarcastically that Ben was right that he hadn't played down the drama, and that "It was, as I recall, a pretty dramatic time."

Woodward was also interviewed by Dylan Byers of *Politico* and said: "It's amazing that it's not in Jeff's piece . . . It's almost like the way Nixon's tapings did him in, Jeff's own interview with Bradlee does him in."

A *Washington Post* story about the *New York* magazine excerpt noted that even Jeff didn't think too much should be read into the decades-old passage. "'I didn't think it was a big deal.' The author says the stir over the 'residual doubts' line is a result of the magazine's excerpting: 'The dangerous thing about an excerpt is they take the gossipiest, sexiest part of your book. I did not intend any implication that it's about anything larger. It's hard for me to imagine the legacy of Watergate changing much.'"

Meanwhile, several reporters tried to contact me, and I went Greta Garbo on them all: dodging their calls, deleting their e-mails, and mostly escaping attention. In most articles, if I was mentioned at all, I was referred to as Ben's secretary or as an unnamed interviewer or researcher.

Ben, who, at age eighty-nine wasn't in any condition to get involved in a public feud, stayed out of the fray. When Ben initially gave Jeff total access to his life, it must have at least occurred to him that it might result in a less than happy ending. Ben knew as well as anyone the land mines an author buries for himself when he writes about the people he loves. A decade after JFK was assassinated, Ben published *Conversations with Kennedy* about his friendship with the late president. Jackie Kennedy Onassis hadn't liked the book and complained to Ben that she felt "It tells more about you than it does about him." After that she froze him out and wouldn't even say hello to him when they ran into each other.

When I asked him in May 1990 whether Jackie's rejection bothered him, I could see the pain in his eyes. It's memorable because his was a constitution that did not hold on to sorrow and was also not built for grudges—either carrying them or being on the receiving end. "It hurts my feelings a lot," he told me. "I don't want to be her best friend, but I think this is shit. She can say, I really wish you hadn't written that book. Probably somebody's fed her some stuff. As it turns out I made quite a lot of money on that book. I have given it and much more to Harvard to the Kennedy School in his honor. Which she doesn't know."

Camelot and Watergate, in sequential decades, each loomed large in Ben's life, legacy, and psyche. For a man who revered the truth as he did, it was, in moments where he was asked to self-reflect, hard to reconcile the possibility of being complicit—even on the periphery—in any mythmaking.

Any chronicler of this town knows the Siamese twins of Loyalty and Betrayal. When I read Jeff's book, I was struck by his recounting of a conversation he had with Woodward, during which they discussed what Ben must have been getting at with his "residual fear" remark. Woodward speculated that Ben must have felt a bit skeptical just because he wasn't privy to everything that went on between Deep Throat and Woodward, how the sanctity of an anonymous source is something that even an editor shouldn't trespass upon, even if that made the editor anxious.

"'Did we get this right, do we have the context right? . . .'

Woodward said. '[Ben] was always kind of nudging me a little about it . . . but you know, and this again is this, that there was a zone of interaction between a reporter and a source where this is, you know it's kind of hallowed ground, and you don't step in there.'"

The phrase "hallowed ground" stung me when I read it. I could hear Woodward's voice in my head as though I had been there in the room with them. I knew the exact pitch of his voice, a bit leavened by his tightly controlled temperament, momentarily modulating with passion and reverence as he spoke about the compact between reporter and source. I was once again left with the unanswered question of why he hadn't extended that to me, a betrayal I've obviously never moved past.

In the summer of 2014, my father recovered from what turned out to be double pneumonia. He returned home after a two-week hospital stay and slowly regained his strength, all the while continuing his political proselytizing. Meanwhile, Ben's health was in steady decline, and there were news reports that he was entering hospice care. On October 21, 2014, news of Ben's passing, at age ninety-three, roiled the Washington media landscape.

Tributes poured in from around the world. Jake Weisberg, president of the Slate Group, asked me if I wanted to write something. I told him I didn't, that I was too upset. Which was true. Besides, so many others had known Ben better and could be more eloquent. And there was this: as public a persona as Ben had commanded, my grief for him felt very private.

Jeff was completely crushed by Ben's death, and by the realization he would never have the opportunity to see him again. Though Ben was not angry with Jeff, the publication of Jeff's book had coincided with Ben's deterioration, and it became impossible for Jeff to visit Ben without Sally's permission. Jeff knew that wasn't going to happen. Jeff certainly was not surprised but was still disappointed to receive word through Sally's camp that he was not welcome at the funeral.

I received my formal invitation to the funeral via e-mail, from the PR firm Campbell Peachey and Associates with the following instructions: "Due to security measures that will be in place for Benjamin Crowninshield Bradlee's funeral service at the National Cathedral, guests will need to proceed through magnetometers upon arrival. The National Cathedral will be open to the public at 9:30 A.M. to allow guests ample time to do so. All guests will need to be in their seats by 10:30 A.M. and will not be admitted after 10:45 A.M."

The event promised to be a Washington spectacle, and I flashed on Mark Leibovich's *This Town*, which my students had just finished reading. The set pieces of NBC icon Tim Russert's and diplomat Richard Holbrooke's funerals paint a portrait of Washington as cynical as anything I have read. In a *New York Times* review of *This Town*, Chris Buckley noted: "These chapters are mini-masterpieces of politico-anthropological sociology. Leibovich does for Russert's memorial service at the Kennedy Center what Tom Wolfe's 'Radical Chic' did for Lenny and Felicia Bernstein's party for the Black Panthers. Holbrooke's valedictory, also held at the Ken Cen, First Secular Megachurch of Self-Regard, reads like the funeral scene in 'The Godfather,' transplanted to the banks of the Potomac."

I didn't want Jeff to be alone, and I didn't want to feel alone among the more than one thousand people at the National Cathedral so I chose to be with Jeff in his house watching the service on C-SPAN. That morning, as I dressed in casual clothes, I was well aware that much of official Washington—politicos and those who cover them—would be donning their power ties and power pearls and heading over to the National Cathedral in cabs or town cars or government-issued black SUVs with tinted windows. I took the Metro over to Jeff's house. We turned on the television and began drinking scotch in Ben's honor, even though it was only 10:30 A.M., and I'm not much of a drinker. But I rose to the occasion.

Soon enough we were downing shots while studying familiar Washington faces as they greeted each other with air kisses and power pats, larger than life on Jeff's gigantic flat-screen TV, the whole thing having the air of the red carpet at the Oscars. Jeff was more tuned into current Washington gossip than I was, and he began to freeze-frame shots when I asked him who was who, and he filled in all sorts of biographical details like who had slept with whom or how this one had gotten that job. We remembered that these sorts of details lit up Ben's face on the rare occasions we knew something before he did, proudly delivering it, like a retriever dropping a rabbit at his master's feet.

The *New York Times* noted that the funeral had the "meticulous orchestration befitting a state dinner, metal detectors, satellite trucks and live coverage on C-Span." The vice president, the secretary of state, and a Supreme Court justice attended. This sense of orchestration was to be expected as Sally attended to the smallest of details and the largest of pomp and circumstance. She had, after all, literally written the book on parties. Word had it that the planning of this memorial service had been in the works for months. Starting out with Barbra Streisand's "Evergreen" and ending with John Philip Sousa's "Washington Post March," the service had the elegiac quality that brought to mind Whitman's tribute to Lincoln's passing, "When Lilacs Last in the Dooryard Bloom'd":

> *With the pomp of the inloop'd flags with the cities draped in black,*
> *With the show of the States themselves as of crape-veil'd women standing,*
> *With processions long and winding and the flambeaus of the night,*
> *With the countless torches lit, with the silent sea of faces and the unbared heads . . .*

Funerals in Washington have always been a pageantry that honors power and separates the insiders from the great unwashed. In Thomas Mallon's brilliant novel *Henry and Clara*, about the young couple who were guests of the Lincolns at Ford Theatre the night the president was assassinated, Mallon notes that Clara, who is a good friend of the widowed First Lady, doesn't get one of the six hundred tickets issued for the president's funeral because only seven were dispensed to women.

With no C-SPAN in those days, the only thing Clara could

do was listen to the drums and dirges as they passed by her residence on Lafayette Square.

The most moving eulogy at Ben's funeral was delivered by his youngest son, Quinn, who has struggled his entire life with health issues and learning disabilities. I had known him as a young boy, and now it was satisfying to see, at thirty-two years old, he had found his place in the world as an advocate for people with similar challenges. There was no one who would miss Ben more than Quinn.

"My father was the happiest man I ever met . . . ," he said. "Everyone who ever met him wanted more of him. They wanted to be his best friend, they wanted to please him. They all reacted the same way. Even though he seemed to give each of them something different . . ."

Watching Quinn heroically make it through this most public of eulogies, I flashed on a moment nearly twenty-five years earlier, when I had asked Ben who his best friend was. This was a man who had counted among his confidants a president of the United States. He had dined with kings and flirted with movie stars.

"I've always had trouble with that question . . ." I remember him saying. But then he stopped and said, "It's probably Quinn. Little Quinn."

I'm pretty sure my eyes welled up with tears then, as they do now.

EPILOGUE

When I first became a ghost, I got a kick out of telling people what I did for a living. But as time wore on, particularly if I found myself in the company of someone who was engaged in what I considered serious work such as foreign correspondence or humanitarian aid, I felt embarrassment admitting how I paid my bills. In their eyes, I imagined, or sometimes sensed, I was a hack. I justified to myself that most of the books I worked on dealt with important topics and that my subjects had many lessons to teach me, either directly or indirectly, and that this ghostwriting business was my own personal tutorial in *The 7 Habits of Highly Effective People*.

Besides learning a lot about the book business, I also learned a lot about Washington—some of it positive but much of it negative. It is a town built on secrets, a place where having the capacity for deception is a marketable skill. It is also a town that people flock to in order to make a name for themselves, but sometimes they lose their identity in the process. That's what happened to me.

In "Washington Confidential," a hybrid literature/journalism class I taught with my colleague and friend Maureen Corrigan, we embarked on a literary quest with our students to find the text that most authentically defined "the Washington story." It proved to be elusive, and by the end of the semester we had yet to settle on our choice. Why was this so

difficult? One of our brilliant students, Caitlin Ouano, made
this observation in her final paper:

> Susan Brownmiller, an American feminist and journalist,
> wrote in her 1984 book *Femininity* that "women are all
> female impersonators to some degree." The question
> of authenticity has been raised in reading Washington
> literature, and perhaps the question can be framed in
> Ms. Brownmiller's terms: aren't Washingtonians all
> Washingtonian impersonators to some degree? Drawing
> this connection in the search not simply for authenticity
> but rather identity in the Washington story, a person who
> can possibly convey the experience of this search is a
> woman: the born impersonator, the individual constantly
> in search for an authentic image of self in a world where
> she is bombarded by multiple representations of her gender
> that are both like and unlike her authentic identity and
> individuality.

As the class tried to determine why it was so hard to maintain an authentic self in Washington, and therefore tough to
create an authentic literary representation, we kept coming
back to the cliché of Washington as a swamp. If you google
"Washington built on a swamp," you will get all sorts of stories and references debunking the myth, noting that only 1
to 2 percent of the actual topography of the federal city is
technically swampland.

In this Google search you will also get helpful disquisi-
tions distinguishing "marshy low ground" from "tidal estu-
ary" from "mudflats." And finally, among all this talk about

why Washington isn't really a swamp, you will find quote after quote noting that the swamp motif is just too good a metaphor to abandon for the sake of geographical accuracy. That's because we're speaking about the intersection of politics, government, and media, and there is no better metaphor to evoke the stench, muck, and impenetrability of a culture that swallows up one's true identity and, often, truth itself. Sometimes we get pulled in, other times we walk in of our own volition.

At the center of my own personal swamp was an African proverb I stumbled onto long ago. It became a constant reminder of a bad time in my life and just the word *village* could send me into a funk. For many years I couldn't see my way out. But life is funny like that—as it turns out, another African proverb served as the inspiration to finally pull myself up out of the muck and write my own book.

"Until the lion has a historian," goes the adage, "the hunter will always be the hero."

Acknowledgments

This book would not have happened without my agent Lauren Sharp of Kuhn Projects. Lauren is a gifted wordsmith, a persistent businesswoman, and a kind soul. My editor Henry Ferris at William Morrow is a magician. I am so grateful to Henry for believing in this project, for his wise counsel, attentive editing, and banana-peel navigation. My thanks to the whole William Morrow team, including Nick Amphlett, Trina Hunn, Laurie McGee, Shelby Meizlik, Kate Schafer, Kaitlin Harri, Mumtaz Mustafa, Bonni Leon-Berman, Dale Rohrbaugh, and Andrew DiCecco.

My first agent, Flip Brophy of Sterling Lord Literistic, worked hard and skillfully on my behalf, through good times and bad. Thanks to her, always, for everything.

Georgetown University has been home to my teaching life for going on twenty-five years. Dean of Georgetown College Chester "Chet" Gillis has shown a commitment to journalism, to our students, and to my efforts like *no one else* at the university. I am indebted to him for his leadership, generosity of spirit, and unwavering support.

Thanks to Andrew Wallender, star journalism student and amazing program assistant; to Jamie Slater, his magnificent predecessor; and to our program manager Leslie Byers, who does the work of three people at Georgetown.

Georgetown has been more than a place where I make

my living; it is also where I have made some of my dearest friends. Maureen Corrigan tops that list. Coteaching "Washington Confidential" has been among the highlights of my teaching career. I have learned so much from her—about books and friendship equally. Her wisdom is infinite. Her cucumber gimlets aren't bad either.

Thanks to David Gewanter, who regularly lends me his shoulder, ear, and wit. To Joy Young, for her steely-eyed honesty and her strong spirit. To Denise Brennan and Doug Reed, for their friendship and for the campfire atmosphere they created, where they encouraged me to tell my stories: May the future hold many more gatherings. To Marybeth McMahon, for listening and encouraging. Gratitude to Rich Yeselson, who at one of these campfires posed a tough but important question and then, when the time came, reassured me I had adequately addressed it. His keen political observations and gentle friendship mean a great deal.

To Aminatta Forna, who shared insight into the memoir process, usually over good wine, great food, and lots of laughs, and to her warm and wonderful husband, Simon Westcott, and their precious Mo, who sees me the way I wish the universe did.

To Carolyn Forché, John Pfordresher, Duncan Wu, Tad Howard, Sanford "Sandy" Ungar, Martha Warner, Maria Donoghue, Penn Szittya, Leona Fisher, John Glavin, John Hirsh, Mike Collins, David Lipscomb, Donna Even-Kesef, Jessica Williams, Jackie Buchy, Ted Gup, Evelyn Small, Liz Kastor, Ann Oldenburg, Garrett Graff, Ellen Edwards Villa, Athelia Knight, Carol Leggett, and Jeff Himmelman.

To Debra Levi Holtz, Barbara Wulff, Judy Hofflund, Katherine Gekker, Mariah Burton Nelson, Sharon Rogers, Monty Tripp, and Don Wolfensberger.

Thank you to Tom Hansen and Tom Ferber.

When students grow up, sometimes they remain in a professor's life and not just because they want a letter of recommendation; I am so lucky that has happened to me: Erin Delmore, TM Gibbons-Neff, Alex Horton, Elaina Koros, Mona Mouallem, JC Sites, and Darona Williams. They all make me so proud.

Thank you to Kitty Eisele, for being there just about longer than anyone else except for those bound by blood or law.

Speaking of blood or law: my sister, Judy Wall, and her husband, Rick Wall, have always supported me. They have lived this book in real time and then submitted to reliving it as its most frequent readers throughout the editing process. Who knew a wood sculptor and a tax attorney could be such great sounding boards? Thanks and love also to my brother, David, and his wife, Jan, and to my niece, Ryan, and my nephews, Michael, Danny, and Jake. And to my father, in his mid-nineties, who passed on a deep love of writing and literature. I wish my mother were still alive to read this book. She taught me to stand up for myself. I'm a slow learner.

Thank you to my husband, Dennis Todd: my best reader, my best friend, and my best everything.

Every Washington writer needs these two things in her survival kit: a dog as loyal and sweet as Nikki and a faraway place to escape to. How lucky we are to have Illa, Jim, and the Maui clan. Soon, please?